B₂B
Data-Driven
Marketing

B₂B
DATA-DRIVEN
MARKETING

Sources, Uses, Results

Ruth P. Stevens
Theresa A. Kushner

RACOM
COMMUNICATIONS

© 2015 by Racom Communications

Published by
Racom Communications
150 N. Michigan Ave.
Suite 2800
Chicago, IL 60601
800-247-6553
www.racombooks.com

Editor: Richard Hagle

Catalog-in-Publication information available from the Library of Congress.
Printed in the United States of America
ISBN: 978-1-933199-17-7

Contents

Acknowledgments

In preparing this book, we gained from the wisdom and experience of many colleagues. We thank them all:

Hallie Mummert
Thorin McGee
Fred Diamond
Tom Judge
Kate Kestnbaum
David Hazeltine
Jason Fischer
Mac McIntosh
John Coe
Eric Gagnon
David Gaudreau
Russell Kern
Marty Sarto
Jerry Reisberg
Blair Barondes
Rick Graham
Jeff Harvey
Carol Myers
Tom Tweedie
Vin Wilhelm
Leo Kluger
Dave Higgins
Sean Clemmens
Al Rosato
Monica Weaver
Anthea Louie
Brendan Edgerton
Louise Guryan

James Johnson
Catherine Carlton
Ann-Margret Crater
Gary Skidmore
Mark Goldner
Elaine Bradshaw
Bill Blundon
Jeff Barela
John Zell
Kirk Schuh
Joseph Puthussery
Derek Slayton
Sheila Donovan
Nitin Julka
Scott Clendaniel
Larry Kaul
Arthur Middleton Hughes
Heidi Tucker
Dave Higgins
Randy Robertson
Chris Pickering
Terry Jukes
Charlie Swift
Michael Veit
Jean Marie Hitcher
Chris Fisher
Craig Rosenberg
John Deighton

And our special thanks to Bernice Grossman, David Knutson, and Cyndi Greenglass for their valuable contributions.

Introduction

In business marketing, customer data represents your single most important marketing asset. Data allows you to reach customers and prospects through campaigns, ongoing relationship marketing, and any kind of outbound and inbound contact. Data also supports the analysis and segmentation that permits effective targeting, and makes marketing communications relevant and productive.

Customer data is a valuable resource for marketing research, to segment customers into actionable groups, to identify business opportunity, to understand trends, and develop ongoing marketing strategies. Finally, data supports your assessment of customer value, enabling strategies to treat customers differently based on their expected future value, and maximize the value of the asset that the customer base represents to the firm.

Information about your customers—their contact information, their buying behavior, their needs, their characteristics—is best assembled into a flexible tool known as a marketing database. The marketing database provides the foundation for business intelligence, business opportunity, marketing communications and customer retention.

In business marketing, the sales process can be long, and the number of customers is often limited, but the value of each customer is likely to be sizable. Thus, B2B data presents certain challenges. Data in B2B is structured entirely differently from consumer data, being built on accounts instead of individuals. Business data tends to degrade faster than consumer data. But, due to the high value of each account, a marketing database that is robust and accessible, and populated with clean, relevant information, is an inestimably important tool in business marketing.

B2B database marketing has been around for decades. Kate Kestnbaum, who with her late husband Robert were pioneers in the field, tells the story of using data analytics to understand the market for HP's first hand-held calculator. Years before the product was launched at retail, it was sold directly to engineers and other professionals. The Kestnbaums surveyed users, analyzed the answers, and reported back the functional preferences among various user segments. The data was so clear that HP eventually launched distinctively different products for business and consumer use. The Kestnbaums also applied data analytics to help IBM determine how to staff its sales territories back in the 1970s, and performed lead scoring for a variety of B2B clients.

But database marketing has evolved rapidly in B2B. Given the new-found interest in data, data analytics, and data-driven marketing communications, both on-line and offline, we decided it was time for an end-to-end treatment of the subject. Herewith, this book, which explains how and why to build a B2B marketing database, how to source the data and keep it clean, and the key applications that generate business value.

Trends in B2B Data-Driven Marketing

As important as the database is to B2B marketers, the tools, applications and approaches are changing rapidly. Driven primarily by the Internet and its impact on buyer behavior, and by emerging technologies, these changes mean that marketers must change how they go to market, using customer and prospect data.

The Internet has been the primary driver of dramatic changes in business buying behavior. Just as no one buys a car anymore without first checking prices and features online, business buyers now research and educate themselves online, months—even years—before ever seeing a sales person.

In the "old" days—just a few years ago—when business buyers had a problem, they'd call in their vendors for advice on how to solve it. So a salesperson was in a nifty position to educate—and influence—the buyer from the earliest stages of the process.

But today, the salesperson has lost control. Buyers don't really want to talk to vendors until somewhere akin to 70% of the way down the road, at the stage of writing RFPs and getting quotes. By then, the possible solutions and the specifications are already set.

But there's more. Business buying processes are getting longer, and—most important—involving more parties than ever before. The so-called Buying Circle in large-enterprise B2B—the influencers, specifiers, recommenders, users, decision-makers—comprises as many as 21 people, according to Marketing Sherpa.

So marketers have to think differently today. First, you need to take an active role in the early stages of the buying process to ensure that your solutions are front and center and that you are in the game of influencing buyers as they educate themselves online. Second, you must gain access to each member of the Buying Circle, so you can understand their needs and interests and deliver relevant messaging to them as they move from stage to stage in their buying journey.

These developments bring front and center five important areas requiring renewed focus from B2B marketers:

1. Complete and accurate data on customers and prospects. To influence the multiple Buying Circle members and get to them early, you need to know who they are. Not an easy task, but more essential than ever.
2. A deliberate contact strategy. Beyond blasting out prospecting campaigns,

marketers must move toward a series of ongoing outbound messages, via multiple communications channels, to connect with multiple parties, over time. Here's where marketing automation becomes an important resource for B2B marketers.

3. Active social media outreach. No longer a mere experiment, social media has become a must-have element of the B2B marketing toolkit. A well-written blog, promoted through Twitter and LinkedIn groups, is a good way to start.

4. A superb website, the core resource for engagement with buyers at all stages of the process. Enhance its interactivity by adding downloadable content in exchange for registration.

5. A library of content assets. Populate your website with white papers, research reports, videos, how-to guides, technical documents, archived webinars, all written in objective, non-salesy language, to help educate buyers and help influence them toward your solution. Be sure to title the documents with plenty of keywords.

All of these new imperatives are either driven or supported by data and tools for accessing and analyzing data. Accountable, revenue-driven marketing engenders new respect and a seat at the table for marketing professionals in B2B firms.

Issues and Challenges

With all this excitement, B2B marketers face new challenges—without having found solutions for their old problems. Of particular importance to data and database marketing are these issues:

- Inattention to data and the database. While most senior marketers and other executives will pay lip service to the importance of customer information, it's rare that they understand what is in their databases and how to maintain and improve it consistently. Neither do they invest in the resources, human or otherwise, to manage the data properly. As noted by Derek Slayton, CMO of NetProspex, "Even companies with data scientists on staff tend to ignore the nuts and bolts of minding the database itself. It's like they have the back pain, but they aren't doing the exercises that would keep the pain at a manageable level."

- Organization and process. Taking advantage of the power of customer data requires deliberate consideration of goals and measurement systems to manage the desired outcomes of effective data management. Jim Bampos, VP of Quality at EMC, recently explained in *DMNews* that his group transformed their organization around data to enhance the customer experience. They built a business case, established a partnership with their IT counterparts, and created a roadmap for the systems needed for data access and analytics. Bampos credits enabling technology, organizational and process changes for their success in transforming the EMC's Total Customer Experience program.

- Everything old is new again. Database marketing, also known as data-driven marketing, is being used across the B2B go-to-market process today, but it may be called something different. It may be "predictive analytics," or "CRM," or "Big Data," or another zillion buzzwords. So classically trained practitioners need to go with the flow and adjust to the new vocabulary. Ken Lomasney, COO of the agency UMarketing LLC provides a handy illustration of this phenomenon. With his clients, he refers to the marketing database as a "knowledge platform," to position it as something that provides real value, becomes smarter over time, and comprises an important company asset. A repositioning we might all learn from.

If you are reading this book, you are already convinced of the importance of data in B2B sales and marketing. As Alex Kantrowitz of *Advertising Age* puts it, data is the "new oil" that provides insight, efficiency and scale. For this century's marketers, it is a new form of currency that gives marketing a seat at the executive table, and the ability to drive shareholder value.

CHAPTER 1

The Marketing Database: The Essential Tool of Business Sales and Marketing

What Is a Marketing Database?

Let's begin with a definition of database marketing:

> An information-driven marketing process, managed through a computerized database technology, that enables firms to gain insights into customer behavior and needs, and develop sales and marketing programs to serve those needs and optimize customer value to the firm.

The marketing database, then, is the tool that enables data-driven marketing. In short, the marketing database is:

> An organized collection of data about individual customers and/or prospects that can be accessed, manipulated, and analyzed, enabling marketing to support both strategic and tactical business decisions across all marketing channels.

In more poetic terms, the marketing database is the *recorded memory of the customer relationship*.

1

How the Database Drives Value for Business Marketers

Business marketers put the marketing database to an enormous variety of uses, among them:

- Capture data about customer behavior from all sales and communications channels, including social media
- Model and predict customer behavior
- Query and perform "what-ifs" to stimulate marketing ideas and actions
- Profile customers to gain insight into their needs (also known as creating "personas")
- Segment customers for differentiated treatment
- New product simulation and testing
- Identify prospects, score them for assessing quality, and nurture a relationship with them until they are ready to buy
- Select customers and prospects for promotional campaigns
- Measure campaign performance
- Track marketing tests and experiments
- Build and sustain customer relationships through ongoing marketing communications
- Calculate the value of a customer
- Track and manage the entire customer experience

B2B marketers share many of these applications with consumer marketers. But one can argue that the marketing database has particular importance in B2B marketing for several reasons:

1. The business buying process is more complex than the consumer process. It involves multiple parties, each of whom has different interests and needs, and plays a different role in the buying process. Thus, each of these individuals needs to be influenced differently. A properly constructed marketing database stores the intelligence that allows marketers to differentiate customer treatment efficiently.

2. Selling to businesses is a business process supported by an extraordinary number of internal and external functions. This means not only sales and marketing people, but also external partners like distributors, resellers, and manufacturers' reps, not to mention sales engineering, customer service, R&D, and finance. The marketing database provides the analytical glue that holds all these moving parts together, to ensure that business goals are being met.

3. Business buying cycles are longer than consumer. The marketing database supports and tracks the multiple marketing touches that keep the process moving toward the close, and supports the customer relationship that will continue to develop over time.

4. Account value and order sizes are usually larger in B2B than consumer, so when data is missing or inaccurate, the financial consequences can be heavy. Rick Graham, co-owner of ComputerCare, an ERP software firm servicing small-to-medium apparel companies, puts it this way: "Like a trusty Rolodex, our marketing database is the tool we use to serve our customers. Each customer is really important to us. Especially in tough times, marketing to our current customers is our survival strategy."

Characteristics and Challenges of B2B Data

Data about business customers and prospects is very different from consumer data. Five important points to note:

1. **The data architecture is often multi-level.** A business record may contain three levels of information:
   - The site, meaning the address of a physical company location, like an office, store, factory, or warehouse. The site level may include multiple addresses, for mailing, shipping, and billing.
   - A parent company, usually attached to a unique identifier like a DUNS number (from D&B), an ABI code (from InfoGroup), an Austin-Tetra number (from Equifax), or an identifier system created internally by marketers.
   - The contacts, meaning the various individuals at the site who are involved in the relationship with you. These would be the names of buyers, decision makers, specifiers, influencers, gate-keepers, end-users, purchasing agents, and others.

2. **The core record is based on a site.** Most B2B marketing databases are organized at the site (business or billing address) level. Around the B2B world, there are many systems organized at the contact level, companies that sell primarily by mail order and e-commerce being a prime example. And most campaign automation systems and contact management systems are built around the contact. It all depends on where the buying relationship exists. Some marketers organize their data at the parent company level if it better suits their business.

3. **Data hygiene is critically important.** B2B data is difficult to gather and maintain since employees move around so much, titles change, and companies come and go. On the other hand, the data can drive enormous

business value. So keen attention to data hygiene is particularly important in B2B. In fact, any effort a marketer can take to keep track of customers as they move from job to job is worth doing.

4. **Data is gathered by hand.** Much business data is available for rent or purchase from service providers, but most B2B companies find that they must fill in the gaps by themselves, especially in niche markets. Thus, business marketers have an extra incentive to place some kind of data "discovery" process; i.e., to populate their databases with important contacts, updated titles and job roles, and additional useful information, like firmographics, buying plans, and budgets.

5. **The data includes both prospects and customers.** Because the B2B sales process is long and involves multiple contacts within a firm, business marketers are very likely to maintain purchased prospect data in their marketing databases, for purposes of nurturing relationships with prospective buyers and influencers. (Consumer marketing databases rarely house prospect data, because it is often cheaper and easier to rent it as needed.)

Essential B2B Data Elements

The data fields shown in Exhibit 1.1 are those typically maintained by business marketers. Each industry and each company will adjust this list as applicable to their specific needs.

Exhibit 1.1: Data Fields Typically Used in Business Marketing Databases

Data Elements	Considerations
Company name, address, phone, fax, website	The site-level company name at a particular site or postal address, plus site-level information, like general phone number, fax, and website. Multiple fields are needed for different addresses, like mailing address, shipping address, and billing address. Multiple names may be needed, such as a DBA or trade style name. Also may include identifiers like Twitter, Facebook, and LinkedIn company page URLs.
Customer number	Either an industry standard, like a DUNS, ABI, or A-T number; a corporate linkage number; or a self-generated customer number.
Contact name (s), direct phone, direct fax, mobile phone, email, Twitter handle, LinkedIn profile URL	Multiple individuals (known as "contacts") and their contact information. In this field, you will use the contact's direct phone number, if available.

Data Elements	Considerations
Contact title, function, buying role	For each contact, an official title plus their true job function. You want to collect both, because titles can be somewhat obscure and meaningless these days. Thus, it is a good idea to identify the job functions that are important to your selling process and to attach a pre-defined, standardized function to each contact. Also useful is an indicator of the contact's role in the buying process, such as decision maker, specifier, or influencer.
Enterprise link	Often, company sites will be part of a larger enterprise, including a headquarters and multiple business addresses. So it behooves you to connect sites to whatever "parent" firm is involved. Of course, some sites do represent stand-alone companies.
SIC or NAICS industrial classification code	The U.S. government is currently in the process of migrating the 4-digit Standard Industrial Classification (SIC) system, a relic from the 1930s, to a 6-digit system called NAICS, or North American Industry Classification System, which was officially launched in 1997. NAICS was developed in cooperation with Canada and Mexico. Read all about it at http://www.census.gov/epcd/www/naics.html. NAICS is a more modern classification system, reflecting the new realities of how our information economy operates. The migration process is proving cumbersome to both businesses and data providers, so progress is slow, albeit steady. At http://www.osha.gov/oshstats/sicser.html you can search for SIC codes by keyword and vice versa. Note: Some companies use their own internally defined industry indicator instead of SIC, or as a supplement to it.
Year started in business	Older firms are more likely to demonstrate stable buying patterns than more recently established companies. A new business, however, may have unique needs that are even more important to some marketers.
Legal structure	Another indicator of buying behavior. May include corporation (parent, division, subsidiary, branch, LLC); government (federal, state, local, military); non-corporate (sole proprietor, partnership, non-profit); and foreign.
Revenue, sales, turnover	In the case of a publicly traded firm, it is relatively easy to find revenue levels. Record company revenue at the site level or the enterprise level, depending on what is more meaningful for your business.
Employee size; total and site	In the case of privately held companies, where revenue numbers are not available, the number of employees can be used as a very powerful substitute indicator of purchase propensity and buying process. But even at public companies, employee size may be a useful data element for predicting marketing opportunity—and often more accurate than revenue estimates.
Purchase history; parent, site, and contact levels	Capturing what products and services the account has purchased in the past, the channel, the date, the amount, the order placement method, the payment method, and the frequency, provides information that is highly predictive of future purchase propensity. Ideally, you want to keep track of each outbound touch and link it to the purchase, for a closed-loop picture. Maintaining return information will add to the veracity of the purchase history.

Data Elements	Considerations
Credit score	Credit score, either an internally generated indicator or a commercially available score from a provider like D&B, Infogroup, or Experian.
Yellow Pages advertising	As odd as it may seem, the extent to which the company actively promotes itself in the Yellow Pages can be a predictive variable for marketers in some industries. This data element is often available because much B2B data was originally compiled from phone book records, and the ad size was listed as part of the publisher's company record. Marketers later found it to have some predictive value, so data compilers continue to make it available.
Product history	The price, category, SKU numbers, and product names of items purchased. Also keep a record if the purchased product was later returned, removed, or uninstalled.
Budget, purchase plans	In some industries, this data may be published by research or analyst firms and made available to marketers. More likely, it must be collected by hand, through customer sales contact or primary research.
Purchase preferences, such as channel; site and contact level	It is useful to record details about how the account likes to buy, their preferred channel, their terms, and other information that may be predictive. By all means, maintain customer preference relating to opting out of receiving communications from you via various channels, particularly email and telephone.
Answers to qualification questions	If your company has developed standard qualification questions around such sales-readiness indicators as budget, authority, need and time frame, and if your company has a scoring system in place, this data will be helpful for sorting and selecting campaign targets.
Answers to survey questions	Information gathered by mail, phone, email, or web-based surveys, such as customer satisfaction, needs, capabilities, and interests.
Promotion history (outbound marketing communications touches)	The frequency, medium, offer code, cost, and type of your outbound contacts with the account can be helpful in two ways: 1) as a predictor of purchase propensity and 2) as part of a customer value analysis. Response history is also helpful here.
Service history	The contacts the customer has had with your service center, such as inquiries, returns and problems, plus their resolution.
Original source of the contact	Indicates where the first contact with this person originated. Some companies also record the most recent source of the contact, which serves as an indicator of campaign results.
Firmographic data	The B2B equivalent of demographics. In business marketing, the two most powerful predictive variables are industry and company size (whether based on revenue or employee size). But other firmographic variables may have value for you, including such factors as fiscal year and number of sites.

Data Elements	Considerations
Industry-specific data	Characteristics that are specific to how you sell or how your customer buys. In technology markets, for example, data about installed technology—how many servers, what kinds of software—is recorded at the site level because it is an indicator of buying needs. An industrial supplies maintenance and repair (MRO) company may find that warehouse square footage is the best predictor of potential.
Uniue identifier	Every record needs a unique identifier. If your data has come from a compiled source, it may come with an ID with each record. Some systems add sequential ID numbers and other use a match code type of ID generated from selected characters in the name.

If you are building a database in support of channel partners, your database will also include the data elements shown in Exhibit 1.2:

Exhibit 1.2: Data Fields Used in Channel Partner Databases

Data Elements	Considerations
Type of channel partner	Most companies tier their channel partners based on various criteria, like their special skills, certifications, and expertise; their performance; or the depth of their relationship with the manufacturer. Another way to classify partners is by their business model, whether distributor, manufacturer's rep, or retailer. Or, the partners may be identified by their territory, or the breadth of their market coverage.
Years as partner	The number of years that the channel partner has been associated with the company gives important clues to the business opportunity. For example, newer partners tend to be more aggressive in their sales and marketing efforts, but are often given a less complete product line to start.
Industries served	Not all channel partners are full service. Some may specialize in specific vertical markets. Recognizing industry specialization allows you to align or link customers to partners who specialize in their industries.
Products covered	Allows you to link SKU and product tables to partners. Not all channel partners carry a full line. Some may specialize in specific technical products or have limited capability to support a full line. In combination with industry information, this field also allows you to link customers and partners by both industry and product interest.
Territory covered	This will identify the actual geography that is covered by this partner according to their agreement with you. The territory indicator could be defined broadly, such as by country in the case of a global partner, or as narrowly as by ZIP code for a local channel partner.
Sales rep assigned	Identifies the link between the channel partner and the internal sales rep responsible for this relationship. It is extremely important when developing marketing programs that impact the channel that you involve the sales rep, to get their buy-in and support.

Types of Data Available to Business Marketers

There are many ways to classify data, but here are five approaches that are particularly helpful to business marketers:

1. Prospect data versus customer data.
2. Internal data versus external data.
3. Behavioral data versus descriptive data.
4. Historical data versus real-time data.
5. Concantenated data versus aggregated data.

Here they are compared and contrasted:

Prospect Data	Customer Data
In larger databases, data about prospects is usually rented or licensed as needed, versus maintained in the marketing database. Why? Because it's expensive and time-consuming to maintain data, and since prospect data tends to be easily available, it's usually better to acquire it specifically for a particular campaign or analytic project.	Usually called the customer file or customer master record, data about current customers and other contacts with whom your company already has some relationship, such as campaign respondents, visitors to your booth at a trade show, or those who have registered at your website. Data about customers and inquirers comprises the heart of any business-to-business marketing database.
But many B2B marketers do maintain prospect data. Examples include:	
• Inquirers and sales leads who are being nurtured along in the expectation that they will convert to buyers.	
• If your target audience is small and you need multiple touches to drive the response, then it often makes economic sense to purchase prospect data for ongoing marketing communications use.	
• In situations where the list is cheaper or easier to license and hold than it is to rent for one-time use when you need it.	
• Contacts in other divisions of an enterprise customer that you would like to penetrate.	

Internal Data

Internal sources like sales contacts, customer service, customer support, billing systems, inventory systems, fulfillment systems and website data are the best place to begin assembling your marketing database.

Keep in mind that just because a contact name is available from an internal source does not mean that it is useful for marketing purposes. It's a good idea to qualify these contacts before adding them in. You also need to arrange for regular updates from these sources to keep your marketing data current.

External Data

Once your database has been built with internal data, it's time to enhance the data from external sources. One method is known as data append, whereby your records are compared to a large external database, and you select for purchase the important extra data elements that you don't have in house. Another source of external data is lists of prospects, whether compiled lists or response lists. Many business marketers find that they need to supplement the usual external data sources with additional data gathered by hand, in a process known as data discovery.

Behavioral Data: "What they do"

Behavioral data refers to elements that record a customer's actions, such as purchase, inquiry, response to a campaign, payment, complaint, website visit, customer service call, communications channels used, etc. Past behavior being a strong predictor of future behavior, behavioral data is generally more valuable than descriptive data for analytical and campaign selection purposes.

Descriptive Data: "What they look like"

Descriptive data refers to elements that describe what a customer looks like. This might be elements like company size, industry, geographic location, and other firmographic fields, like legal structure and number of years in business.

Historical Data

Most marketing databases are built based on past customer behaviors, plus descriptive attributes, as discussed above. The customer record is built up over time, enhanced, and kept as current as possible. Updates are usually imported in batch mode, on regular occasions, like daily, weekly, or monthly. This rich historical record allows marketers to analyze the customer over time and make decisions about how to drive customer profitability going forward.

Real-time Data

In recent years, a large portion of customer interactions takes place online, giving marketers the chance to react quickly, on the spot. These interactions include form fills and downloads, but also tweets and anonymous behaviors. Still in its infancy, real-time data-driven marketing is focused on A/B split testing and struggles with multi-touch campaign attribution issues. The potential for marrying the historical record with real-time data is tantalizing.

Concatenated Data

Concatenated data usually refers to large data sets that need to be associated to your data. For example, you may want to associate the data about hospitals (number of beds, associated doctors) to your list of companies in the healthcare industry. This usually requires a link of some kind, like a DUNS number, to help you pull this information together.

Aggregated Data

Aggregated data refers to data that may be found in disparate sources but, in order to be useful, must be aggregated and associated to a company. For example, you may have a field associated with a business partner indicating how many customers that partner has. This could be a number aggregated from your own internal records of customers who prefer that partner. Or, you could aggregate instances of social media contact to rank how active an influencer is inside a company.

What a Marketing Database Is Not

When you ask business marketers the question, "Do you have a marketing database?," they will inevitably say, "Yes." But dig a little deeper, and you may find that the database in question is really something else. Most likely, what they have is an operating system, an accounting system, a sales force automation system, or a contact management system, versus a marketing database designed to support a wide range of marketing tasks.

Operating Systems

An operating database is designed to run business operations, like accounting, inventory, shipping, payroll, and supply chain management. Examples include enterprise resources planning tools (ERP) and e-commerce tools. Often, such systems contain customer information for billing and fulfillment purposes, and thus contain information essential to marketers.

However, if you try to use such a system for marketing purposes, your frustrations will be immediate:

- Operating functions take business precedence, for good reason, so marketing requests can be delayed, often for days.
- Operating systems tend to send older data off into an archive, which severely limits marketing's ability to analyze long-term customer behavioral history.
- The system is not designed to support the "what-if" queries that marketers depend on to stimulate their thinking and to plan effectively.
- You are unlikely to be able to analyze the data quickly and easily, without additional coding, external processing, or the services of your IT department.

Accounting Systems

Many small businesses keep their customer lists on their accounting systems, like QuickBooks or FreshBooks. Certainly, these systems allow a certain amount of data accessibility and sortability, but they provide next to no query or selection capabilities, and are not set up to house the data elements a B2B marketer needs to segment and analyze the data effectively. For example, they do not capture historical promotional behavior, nor do they provide marketers a good understanding of the customer's experience with their company. If forced to use an accounting system for marketing purposes, you will end up with either tunnel vision or an excessive amount of manipulation by your IT department.

SFA and CRM Systems

Systems designed to manage a prospect pipeline, like sales force automation (SFA) and customer relationship management (CRM) systems, are frequently confused with marketing databases. In B2B, where a sales team is the primary "owner" of the customer relationship, these tools are of paramount importance to sales force productivity and thus to revenue generation.

A sales force automation and contact management system is not a marketing database. Why?

- They are not designed to support the kinds of queries marketers need to ask to gain insights, predict behavior, and plan campaigns.
- Neither are they designed to hold the kinds of information—detailed purchase history and promotional history, for example—that marketers need for analysis.
- The content is organized to support the day-to-day needs of a salesperson, with an emphasis on follow-up, forecasting and pipeline management, and reporting.
- They allow most, if not all, users to enter data. This feature is essential to salespeople, but anathema to marketers, since it means that data standards on accuracy and completeness are impossible to maintain.

However, the fact is that many companies, especially smaller firms, are relying on their contact management systems, such as Salesforce.com, Microsoft Dynamics CRM, SugarCRM, NetSuite, or Saleslogix, for marketing purposes. Many SFA providers have integrated marketing automation, data analysis/reporting, campaign planning, and project management modules into their core CRM product. For smaller companies, especially those without a good customer file design, this may be just what they need. Or, the CRM system may function as a reasonable interim tool until they have enough volume and urgency to demand a fully functional marketing database.

The Characteristics of a B2B Marketing Database:
A Practitioner's Perspective
by Susan Fantle, The Copy Works

Sales force Automation (SFA), Customer Relationship Management (CRM), and Point of Sale (POS) are all software solutions created to specifically track interactions and transactions with individual prospects and customers. With a database attached to each of them, it can be very tempting for B2B marketers to just tap that data for marketing purposes.

In fact, through interaction with my own clients, it seems like the majority of B2B marketers do just that. They pull records right out of their Salesforce.com data, SAP or Oracle/Siebel data, or other transactional data. But that's not a best practice. Using these non-marketing databases removes some very essential insights from the marketing process.

My colleague James Pennington, VP of business development at Anderson Direct Marketing, has been railing on this issue for a long time, so I asked him to clarify why sales, CRM, or transactional databases are not appropriate for use in marketing. Here is a summary of his response:

SFA is made up of a list of people who have responded to various marketing offers via email, direct mail, social media, or other channels. The business rules and the logic built into those programs do what they were designed to do—show individual salespeople where leads, customers, and prospects are in the buying cycle. The reports available from this software show management basically the same thing, but group that information by salesperson, territory, and products, showing such important data as the length of the buying cycle.

CRM is different in the fact that acquisition information isn't part of the software. CRM solutions are designed to help with customer retention, cross-selling, and upselling individual customers.

POS and other transactional solutions report what individual companies have bought and how long they have been customers. It flags opportunities to sell more and trends showing that a customer could be lost. These systems link directly to the back office and can track types of transactions by sales source and other important data.

But none of these databases do what marketing needs to do—look at groups for insight, not at individuals.

A marketing database needs to reveal the impact made by marketing in the simplest terms. This requires:

- Before-and-After Snapshots: Showing what a group of prospects looked like before they were targeted by a B2B marketing campaign. Basically, marketers want to take a snapshot of the records, market to those records, then take another snapshot of the data to see what changed. For example: Market to a group of prospects targeted by industry, company size, and other appropriate factors. None are customers. Retain that snapshot of that group. Then compare the first snapshot to a snapshot of the result of that marketing, e.g., 3 percent responded and .5 percent became customers. Marketing should be the reason those numbers changed. SFA, CRM, and transactional databases don't track the information needed for this insight. In addition, these snapshots need to be retained in the database.
- Response Mechanisms: Tracking how that group responded—mail, web form, email, phone, fax.
- Outcome: Showing what those responders downloaded, left behind, or bought.
- Retention of Data: Retaining a pre-marketing snapshot of the data so it can be compared with a post-marketing snapshot of the data.

- Patterns: Tracking groups of contacts over time with historical data to show if they have been contacted once, twice, three times and how those groups have responded.

Marketing data is all about the big picture, not the individual. For B2B marketers to improve their success rates, internally and externally, they should start by gaining access to the full measure of their customer and prospect data.

Marketing Automation Systems

Sales contact management systems, also known as sales force automation (SFA), and now, more often referred to as CRM systems or CRM software, have been with us for more than a decade. In the last few years, advances in marketing software, and demand within the B2B marketing world, have resulted in the emergence of a new set of tools, generally known as marketing automation.

Marketing automation may have developed on its own, but it is now increasingly integrated within CRM software. The current marketing automation leaders are Eloqua (now part of Oracle) and Marketo. Other players are coming up, like Act-on, Salesforce Pardot, Silverpop, Infusionsoft, Leadlife, and Adobe Campaign, many of which also specialize in lead management. The very popular MailChimp is frequently used as a low-cost alternative to full-bore marketing automation.

Marketers now refer to these technologies as part of a marketing "stack," illustrated in Exhibit 1.3, which includes a variety of capabilities, each bolted together to achieve marketing objectives.

Increasingly, B2B marketers are using their marketing automation systems, combined with their "CRMs" (sales contact management systems) as their marketing databases.

Rita Selvaggi is an articulate proponent of this approach. Having headed up marketing at two tech companies, Solarwinds and now Alienvault, Selvaggi is a committed inbound digital marketer. "We need to connect with buyers and influencers. We find their trusted sources of information, and that's where we want to be. We acquire a relationship with them using multiple channels, like paid search, content syndication, display advertising and organic search. We don't buy lists—that feels like a cold call." The inbound contact is nurtured via Marketo, and eventually transferred to Salesforce.com.

Today's marketing automation systems are designed to move prospects through the B2B marketing funnel, from inquiry, to lead, to qualified lead, and on to the sales team for conversion to buyers. But, unless integrated with a fully functioning CRM system, they are suboptimal for the larger marketing mission in several respects:

- For market analysis, the kind of querying and "what-if" interaction so important to market and customer development.
- For control over the data architecture. The marketing automation vendor determines important aspects that impact your ability to manage such challenges as attribution, hygiene, and data quality.
- For flexible management. Marketing automation tools are typically set up at the contact level. CRMs are set up at the account level.
- For customer development post-sale. It may be difficult, for example, to import customer purchase history.
- For building predictive models, like look-alike analysis, and purchase propensity.

Spreadsheets

Some companies maintain their customer data on simple spreadsheets, like Excel. Spreadsheets are designed to let you sort the data, and even do fairly complex analysis, like regression. The next step up might be a database tool like Access or FileMaker Pro, which allows the handling of larger files. But, as your business grows, you will find that you need a relational database to support your marketing effort.

Data Management Platforms

In the ad tech world, data management platforms (DMPs) have sprung up in recent years to manage structured and unstructured data from multiple digital sources, like cookies, mobile web, mobile app, web analytics tools, CRM systems, point of sale, social media, online video, and anything else you can think of. Primarily targeted to the needs of e-commerce marketers and large advertisers to manage cookie-based interactions in coordination with other communications, like e-newsletters, DMPs help keep track of reach and frequency, plus deeper audience analysis, to understand trends, profiles, segmentation, and other customer insight and opportunity. Examples include Demdex (now owned by Adobe), Core Audience, and Krux. DMPs usually strip out personally identifiable data (PII), rendering them unusable for the kind of data-driven marketing that's needed in business markets.

Exhibit 1.3: Example of a Company's Marketing Stack

Bizo, a B2B marketing services company, presents its marketing stack in info-graphic form. Bizo was later acquired by LinkedIn. Used with permission.

How to Tell If You Really Have a Marketing Database:
A Data Processing Test

by Jim Wheaton, Wheaton Group LLC

To determine if you have a marketing database, take the following data processing test. If you can execute the five steps within the test easily and rapidly, with no outside-the-system processing, then you will know for sure that you have a marketing database.

FIRST, examine the history of each of your customers as of one year ago. For the sake of illustration, let's assume that "today" is December 1, 2015. The initial challenge is to define who your customers are. This is more difficult in B2B than it is in B2C because you have three options:

- Define your customers at the company level, which often involves multiple locations, as well as multiple individuals within each location.
- Define your customers at the location level.
- Define your customers at the individual level.

A best practices marketing database allows you to define your customers at any of these three levels, on the fly, as the circumstances warrant. However, the definition of best practices is a topic for another discussion. So, for the sake of illustration, let's assume that you use the location-level definition.

If you cannot access the history of your location-level customers as of one year ago (December 1, 2014), then, by definition, you do not have a marketing database. The history of your customers as of one year ago is what is known in the analytics world as a past-point-in-time ("time-0") view. A past-point-in-time view will be impossible to recreate if any of the following is true:

- Some of your customers as of December 1, 2014, are no longer in the system.
- Some of the historical data previous to December 1, 2014, for some or all of your customers, has been deleted or overwritten.
- You cannot exclude from your examination all of the historical data subsequent to December 1, 2014.

SECOND, rank your customers from best to worst, as they would have been ranked one year ago. If you currently use a statistics-based predictive model to rank your customers, then run it off the year-ago customer view.

If you do not have a statistics-based predictive model, then implement a basic RFM scoring system. RFM is the very effective approach pioneered by direct marketers to create a hierarchy of anticipated upcoming customer quality, as follows:

- R, which stands for Recency, indicates the time since a given customer's most recent purchase or other interaction. Often, the unit of measurement is days.
- F, which stands for Frequency, indicates a given customer's total number of purchases within a given period of time. Often, the period of time is over the past year or two.
- M, which stands for Monetary, indicates a given customer's dollar amount of the average purchase within the same period of time as the Frequency variable.

I recommend that you execute the generic but powerful RFM model that was published in 1988 by Connie L. Bauer, Ph.D. The following is a version of Bauer's model that currently is used by several companies:

Likelihood to Purchase = $((M+1).75 \times (F+1)) / ((R/30.4)+.9)$, where M = lifetime dollars,
F = number of orders in the past 12 months, and R = number of days since the most recent order

THIRD, divide the ranked customers into deciles, that is, into ten equal groups. Decile 1—the customers with the highest calculated Likelihood to Purchase—will represent your best customers, and Decile 10 your worst.

FOURTH, for each decile, calculate from one year ago, that is, from December 1, 2014, the average per-customer revenue and the average per-customer promotional spend. Please note that the second will be impossible to calculate if you do not maintain promotion history. The following are examples of promotions:

- A face-to-face visit by a sales rep
- An outbound contact by an inside sales rep
- A mailed catalog or advertising flyer
- An email communication

FIFTH, simultaneously for each of four past-points-in-time—one, two, three, and four years ago—create a standard File Inventory Report. The specifics will vary by the type of business that you are in, but invariably will include:

- Permutations of customer counts, purchase rates, and dollar amounts
- Year-over-year absolute as well as percent changes

Components of your File Inventory Report should also double as Key Performance Indicators (KPIs) that are closely tracked throughout your organization.

If you can execute all five of these steps of the data processing test easily and rapidly, with no outside-the-system processing, then congratulations: You really do have a marketing database.

Furthermore, you probably understand why a marketing database needs to be able to do all of this. Sophisticated data-driven marketing is driven by deep-dive analytics. Analytics require the ability to rapidly recreate past-point-in-time ("time-0") views, and then manipulate and report on the data within these views. In fact, multiple such views will have to be recreated simultaneously. Without this ability, you will not, for example, be able to quickly turnaround any cohort analysis, including lifetime value. Nor will you be able to build any statistics-based predictive models.

Whither the B2B Marketing Database?

The status of the marketing database is in rapid flux these days. Large companies are frustrated at the enormity of gathering, maintaining, and making accessible marketing data across the enterprise. Smaller companies are finding work-arounds, relying on marketing automation and CRM tools to manage their customer—mostly their prospect—information.

Why has this happened? "We did it to ourselves," says Cyndi Greenglass, president of Diamond Marketing Solutions, a leading Chicago B2B agency. "We made it too hard to manage data across silos. The marketing database takes forever to build, and by the time you go live, the database is outdated—and far too expensive."

So marketers are going in innovative new directions. In B2B today, the easier sell is sales force automation, which provides the control, the sales pipeline metrics, and the forecasting. Marketers are using this essential tool as the base, building file structures and data dictionaries around it. Marketing automation tools like Pardot or Marketo are added on top, while email may be deployed through ExactTarget, SilverPop, or MailChimp. Pulling together the pieces they need, they are getting the job done, but without the robust analytical capabilities of a traditional relational database.

Whatever tools they select, marketers must still understand the principles of database marketing—analysis, segmentation, targeting, campaign selection, predictive modeling. They still have to confront the age-old B2B database marketing challenges like sorting among enterprise, site-level, and contact-level data. And they must take up new challenges, like how to integrate unstructured data from social media. "Marketers must understand the fundamentals," says Greenglass. "They just need to apply them faster. Ninety days is the new normal."

Data is used all over the B2B sales and marketing function, so the confusion about what is "really" a marketing database is to be expected. In fact, you could argue that there are myriad kinds of tools that can legitimately be called marketing databases, since they contain information about customers and/or prospects, and can be sorted and analyzed. To get some clarity on the variety of databases used for B2B marketing purposes, David Knutson, principal at Direct Business Systems, has compiled an explanatory chart, shown in Exhibit 1.4.

Exhibit 1.4: Types of Marketing Databases

Type of Database	Description
Analytical database	The analytical database houses the complete record of the customer relationship, and allows the data to be accessed and analyzed for marketing purposes. In this book, this is what we mean by "marketing database."
Customer file	For most organizations, the base building block of a marketing database. Contains all customer-specific fields, for billing, shipping, and for contacts. May also include summary sales data and links to order history.
Prospect and inquiry file—in-house	Includes inquiries and other leads from multiple channels, generated from a variety of sources. Ideally, a subset within the customer file, but may be kept within a marketing automation or CRM system until the first sale is made.
Prospecting database—external	Usually assembled by a list brokerage company, and may be housed at a service bureau. The customer file may also be loaded into the prospecting database, for both matching and suppressing customers from prospect marketing.
Co-op prospect database	Multiple companies pull their customer file data together, and a service bureau combines and de-duplicates. Participating companies agree to mutual use, for prospecting. Typically organized by large list brokerage and management firms.
Marketing automation tool, aka campaign automation	Software for campaign planning and execution. May be hosted internally and be fed by customer file information, ideally, as part of a marketing database. Usually includes full promotion history. Can also be administered by third-party marketing services companies, in the cloud. Used for lead generation, new customer acquisition, and for increasing revenue from existing customers.
Sales force automation (SFA, also sometimes called CRM)	Enables salespeople to manage their contacts, opportunities and accounts, set daily action plans, and keep a record of their interactions. Some SFAs include the customer file as part of their function.
CRM	Enables marketing to manage customer relationships at the contact level, from initial inquiry through upsell and cross-sell.
Customer service system	Tracks customer inquiries, complaints and problems, as well as the company response. Provides easy access to both customer and order history. Ideally, provides a closed loop process to ensure all inquiries are properly handled. Usually a component of the customer file, but can also be a part of some SFAs.
Reactivation database (archive)	Dormant customer records that have gone three to five years since last order may be removed from the customer file on an annual basis, but saved as a separate database. In spite of their age, these accounts usually perform better than a good external prospect. A response generated from marketing to reactivation records can turn into a new lead, or a new order, moving them back onto the customer file.

CHAPTER 2

Data Sources: Where to Get Customer Information

The importance of data sources to a B2B company's marketing database cannot be stressed enough. Without a continual stream of data from reliable and robust sources, a B2B marketing database soon loses its value. So, where do business marketers find their data? Some of the most typical sources are shown in Exhibit 2.1.

Trade shows and other activities are 25%. Third-party media buying is 22%. Call to action on website and email are 21%. Not sure is 17%. Partner and channel promotions are 15%.

Exhibit 2.1: Where Business Marketers Get Data

Respondents were asked: "What is the primary method by which you grow your house database?"

Trade shows and other activities	25%
Third party media buying	22%
Call to action on website and email	21%
Not sure	17%
Partner ana channel promotions	15%

Source: Executive Benchmark Assessment, Frost & Sullivan and Bulldog Solutions

---

What data sources feed your B2B marketing database? Following are the key sources of information about current customers, inquirers, and prospects, beginning with internal sources.

Internal Data Sources

Begin by populating your database with internal sources, which have the benefit of being already on hand, and also likely to be the most up-to-date information on your valuable current customers and prospects. It can sometimes be difficult to identify and assemble data from internal sources, but well worth the effort.

Sales Contacts

Sales contact files can range from paper Rolodexes and Outlook contact lists owned by the sales reps to your contact management systems like Microsoft Dynamics CRM or Salesforce.com.

Field sales and inside sales teams are likely to have the most accurate and current information about customers and prospects. This is an extremely valuable company asset. However, salespeople are often reluctant to give information up to the marketing function. In fact, it is often hard enough to get them to key-enter data into their own sales contact management system. Persuading sales teams to participate requires some combination of carrot and stick strategies.

Once the data is in a sales contact management system, it is usually relatively straightforward to transfer data from there to the marketing database. Contact automation tools are typically designed for easy data transfer, in and out. A large enterprise with thousands of sales reps may have a system that can be set up to feed data regularly to the marketing database. Smaller companies are likely to use off-the-shelf tools, even spreadsheets, and these can be supplemented with interfaces to allow data to transport easily.

How One Firm Used Both Carrot and Stick to Extract Sales Contact Data

The head of corporate marketing at a large HR consulting firm, while requesting anonymity, shares a vivid tale of effective techniques for motivating salespeople to contribute contact information. This company has been using a sales contact management system and is in the process of adding a CRM system.

We begin by enlisting the senior salespeople. In a nutshell, we drive a consciousness of customer/prospect contact and other data by having our sales leaders use the system itself for both monitoring sales progress and doing forecasting. When the sales team knows that their leader is looking at the data, asking them for updates about their progress, and passing along forecasts to the head of sales, there is much more attention paid to the accuracy and completeness of the data.

Also, to create a clear line of sight to the implications of poor data, we have provided the sale group with examples of what has gone wrong in the past. For example, we make them aware that we have received returned mail from their clients as a result of incorrect address or email. Or we show them that their client/prospect received a personalized letter with the wrong name spelling or some other error, or that a client received information about an unwanted product because their interest was incorrectly identified in the database. We also let them know about situations when contacts who are not in the system miss out on receiving a key invitation, or a thought leadership piece, or being included in an opportunity to benchmark with peer organizations. Usually, these situations come up when someone else in the organization reviews a mailing list and then the salesperson will be asked why a specific contact was not on the list. All of these things make the sales rep feel the pain more directly.

We're configuring a new CRM system at the moment. Our sales leaders are part of the design team, along with representatives from marketing, inbound/outbound telemarketing, and our solution groups. Everyone is focused on the few best pieces of information, to make it easier to input and extract in the most useful ways. The new system is going international so we can see the sales funnel and contact information for the entire company in one system.

Billing Systems

The marketing database can receive critically important data from accounting systems, primarily relating to purchase history. Billing systems can also tell you how, when, or if customers pay—data that gives valuable insight to account preferences and creditworthiness.

While the transactions will relate accurately to the account, be careful of the contact-level data from these systems, which is likely to be from a person in an administrative function, rather than a decision maker. If you associate this contact with large order values, you may be focusing on the wrong party for outbound marketing communications.

Operations and Fulfillment Systems

Operations systems may provide valuable data about an account's channel preferences and communications needs. Whether the customer is most comfortable communicating by mail or phone—or through a sales resource like a field rep or a distributor—this is information that can predict behavior as well as indicate the best channels for campaign communications.

The customer's preference in shipping method may also be useful. For example, someone who consistently requests overnight delivery may be signaling some additional needs, not to mention providing an indicator of the cost to serve the account. Finally, operating systems supply frequency data, which can give insights into customers' purchase patterns and preferences.

Customer Service Systems

Information about problems and customer service contacts provide much value to the marketing database. Complaints are generally recorded by type, using a coding system, and a complaint code may give insights into the nature of the customer and the relationship with him or her. Marketers are very likely to discover that a customer whose problem has been resolved will turn into a very loyal buyer.

Be careful about importing open-ended comment fields. Most contact management systems allow for comments by salespeople. Many customer service systems allow comments, as well. But comments must be text-mined before being imported into a database for use in modeling or other applications.

Inquiry Files

A prospect who has indicated interest in more information or perhaps a sales call—aka an inquirer—is a prime prospect for further attention. Inquiry files are fed by the results of marketing campaigns of all types, like content syndication, email, direct mail, banner or SEM advertising, or trade shows and webinars.

Website Data

Your website is a fertile environment for generating prospect data. This generally comes from three sources: cookies, IP address identification, and registration.

Cookies dropped on the browsers of site visitors will allow you to recognize return visitors, as well as conduct marketing interactions when the person behind that browser visits certain other sites. Banner ad and search ad retargeting is a good example of the kind of use marketers make of cookie data.

The visitor's IP address can be identified through various software solutions, Google Analytics being the cheapest, but not necessarily the easiest. Other software vendors, like VisitorTrack, Visitstat, VisualVisitor, Demandbase, and Profound Networks, offer IP address identification solutions with such features as alerts on visitor behavior, plus publically available names and contact information of senior and mid-level managers in the company whose employee visited.

The most valuable and actionable website data comes from registrations. It's a good idea to include a registration request at your website, with a motivational offer like a white paper or case study download, to convert anonymous visitors into contacts that you can add to your database, and begin to build an ongoing relationship.

If you are conducting e-commerce, your web data will include not only contact data, but also purchase history and other behavioral indicators that serve as an even more important source of information for your marketing database.

External Data Sources

External data will be the most productive source of potential new prospects. The average costs of the lists that you might use to help your company find new business are shown in Exhibit 2.2.

To Gate or Not to Gate,
That Is the B2B Content Marketing Question
by Ruth P. Stevens

There's a spirited debate in B2B marketing about whether it's best to give away information (aka "content," like white papers and research reports) to all comers, versus requiring web visitors to provide some information in exchange for a content download. In other words, to gate your content or not to gate. The debate involves aspects of both ROI and philosophy. Myself, I lean toward the "gate it" camp, and here's why.

I know that plenty of very smart and well-respected Internet marketing experts line up with dear old Stewart Brand, founder of the Whole Earth Catalog, who famously said in 1984 that information "wants to be free." The underlying assumption there is that people buy from companies that they trust—a valid point, to be sure. Casting a net through free—unimpeded—distribution of content encourages both trust and, perhaps more importantly, wide dispersal and sharing of information. You'll get to a much bigger audience, who will be educated on the solutions to their business problems, will be grateful for the free info and, one hopes, will think of you when they're ready to buy. So far, so good.

The problem is that this model—which lives under the umbrella concept known as "inbound marketing"—leaves marketers in a serious quandary. We don't have any way of knowing who is reading our informative, educational, and helpful content. We are left sitting on our thumbs, unable to take any proactive steps toward building relationships with these potential prospects. All we can do is wait for them to contact us and, we hope, ask us to participate in an RFP process, or, more likely, give them more info and more answers to their questions. Is that any way to sustain and grow a business relationship—not to mention meet a revenue target? In my view, it leaves too much to chance.

Let's look at the numbers. The ROI model for inbound marketing says that distributing the content to a wide audience will eventually result in more sales than gating the content and marketing proactively to a smaller universe. Let's look at how these numbers might actually work.

To start the conversation, say that wide distribution would put your content in front of 10,000 prospects, via free downloads and pass-along.

In contrast, we might similarly assume that by gating, and requiring some contact information in exchange for the content download, we would only get 1 percent of that distribution: 100 prospects. These are now legitimate inquirers, and we can conduct outbound communications to them. By applying typical campaign conversion rates, we could predict that of 100 inquiries, 20 percent will qualify—producing 20 qualified leads. Of those, we'll be able to contact 50 percent (or 10), and of those 20 percent will convert, resulting in two sales.

But how many sales will we get from the 10,000 with whom we have no direct connection? It's hard to say. When inquiries come in, we can ask where they heard of us, and certainly some will say they read the white paper, or whatever content we put into circulation. But this data tends to be unreliable. Inquirers usually don't remember how they heard of you, or they just make up an answer to get the question out of the way.

This is exactly why business marketers debate the subject with such vigor. We have data, and thus proof, on the gating side. But we only have conjecture on the other. So it boils down to which side you believe. It's tough to do sustainable marketing on faith. Myself, I grew up as a marketer in the world of measurable direct and database marketing. So it's no surprise that I favor the gating side of the fence. I like marketing campaigns that provide predictable results. Where I can stand up in court and show a history of my campaign response rates, conversion rates, and cost-per-lead numbers. And most important, where I can reasonably expect to deliver a steady stream of qualified leads to my sales counterparts, who are relying on me to help them meet their quotas.

So that's my argument for gating content in B2B marketing. I understand the logic of the other side. And I see clearly situations where it makes sense to let the information run free—as a teaser, for example, to persuade prospects to come and get the richer information that is so useful that they'll be falling all over themselves to give me their name, title, company name, and email address. The debate is most likely to rage on forever.

Exhibit 2.2: Business List Prices, by Type

List Category	Average Price per Thousand
Business magazines, controlled circulation	$133
Business magazines, paid circulation	$129
Business merchandise buyers	$116
Permission-based email, small businesses	$112
Permission-based email, large businesses	$212
Data purchase, small businesses	$415
Data purchase, medium-large businesses	$527

Source: Worldata Fall 2014 Price Index

Prospect Lists

Prospect lists are typically rented through specialized brokers. In the U.S. there are more than 34,000 business lists available for rent (see Exhibit 2.3), at prices ranging from $50 per thousand (M) to more than $200/M. Business lists often focus more on the job title or function than the individual person. They come in two general types: compiled files and response files.

Compiled files

Compiled lists are those created from directories, or other public and private sources, for the purpose of resale or rental to marketers. The names on compiled files have some characteristic in common, whether it's geographic or demographic, or related to industry, job function, or product type.

The two largest compilers of original business data are D&B and Infogroup.

D&B data was originally compiled to assess company creditworthiness, so D&B data tends to be most complete when it comes to medium and large firms. Infogroup data was originally compiled from Yellow Pages phone directories, so it tends to offer broad market coverage, even among small firms, but may provide less richness about any given company.

Compiled data is often sorted, repackaged, and sold by other companies, like Experian, Harte Hanks, and Acxiom. Compiled files are also available via list brokers. These days, most large data providers have similarly rich data about U.S. and Canadian businesses. However, they vary in coverage, accuracy, and completeness, so it is worthwhile to try more than one compiler to find out which produces the best results in your target market.

Compiled files tend to be rented at a relatively low rate, usually $70/M (thousand) to $150/M. They generally offer good generic selectability of variables, like SIC (Standard Industrial Classification code), NAICS (North American Industrial Classification System), phone number, and details about the location and its relation to a corporate entity. This data is often sourced from larger compilers and appended as an enhancement to make the names more valuable to list renters.

In recent years, many compilers have been making their data available for purchase via an online interface, vastly enhancing the speed and flexibility of ordering. For a study on the accuracy and completeness of data available from B2B compiled data vendors, see Appendix 4.

Exhibit 2.3: Business-to-Business List Availability in the U.S.

List Category	Number of Lists Available
B2B postal mail lists	34,319
Lists offering telephone numbers	24,758
Lists offering email addresses	23,538
Mainstream postal lists (regular usage by mailers)	1,200
Very actively used postal lists	400

Source: Jeff Adee, Infogroup Media Solutions

Exhibit 2.4: Examples of Industry-specific Compiled Lists

Target Audience	Compiled List Vendor
Government buyers	Amtower & Company, MCH
Schools	MDR, MCH, Agile
Installed technology at companies	Harte Hanks Ci Technology Database, HG Data
Pension and benefits managers	Judy Diamond Associates
Hospitals and institutions	MCH, HIMSS Media
Marketing professionals	The List, Inc.
Law enforcement, fire chiefs, public health administrators	Public Safety Information Bureau

Exhibit 2.5: What Do Lists Cost?

List Type	Price per Thousand Names
Compiled	$70-$150
Office supplies	$80-$100
Seminars/training	$100-$125
Technical publishing, paid circulation	$125-$250
Technical publishing, controlled circulation	$125-$250
General business publishing	$125-$195
Business newsletters	$100-$125
Industrial	$100-$250
Back office products	$100-$125
Food/gift	$100-$125
Email	$250-$400
Telemarketing	+$50-$75

Source: Jeff Adee, Infogroup Media Solutions

Compiled files can also be found in relatively small niche target categories. (See Exhibit 2.4 for examples of industry-specific compiled lists and Exhibit 2.5 for average list costs.) Look for trade associations, professional associations, and trade publications in your target industry or segment. Some list managers and brokers specialize in particular industries.

Response files

Response lists are created as a by-product of other businesses, like catalog sales, seminars, trade organization memberships, or magazine and newsletter subscriptions. Response files tend to be more current and accurate than compiled files, and they usually contain some useful information about product interest or buying authority.

The fact that the people on response lists have joined, subscribed, or otherwise taken an action in the business world indicates that they are "responsive" and may be better prospects for lead generation than someone whose name was merely copied from a directory.

On the other hand, response files represent a self-selected group, and thus cannot be counted on to serve as complete universes of all the potential prospects in a category. Also, they are less likely to have additional data available for targeted selection, unless they have been enhanced with data append. So most B2B marketers will use a combination of complied and response files to cover their target markets as effectively as possible.

Response files are, not surprisingly, priced higher than compiled files. Response files range from $100 per thousand (M) to $150/M, with hi-tech industry lists priced at a premium, in the $125/M to $350/M range.

Sourcing Response Data from Distribution Channel Partners

B2B companies that deal with two-tier distribution face an important issue: determining which campaign targets are responding to their outbound marketing communications. This is especially troublesome for manufacturers if the responses are designed to flow to dealers or resellers who can respond more quickly to customer requests. A 2014 study from Ascend2 showed that nearly half (46 percent) of marketers rely on data from channel or marketing partners.

Recently, some distributors are getting extra smart about these responders. Many distributors are managing their own marketing operations and analytical databases so that they can provide information to both the manufacturers they serve and their resellers. Sensing that they play an important role between manufacturer and reseller, some distributors have begun to take steps to calculate the value of the response data. Often this information has so much value that the smarter distributors are packaging it for resale to manufacturers, who are willing to pay handsomely for it. Distributors are also using the data as a competitive value-added "reason to engage" with their resellers.

In recent years, some list managers and owners are aggregating a variety of lists into large databases of response files from multiple list types, like publications, event attendees, buyers, etc. (see Exhibit 2.6). An example is Penton Media, which manages a combined file of 16 million names in such industry sectors as agriculture, manufacturing, and transportation.

List categories may come on and off the market over time. For example, during the go-go 1990s technology boom, a number of PC-related lists were active, among them Adobe, Intuit, Symantec, and Iomega. All of these companies have removed their lists from the market. More recently, the major office supplies companies have taken their lists off the market, among them Staples, Office Max, and Office Depot.

List Rental versus List Licensing

B2B lists, like consumer, are available for either rental or license, depending on the preference of the list owner and on the marketer's ability to negotiate. To summarize the difference between these types of deals:

- Rental agreements typically require that the list owner approve the renter, to protect the list from competitors. The renter then agrees to use the list just once. The list owner enforces this rule by seeding the list with decoy names, and reporting any divergence from the one-time usage agreement. Any respondents to campaigns mailed to rented lists become the property of the marketer.

Exhibit 2.6: Key B2B Response List Categories and List Suppliers

Major B2B Response List Categories	Examples of List Suppliers
Office supplies	Pitney Bowes, Vistaprint
Seminar and training companies	Fred Pryor, American Management Association, National Seminars, Skillpath
General business publishing	Business Week, McGraw-Hill, Advantage Business Media
Technology publishing	IDG, UBM Tech, 1105 Media, 101 Communications
Newsletters and magazines	Clement Communications, Briefing Publishing, Aspen Publishers, Harvard Business School Publishing
Back office supplies	SmartSign Identification Products, Seton Identification Products, C & H Distributors, National Business Furniture
Food and gift	B2B files of Omaha Steaks, Mrs. Beasley's, Oriental Trading Co., LL Bean
Industrial products and trade publications	CFE Media, MSC Industrial Supply, New Pig, Packaging Digest, Advanced Packaging, Adhesives & Sealants Industry
Compiled information	Infogroup, D&B, Harte Hanks Ci Technology Database

Source: Jeff Adee, Infogroup Media Solutions

- License deals typically cover unlimited use of the names for one year, although additional years can be negotiated. Some people refer to this kind of deal as a "data purchase" versus a rental, but because of the one-year time limit, technically the deal is a license. The data may be imported into the marketer's database and used for communications or analysis. Pricing for licensing deals is usually around two times the base list rental price, so they generally make economic sense for multi-touch campaign strategies. However, not all list owners are willing to offer names for license.

Any kind of deal may be possible, but as a general rule, business marketers find that response lists are more suitable for one-time rental agreements and compiled files may work for rental or license, depending on the quality and relevance of the data.

As examples of situations where the decision must be made about rental or license, consider these hypothetical scenarios suggested by David Gaudreau of Infogroup:

- A controlled-circulation trade magazine serving the business insurance industry is seeking new subscribers. They are not looking for buying behavior or evidence of past purchase. They simply want every possible middle manager in the business insurance world, and they want to penetrate the audience as deeply as possible, with multiple touches. So they cut a deal for a multi-usage license with owners of lists based on firmographic data, pulling all the names at particular companies with particular titles.
- A seminar promoter wants to find new attendees and the best way to identify prospects from a large database of business people is via modeling. So they import a large number of names under license, building predictive models, and then mail the most promising prospects.
- An office products company knows that response lists are most productive, but needs to augment the available universe of names to optimize its catalog production volume. So they take compiled names on a rental basis to round out the mail quantity.
- A marketer targeting the machine tools industry wants to be sure it has every possible target site and all possible contacts at each site on its database for ongoing marketing purposes. So it brings in compiled data, matched first at the site level and then at the contact level, experiencing a 65 to 70 percent match rate against its house file, and populates the database on a three-year licensing basis, paying per element matched.

Should You Put Your Customer List on the List Rental Market?

When looking over the kinds of B2B lists available for rent, you'll notice that most of the categories comprise traditional mail order or subscription businesses. Essentially, these are businesses that grew up communicating directly to customers via mail, whether for selling or for product fulfillment. For these companies, list rental is a natural business process. Some may decide not to put their names on the market, for various reasons, but all are large users of mailing lists, and are at least familiar with the business—and comfortable with its practices.

But there are plenty of marketers whose core business has nothing to do with direct mail, or even e-commerce. These are the millions of companies who sell through person-to-person contact, whether through field sales, telesales, distributors or resellers. In B2B, these companies are the mainstream. Compared to consumer marketers, these businesses are likely to have relatively fewer accounts, but each will represent much higher value.

Consider companies like, say, Pricewaterhouse Coopers, Siebel Systems, or Cummins Engine. Companies selling products and services to other businesses, and who have sizable customer files—even substantial prospect files—for whom the notion of list rental is a tricky one. Why should companies like these even consider putting their files on the market?

Why put up your list for rent? The arguments in favor.

For some, the leading argument in favor of renting your customer list is sheer lucre. When you consider that after brokerage, management, and data processing expenses about 65 percent of the rental revenue goes directly to your bottom line, the benefit of rental can be compelling. If the file turns sufficiently, you can expect to net between one and five dollars per name, per year, on postal files alone.

A more philosophical argument has to do with the true nature of customer relationships. Marketers frequently get starry-eyed about "their" customers, deluding themselves that the relationship is somehow exclusive. But mail-order companies gave up on that idea decades ago, when they recognized that it's a rare mailbox that is "owned" exclusively by one marketer. They found, instead, that their own best customers are often excellent customers of other marketers as well. In fact, when they shared these names, even with their competitors, everyone was better off.

Business marketers, especially those in industrial and services markets, are unlikely to go that far. But they should consider that an account with a large budget that is "open to buy" will make an attractive prospect for suppliers of all sorts. Furthermore, competitive concerns are entirely manageable, because list owners may approve—or reject—rental requests from any company for any reason.

But it may be that the most compelling argument in favor of renting your file is that of fairness. Assuming you are building your business by renting names from other companies, it hardly seems cricket to withhold your own names from others. One way to approach this is via exchanges or reciprocal agreements.

The arguments against renting your list.

The main reason business marketers give for keeping their lists off the market is potential harm to the customer relationship. CDW, a publicly traded direct marketer of computer equipment, for example, rents lists regularly, but refuses to make its own list available to other marketers. A CDW spokesman, Clark J. Walter, explained their position this way: "We don't share our list. We believe our customers are our greatest asset. Our customers trust us. We don't want to risk the hard-fought relationship we have with them in exchange for income."

The other reason is irrelevance. When you are selling millions of dollars of products and services, a few dollars of list rental revenue may be too small to justify management attention.

Another issue is the state of the customer data itself. As Linda Klemstein, president of the list management firm TriMax Direct in St. Paul, Minnesota, points out, many B2B house files are simply unready to take to market. "We often find that the data has been entered incorrectly, or without any entry date, that the duplication rate is high, or there is no sales channel identified. We are usually asked to clean up the data, add overlays, and then maintain the files at TriMax and do the list pulls from here. In some cases, the marketers back at the client ask us to share the file with them, because it's in better shape than they can get from their own IT departments."

Some marketers feel that their lists are too small to be of interest to other marketers. But with the arrival of prospecting databases, this issue has gone away. According to Linda Klemstein, a file as small as a few thousand names can be successful when mixed into a database. "If the names are unique and represent an unusual market segment, we can make them work. Of course we won't know until the names have been tested. But the rental revenue will be all profit to the list owner."

In most cases, the list-rental decision is rooted in the corporate culture. You can look at the rational factors—the revenue, the competitive intelligence, the opportunity for exchanges—and still decide to stay out of the game. Open-minded business marketers will weigh the pros and cons, and make the right decision for themselves.

Prospecting Databases

In recent years, some large mailers (for example, with mail volumes of more than 10 million annually) have experimented with developing proprietary prospecting databases as a way to lower costs and increase the list options available to them. Typically, a private prospecting database will be built and maintained by your list broker or manager, using the rental lists that are most productive for you. The benefit to you is fast and convenient access to pre-deduplicated names that have appropriate appends in place, and with approvals already secured.

The other prospecting database route is to access the commercially available prospecting databases of business names. These come in several flavors:

1. Member databases, meaning that in order to take names out, you must also contribute your names to it. The leader today is the Abacus B2B Cooperative Database, comprising 120 million contacts at 50 million sites, with 4.8 billion transactions, contributed by over 500 member companies. Also available are the b2bBase, a joint venture of MeritDirect and Experian (8 million multi-buyers), and Pinnacle from MeritDirect, which is an extension of b2bBase, with an emphasis on site-level targeting.

2. Open cooperative databases, deduplicated from multiple lists, where you pay only for what you use. Two big players in this category are MeritDirect and Infogroup. MeritDirect's MeritBase has 60 million net names from over 1,800 lists. InfoGroups's b2bdatawarehouse offers over 100 million busi-

ness contacts, 30 million business locations from over 1,500 list sources. Their Sapphire database has over 50 million addresses and phone numbers, plus 17 million email addresses, consolidated from response lists.

3. Mash-ups, as coopetition becomes advantageous in the list industry. B2BAdvantage, for example, is a product from Infogroup that combines their b2bdatawarehouse product with Epsilon's Abacus cooperative transactional data.

Email Lists for Prospecting

Email lists are hugely popular with marketers of all sorts, and B2B is no exception. Just tread with caution, since spam has significantly impacted the productivity of email for prospecting. Many business marketers are reporting better (lower) cost per lead results using direct mail versus email, since buyers tend not to open email from unknown sources. Most list brokers include email list recommendations among their offerings and serve as a useful one-stop shop for what's available in both postal mail lists and email lists.

Keep in mind that email is still a hugely productive tool for current customer marketing—for lead nurturing and for up-sell, cross-sell, and retention. But for cold prospecting to targets with whom you have no prior business relationship, email is no longer as productive as we would like.

How to Increase the Email Coverage of Your Customer Base

When you compare the cost of postal mail—about a dollar per piece—to the cost of email—about a penny per piece—any B2B marketer is going to prefer using email as the medium for staying in touch with current customers and inquirers.

But here's the rub: Most B2B companies have email addresses for only a fraction of their customers. And even worse, if their privacy policies call for opt-in, only a fraction of that fraction are emailable.

Consider the case of Cicso Systems, the networking hardware giant. While 45 to 50 percent of Cicso's global house file contains email addresses, only 29 percent of those are opted in. Doing the math, that's a mere 14 percent of the file that can be contacted via email.

Out of email contact: The root causes.

Clearly a dire situation, when you're trying to cut costs. How did we get into this mess? There are a number of contributing factors, among them:

- Data decay. We all know how volatile data is, especially in B2B. Email addresses are one of the most volatile elements of all.
- Consumer-like privacy policies. Business buyers need information to do their jobs, so they generally welcome relevant email from their suppliers. But in the 1990s, when email policies were first being established, companies—especially large corporations—tended to settle on opt-in as their guiding policy.
- Blanket opt-in. In companies with many product lines, an opt-out of email for one category may be applied to communications about all products, further depleting the available email addresses.
- Global standards based on lowest common denominator. Many firms have decided to comply everywhere with the most restrictive policies from any geography—usually Europe—in an effort to do business consistently worldwide.

So, what are the options for business marketers to increase their customer coverage via email?

Email data append.

The cheapest and fastest route to jumpstart your email address collection is via data append. For pennies per record, you can expect to append valid email addresses to around 10 to 30 percent of your file. Some best practices:

- Select a reputable vendor, such as FreshAddress or TowerData.
- Only try appending on names with whom you already have a business relationship, like customers or inquirers. Appending email addresses to prospect names, while tempting, should be avoided.
- Don't ask the vendor for email addresses of additional contacts at sites where you do business. Stick to the contact names already on your database.
- Once the appended email addresses have arrived, treat them with care. The email expert Regina Brady, of Reggie Brady Marketing Solutions, suggests that your first few communications should explain why they are hearing from you and state the opt-out prominently at the top of the message.

Permission policy revision.

Just as the B2B world has ducked the Do Not Call list, it may be time for business marketers to rethink their early decision to apply opt-in policies to their email communications.

If you attend a trade show and exchange cards with a vendor, you fully expect to receive email—as well as postal mail—from that company. As a business buyer, that's how you stay informed. So, as long as opt-out is offered, and respected, you could argue that a business relationship implies willingness to receive email, and that the well-established standards of opt-out ("notice and choice") should be the rule of thumb for business marketers.

Dave Lewis, CMO of Message Systems, believes that the better approach to permission policies should be based on neither opt-in nor opt-out, but on customer behavior. "The rule should be whether the customer is engaged," he says, "as indicated by such behaviors as clicks, downloads, purchases, and answering survey questions. For too long our focus has been on list size. We need to move toward list quality."

Proactive address collection.

When you look at the cost savings, the business case for aggressive email address collection is very clear. So educate your customer-facing personnel on the importance of gathering email addresses, and weave a collection program into your current business processes.

Cisco Systems, according to Robert McCarty, manager of marketing foundation data services, has a standard practice of outbound phone calls to its SMB (small/medium business) customers to gather email addresses. The SMB marketing team also works with distributors and resellers, asking them to allow Cisco messaging to go out to customers from whom the distributor has email permission. In the large accounts, the calls are made by the named account managers who cover that company, but marketing provides them with suggested topics to improve the call's effectiveness.

Some tips on email collection best practices:

- Explain to your customer the benefit of providing the email address. Give a good business reason, like "We want to keep you up to date on new technical developments."
- Service touchpoints may actually be the most effective collection points, versus outbound marketing communications.
- Create a web-based preferences page, where customers can manage their subscriptions and indicate what kinds of email, mail, and phone calls they'd like to receive.
- Avoid blanket permissions that apply across brands or business units. Says Dave Lewis, "The more options you give them, the happier both sides will be. You may find that they'll opt to receive things they didn't know were available before."
- Place an email collection device on your home page, and elsewhere in your site as well. Says Reggie Brady, "Thanks to search engines, you never know where people will enter your site, so be sure the email sign-up is everywhere, including landing pages."

Relevant communications.

Stop "blasting" emails to your entire file. Once you have an email address, your mission shifts to maintaining its status—preventing customers from opting out. Relevant, timely, targeted communications are the key. We all know this, but not all of us are executing it.

Tektronix, an engineering instruments company in Oregon, solved the relevance problem by communicating with customers through a strategy they call "incremental profiling." Based on product interest, Tektronix sends an email, or makes an outbound call, with an information-based offer.

For example, for customers who have indicated an interest in spectrum analyzers, they'll offer a paper called something like "Fundamentals of Real-time Spectrum Analysis." If the customer bites, Tektronix asks for more detail about product interests: Are they looking for radar, surveillance, WiFi, RFID, or other sub-topics within spectrum analysis? The result is better segmentation, greater relevance and, best of all, response. The program resulted in 46 percent click-through rates and 9 percent response rates, meaning the customer opened, clicked and took some action to continue the dialogue.

The email append process.

The email append process has matured dramatically since its somewhat sketchy early days. According to Bill Kaplan, CEO of FreshAddress, the process involves three possible approaches:

1. Send your email house file to the vendor for matching against a large database of opted-in names. (These are businesspeople who have given permission at some point to share their names, typically by having either checked—or not unchecked—a box saying something like "I am interested in receiving email from selected marketing partners.") The match is done based on first name, last name, company name, and company postal address.

2. The still unmatched names can then be appended through corporate domain pattern matching; for example, first.last@us.ibm.com. Vendors may have different approaches to pattern matching. At FreshAddress, for example, this is an optional part of the process. But TowerData's B2B append process consists primarily of imputed address formulation. You will have to decide whether your company is comfortable with this practice.

3. The last option is a match against an opt-in consumer email address file. FreshAddress, for example, has 835 million consumer records, many of which turn out to be SOHO (small office/home office) people or corporate employees working from home.

After the match, the next step is clean-up and validation. FreshAddress runs the matched email addresses through as many as twenty hygiene and suppression processes, comparing the addresses to the FCC's wireless blocked list, the DMA's Do Not Email file, spam traps, and of course your own house file opt-outs.

Finally, the vendor sends out an opt-in email on behalf of the client, offering the option to unsubscribe. The unsubscribes are tracked and the net names are then run through the suppression process again, to ensure that they are as fresh as possible.

What append rates can you expect? FreshAddress averages 10 to 30 percent on B2B files, broken down as follows:

- 3 to 7 percent from matching against opt-in names
- 6 to 18 percent from corporate domain pattern matching
- 1 to5 percent from consumer/SOHO matching

New Data Sources

The world of B2B prospecting data has exploded in the past decade with innovative ways to capture and collect information useful to marketers. Early examples of this exciting new trend were Jigsaw, a business-card swapping tool that allowed salespeople to trade contacts, and ZoomInfo, which scrapes corporate websites for information about businesspeople and merges the information into a vast pool of data for marketing use.

One big new development today is the trend away from static name/address lists to dynamic sourcing of prospect names, complete with valuable indicators of buying readiness culled from their actual behavior online. Companies such as InsideView and Leadspace are developing solutions in this area. Leadspace's process begins with constructing an ideal buyer persona by analyzing the marketer's best customers, which can be executed by uploading a few hundred records of name, company name, and email address. Then, Leadspace scours the Internet, social networks, and scores of contact databases for look-alikes and immediately delivers prospect names, fresh contact information, and additional data about their professional activities.

Lattice, another dynamic data sourcing supplier with a new approach, also analyzes current customer data to build predictive models for prospecting, cross-sell, and churn prevention. Lattice differs from Leadspace in that it builds the client models using their own massive "data cloud" of B2B buyer behavior, fed by 35 data sources like LexisNexis, Infogroup, D&B, and the U.S. Patent and Trademark Office. According to CMO Brian Kardon, Lattice has identified some interesting variables that are useful in prospecting. For example:

- Juniper Networks found that a company that has recently "signed a lease for a new building" is likely to need new networks and routers.
- American Express's foreign exchange software division identified "opened an office in a foreign country" suggests a need for foreign exchange help.
- Autodesk searches for companies who post job descriptions online that seek "design engineers with CAD/CAM experience."

Lattice faces competition from Mintigo and Infer, which are also offering prospect scoring models—more evidence of the growing opportunity for marketers to take advantage of new data sources and applications.

Another new approach is using so-called business signals to identify opportunity. As described by Avention's Hank Weghorst, business signals can be any variable that characterizes a business. Are they growing? Near an airport? Unionized? Minority owned? Susceptible to hurricane damage? The data points are available today and can be harnessed for what Weghorst calls "hyper segmentation." Avention's database of information flowing from 70 suppliers, overlaid by data analytics services, intends to identify targets for sales, marketing, and research.

Social networks, especially LinkedIn, are rapidly becoming a source of marketing data. For years, marketers have mined LinkedIn data by hand, often using low-cost offshore resources to gather targets in niche categories. Recently, a gaggle of new companies—eGrabber and Social123 among them—are experimenting with ways to bring social media data into CRM systems and marketing databases, to populate and enhance customer and prospect records. SalesLoft Prospector enables sales reps themselves to search for and import prospect names into their contact management systems.

Then there's 6Sense, which identifies prospective accounts that are likely to be in the market for particular products based on the online behavior of their employees, anonymous or identifiable. 6Sense analyzes billions of rows of third party data, from trade publishers, blogs, and forums, looking for indications of purchase intent. If Cisco is looking to promote networking hardware, for example, 6Sense will come back with a set of accounts that are demonstrating an interest in that category, and identify where they were in their buying process, from awareness to purchase. The account data will be populated with contacts, indicating their likely role in the purchase decision, and an estimate of the likely deal size. The data is delivered in real-time to whatever CRM or marketing automation system the client wants, according to founder Amanda Kahlow.

Just to whet your appetite further, consider CrowdFlower, a start-up company in San Francisco, which sends your customer and prospect records to a network of over five million individual contributors in 90 countries, to analyze, clean, or collect the information at scale. Crowdsourcing can be very useful for adding information to, and checking the validity and accuracy of, your data. CrowdFlower has developed an application that makes it possible for you to manage the data enrichment or validity exercises yourself. This means that you can develop programs to acquire new fields whenever your business changes and still take advantage of their worldwide network of individuals who actually look at each record.

The world of B2B data is changing quickly, with exciting new technologies and data sources coming available regularly. Marketers can expect plenty of new opportunity for reaching customers and prospects efficiently.

Appended Information

A 2014 study from NetProspex called *The State of Marketing Data* showed that 88 percent of business database records lack firmographic data (like industry, company revenue, number of employees) and 64 percent of records did not include a phone number.

Business marketers can enhance their customer information by appending certain data elements purchased from third-party data vendors. Owners of large complied business databases often make their information available for appending to your house file. You can overlay your file with such important data fields as industrial classification code, title, phone number, credit rating, executive contacts, and company size. Append is priced very reasonably, ranging from $50/M to $150/M, depending on the number of records input, number of records matched, and number of elements appended.

Compared to collecting the data directly from customers and prospects, data append is a fast, inexpensive, and convenient way to enrich your database for purposes of research, analysis, modeling, and campaign selection.

Keep in mind that matching B2B files is far more difficult than consumer files. B2B files can have a company name, a title, or an individual name on line one. So, while this inconsistency causes no problem with postal delivery, it does mean that computerized matching of the company name on your file to the company name on the append file requires specialized software.

As a process, data append in B2B is no different from that performed on consumer files. Before you begin, you must decide on the fields you want to append. While appended data is cheaper than proactively collected data, there is still a cost associated with it. So only buy the data elements that will drive measurable value for your firm.

Most B2B marketers find the greatest value from knowing the *size* and *industry* of their customer and prospect companies. But there are scores of business data elements available for purchase. Consider this list, provided by Infogroup:

Actual Number of Businesses at Multi-Tenant Code

Affluent Neighborhood Location Indicator

Block Group

Business Status Code (Headquarters, Branch, Subsidiary, Single Location Businesses)

Census Tract

City Population Size

Contact Name, Title, Salutation, Gender, Ethnicity

Credit Rating

Entrepreneur Indicator

Fax Number

Female Executive/Owner Indicator

Foreign Parent Indicator

Fortune Magazine Ranking

Geocode

Government Segment Code (Federal, State, County, Municipal)

Growing/Shrinking Indicator

High Income Executive Indicator

High-tech Business Indicator

Inport/Export Code

Location Property Manager

MSA (Metropolitan Statistical Area) Code and Description

NAICS and Description

New Business Code

Number of Employees (Site and Total Company)

Number of Personal Computers

Office Size (Employees, Square Footage)

Own/Lease Code

Phone Number

Population Density

Post Office Box

Public/Private Indicator

Public Filing Indicator (Bankruptcy, Lien, Foreclosure)

Sales Volume (Site and Total Company)

SIC and Description

Size of Yellow Pages Ad

SOHO Business Indicator

Stock Exchange Ticker Symbol

Toll-free Number

Web Site URL

White Collar Indicator

Year Established

Many of the kinds of data that B2B marketers append to their files are not particularly fast-changing data elements. So, the frequency of appending or updating appended data is a function of how often you update your marketing database, the cost/benefit of updating, and the uses to which the data will be put. For example, if you are profiling your customer base in order to develop your marketing strategy, you will be able to work with data that hasn't been refreshed in several months. On the other hand, if you are selecting campaign targets, you will want to refresh your appends regularly, for attachment to new records that have come onto your file.

You should also look at the cluster codes available for append from suppliers like D&B and Ruf Strategic Solutions (see Exhibit 2.7). Similar to consumer cluster systems like PRIZM from Claritas, these codes provide a fast way to add profiling information to business records. For a reasonable fee, an appended cluster code

Exhibit 2.7: Sample Profile from Ruf's Connex Business Clusters

ⒸRUF
STRATEGIC SOLUTIONS

BUSINESS SITE CLUSTER DESCRIPTIONS
CLUSTER A01

	Business Count	Business Percent	Business Rank
U.S.	281,380	2.81%	4 of 114
Family	1,268,171	22.19%	1 of 13

Business Demographics

Averages:	Cluster	National	Index	Strength
Employees/Business	2.30	12.40	18.50	(-)
Sales/Business	166.00	1902.00	9.80	(-)
Sales/Employees	80.87	163.39	52.70	(-)
Yrs on File/Business	3.27	7.96	41.10	(-)(-)
AD Size/Business	1.64	1.67	98.20	(0)
Population/Business	59.17	208.91	28.30	(-)
Credit Rating/Business	2.92	2.52	96.28	(-)

Percents:	Cluster	National	Index	Strength
Headquarters	0.00%	0.28%	0.00	(0)
Branch	3.90%	12.12%	32.20	(-)
Subsidiary HQ	0.00%	0.26%	0.00	(0)
Franchise	3.60%	12.60%	30.20	(-)
Individual Establishment	4.42%	5.58%	79.20	(0)
Homebased Company	0.00%	10.43%	0.00	(-)
Professional	1.28%	4.34%	29.50	(0)
Institution/Government	0.48%	11.53%	4.20	(-)
Public Firm	0.48%	1.06%	45.30	(-)
Growing Company	0.00%	3.18%	0.00	(-)
White Collar	35.60%	64.46%	55.20	(-)(-)

Geographic Based:	Cluster	National	Index	Strength
Wealthy Area	30.86%	27.62%	111.70	(+)
Unemployment rate			90.10	(-)(-)
Personal Crime			80.21	(-)
Property Crime			86.81	(-)

Purchase Propensity	Index
Construction	(+)(+)
Lumber, wood prod., fruniture	(+)(+)
Hotels, recreation, motion pictures	(+)(+)
Stone, clay, and glass products	(+)(+)
Motor vehicles and equipment	(-)(-)
Mined minerals, except fuels	(+)(+)
Printing and publishing	(-)(-)
Personal services	(+)(+)
Business services	(+)(+)
Retail trade	(-)(-)
Forestry and fishing products	(+)(+)
Real estate	(+)
Paper and allied products	(-)
Fabricated metal products	(+)
Chemicals, petroleum, and coal	(+)

Top SIC Absolutes	Cluster Pct	Index
Special Trade Contractors	18.79%	431.02
Business Services	14.79%	287.68
Personal Services	12.81%	237.48
Gen Building Contractors	10.84%	465.42
Real Estate	9.00%	248.69
Eng/Acct/Rsrch/Mgmt Svcs	7.57%	214.87
Recreational Services	6.64%	386.39
Misc Repair Services	6.30%	436.48
Agricultural Services	3.36%	223.96
Misc Retail Stores	2.75%	43.40

Top SIC Relatives	Cluster Pct	Index
Miscellaneous Services	1.07%	533.00
Gen Building Contractors	10.84%	465.42
Misc Repair Services	6.30%	436.48
Special Trade Contractors	18.79%	431.02
Recreational Services	6.64%	386.39
Real Estate	9.00%	248.69
Personal Services	12.81%	237.48
Agricultural Services	3.36%	223.96
Eng/Acct/Rsrch/Mgmt Svcs	7.57%	214.87

Pie chart legend: Agriculture Pct; Mining Pct; Construction Pct; Manufacturing Pct; Trans/comm/utilities Pct; Wholesale Trade Pct; Retail Trade Pct; Fin/ins/real Estate Pct; Services Pct; Public Admin Pct; Nonclassifiable Pct

Relative to National Average: (+)(+) = Much Greater Than; (+) = Greater Than; (0) = Little Difference; (-) = Less Than; (-)(-) = Much Less Than

Businesses within Cluster A01 are typically smaller contractors that sell into the construction industry, and have been in business on average 3.27 years, shorter than the national average of 7.96, and with relatively strong credit ratings. Once a market penetration study is done matching your customer file to the clusters, you can see the percentages of customers that fall into a particular cluster versus the other 114 homogenous segments. This cluster also contains more than 281,000 additional businesses in the market universe that are "clones" of your best customers, and ideal for prospecting.

provides you with an instant profile for the sites on your database, giving you potentially useful insight into their buying behavior and their needs. You can also use the clusters to identify prospects with characteristics similar to your best customers.

How to Append Data, Step by Step

Step 1: Clean up your file

Your append efforts will be much improved if you begin with clean data. Inaccurate data is harder to match, and will result in lower append rates. To clean up your file, perform the following standard hygiene steps:

- Ensure that your data-entry standards are solid, so that the data is entered properly in the first place. For example, you want to ensure that COMPANY

NAME is entered always in the same place, TITLE is always in the same place (and never in the name field), and that individual names are always FIRST NAME, LAST NAME.

- Run your own standard in-house hygiene protocols.
- Ask your vendor to run their hygiene processes, like NCOA (national change of address), correction of state abbreviations, ZIP Codes and ZIP+4, append of directionals, etc.
- Review your data. There may be anomalies that are identifiable to the naked eye that would be missed—or mangled—by a computerized process. For example, you may know that *Avenue Magazine* would not appreciate being addressed as *Ave Magazine*, which is how an automated hygiene process might standardize it.

Step 2: Create a list of vendor candidates

There are several large and mid-sized data vendors with B2B expertise. You need to identify the one that will perform most effectively with your data. To find the right vendor, conduct the following steps:

- Create a short (3 to 5) list of vendors. Make sure they have B2B experience.
- Ask them for a list of fields they can append, since there will be differences by vendor. Make sure your chosen fields are available.
- Ask how recently their data has been collected, by field, and the source of their data.
- Ask them to show you a sample of the results of their matching process, so you can get a feel for its flexibility and appropriateness to your data.

Step 3: Perform a test of several vendors

The effectiveness of any given vendor is a function of how the vendor performs on your data, not on any one else's files. So the only way to identify the best vendor for you is to conduct a live test. Here is the process:

- Explain to the candidate vendors that you want them to run their append process on a sample of 10,000 names from your file. Depending on the size of your file, you may want to select a somewhat smaller or larger sample.
- Seed the file with some companies about which you already have detailed—and correct—information. This will allow you to do a quality check on the returned append input.
- Ask the vendors not to run any data hygiene or de-duplication for this test. This will allow a better apples-to-apples comparison of the data append process on your records.
- Give the participating vendors several weeks to do the work, and ask them not to charge you for the test. However, do ask them for a bid on the whole

project so they know that you intend to pay for the service once the project is awarded.

Step 4: Determine your evaluation criteria

How will you recognize success when you see it? There are four criteria by which to judge the relative performance of the vendors:

- Match rate. Defined as the number of your records identified as also appearing in the vendor's database, divided by the number of records the vendor received from you. Match rates of 50 percent are not uncommon in B2B data environments.
- Hit rate. Defined as the number of matched records that also had the required fields available for append, divided by the number of records the vendor was able to match against the vendor's database. Hit rates range widely, depending on the data element required. You may experience a 100 percent hit rate for a easy-to-find data element like SIC, while the more esoteric elements like Size of Yellow Pages Ad will be much lower.
- Accuracy. Expect a certain amount of incorrect data to be part of the append process. It's inevitable. The only way to measure the accuracy of the appended elements is by seeding your file with names of companies about which you already know the correct answers and comparing the results.
- Price. Price appears as the last criterion for a good reason. Assuming you are purchasing data that will drive real business value for your company, the amount of correct data you can expect to get will be the most important factor. However, prices can vary dramatically, and you may have budget constraints, so price is a factor you need to consider.

Step 5: Assess your test results

Based on the vendors' performance against your selection criteria, your selection decision should be fairly straightforward, as a combination of performance and price. Some points to keep in mind as you make your decision:

- Not all vendors have the same data, despite what they may tell you. Similarly, not all vendors collect data in the same way and from the same sources.
- Don't be surprised if less than half of your file will be matched. In short, B2B data is a bear.
- Beyond that, only a percentage of the matched files will be appendable.
- Your files will have their own unique hit rates, which is why you need to conduct the experiment.
- You may not be able to get every data field you need. While third-party data append is the lowest-cost source of business data, it's only the first step in a longer process of making your database as useful as it can be.

For a comparative study of actual data append results from three prominent vendors, see Appendix 5.

Data Discovery

Most business marketers are focused on a relatively narrow target audience—optical engineers, for example, or owners of apparel importing companies. When your entire universe of prospects is narrow, you want to be sure you have access to every possible company or contact in the target. Furthermore, you may want to ensure that your database is populated with specific, important data elements about each account.

This kind of breadth and depth is rarely available from commercial data sources. So many B2B marketers rely on a discovery process, whereby they call into key target accounts and gather up the needed data by hand. This process is sometimes called "contact discovery" or "list enhancement."

The first rule of contact discovery is: Don't do it until you have exhausted other, less expensive, routes, like data append.

Dennis Totah, the founder of Catapult Target Profiling and a pioneer in the field of contact discovery, recommends the following process for identifying the areas where data discovery is needed:

1. Determine what companies are truly in your target market. Be very specific as to company size and industry sector. Don't settle for blanket statements like Global 2000 or Fortune 1000.
2. Determine exactly what contacts in these firms you want to be selling to. Identify them by their role in the buying process (decision maker, influencer, user, etc.) and/or by title.
3. Perform a count of the contacts you have in the target accounts in your database.
4. Assess these contacts by: a) buying role/title, and b) freshness. Contacts with no interaction after a year may need to be recontacted before you continue to market to them.
5. Summarize the results by percent. For example, you may find that have 50 percent of the relevant VP-level contacts in your target accounts, but only 25 percent of the director-level contacts. With this information, you can determine that you need to add 50 percent of the VPs and 75 percent of the directors to the database, using contact discovery methods.

To fill in the blanks in your database, Totah recommends the following overall process:

1. Buy first. Get what you can from third parties before investing in any hand work.
2. Identify the holes, and verify or validate the data in your database. This can be done relatively cheaply via Internet searches, and web-based sources like LinkedIn. Or you may choose to verify using the more expensive method of outbound calling. A key advantage of phoning is that you not only find out whether a contact is still at the firm, you also can capture the name of the replacement executive in the case where the person has left the job.
3. Build, adding contact names, titles, and other key data elements, using outbound telephone calls.

Determine very clearly what data elements you need. For example, you may be looking for people who have particular titles, but most B2B marketers are really looking for people who play particular roles. So identify in advance the characteristics of the target. What are the specific responsibilities of the person you are looking for?

Not surprisingly, Totah recommends using a third-party firm to do the outbound discovery work. "You don't want to take up the time of your salespeople with market testing," he says. Expect to pay $7 to $25 per discovered contact, depending on the qualifications needed. Besides Catapult, other firms specializing in contact discovery include ReachForce and Salesify.

What Data Not to Collect

Give careful consideration to the data fields you will gather and maintain. It's tempting to want it all. But there are considerable costs to data acquisition and maintenance, so be absolutely sure it will have solid business value before you decide to collect it.

The issue is not data storage, which is inexpensive these days. The real expense results from data degradation. Inaccurate data is worse than no data at all. So before you decide to focus on a data element, make sure it is available, that you can maintain its accuracy, and that using it will drive business results.

Irresponsible data collection is a pet peeve of Carlos Hidalgo of Annuitas, who specializes in helping B2B marketers get their demand generation processes structured and organized. "It makes me mad," he says. "Marketers don't put their data into a strategic context. Often, they are just guessing about what they are planning to use the data for. They need to consider how the data will provide greater pipeline and higher ROI for the firm. Just because you can collect it doesn't mean you should."

Beware of Dubious Data Providers: A Nine-Point Checklist

The truth is, there are some bad apples in the data business. These days, marketers are hounded by email pitches offering access to all kinds of prospective business targets. How do you assess the credibility of these sources?

Here is a nine-point assessment strategy to help marketers determine the likely legitimacy of a potential vendor, using yes/no questions that can be examined fairly easily, without any direct contact with the vendor. Thanks to Tim Slevin and Ken Magill for the ideas they contributed to this list.

1. Do they have a website you can visit?
2. Do they provide a physical business address?
3. Do they have a company page on LinkedIn?
4. Are the names of the management team provided on the website?
5. Is there a client list on the website?
6. Is there a testimonial on their website with a real name attached?
7. Do they claim some kind of guaranteed level of the accuracy for their data?
8. Do they require 100 percent pre-payment?
9. Is the sales rep using a Gmail or other email address unrelated to the company name?

For questions 7, 8, and 9, a "no" is the right answer. For the first six, a "yes" is what you're looking for. We suggest that any vendor who gets more than one or two wrong answers should be avoided.

CHAPTER 3

Data Architecture:
Setting It Up Right

Bernice Grossman, a longtime builder of B2B databases, describes database architecture this way: When building a house, you think about the number of rooms your family needs, what kind of design suits your lifestyle, and how the layout of the rooms ensures easy movement around the house. But the first task when building a home is to decide on your strategy. Where should we build it? In the suburbs or the city? What is our main goal for the house? Ease and convenience for the family or great spaces for entertaining guests? These questions need to be answered well before you call in the architect.

When building a B2B marketing database, many of the same considerations come into play. First you develop a data strategy. What is it that you want your data to do for your business? Is your primary goal to create leads for sales or to enable market and competitive intelligence? One or all? In short, these decisions should drive your data architecture. Then you need to develop a "data architecture," which defines how the information will be organized and presented to its users. The strategy supported by the architecture has vast implications for how well the data will support your marketing objectives.

The data architecture decisions you make ensure that:

- The information is accessible, actionable, and measurable when the user needs it
- You can report results the way you and your company need to

- Interactions with the data can be accomplished at the speed you need for your business, at the cost you can afford
- Data is effectively and efficiently dataoptimized against your requirements, whether it's analytics, campaign list building, updates or whatever functionality is critical to your business

This chapter is designed not to make you an expert on how to build a marketing database, but to give you enough information to ensure that you provide clear direction to the IT department or to an information technology consultant that you engage to help you.

Who Is Your Customer, Really?

When considering the architecture of your data, the first question you have to answer is: Who is your customer? In other words, what kind of entity embodies the primary customer relationship?

In B2B, there are many choices, depending on what you sell, where your products can be bought, and the size of your company. Typically, the customer is an individual at a site or single location, a buying group at a site, or a corporation as a whole with all its subsidiaries and sites.

For example, if you are Staples, your customer can be an individual businessperson, or the purchasing group at a site, or a corporation that is buying from you on an enterprise-wide contract. If you are an engineering firm selling waste-energy capture devices to industrial boiler plants, your customer is the group of plant engineers, plant managers, and project managers at the site housing the boiler. If you are an HR software vendor selling to large enterprises, then your customer likely comprises the HR and IT professionals at the corporate headquarters, but you will also need to maintain contact with such professionals at various regional sites. If you are Boeing, you are selling airplanes to a relatively small number of enterprises, but a relatively large number of companies buy your parts. In addition, a large number of individuals within the companies as well as regulators outside the companies you sell to can influence the buying decisions.

A customer is ultimately someone who gives you money in exchange for a product or service. But in B2B, the money line can be confusing and multi-tiered. For example, a software or hardware manufacturer that sells through partners or independent software vendors could have many "customers" who provide currency in exchange for product or services. Determining the "customer" is not always easy. Exhibit 3.1 shows just how complicated this can be.

Exhibit 3.1: The Possible Customers of a Hardware-Software Manufacturer

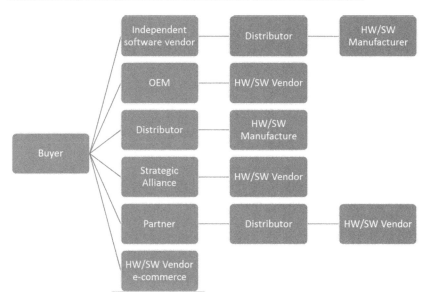

So, one of the first decisions that you need to make about "customer" is how you want to represent these different aspects of the customer with your data.

Seven Goals of a B2B Database
by Robert Bloom, Business Development Solutions, Inc.

Harnessing all relevant data into a B2B database is essential in business today. With that in mind, let's take a look at the goals involved in building and maintaining a B2B database. Often a database building effort may be initially driven by one of these goals, but the other goals will quickly come into play. Here are the typical goals:

1. Improve Analytical Insights into Customer, Product, and Market Behavior
   A database should enable the creation of accurate and complete reports. This includes the ability to compile all sales revenue and transaction activity, over time, including all contacts and locations. The database should become a framework for analysis, easily accessed and used by all who need to know.
2. Develop a Complete View of the Customer and Prospective Customer
   Marketers need to have a complete view of the customer relationship. Sometimes this is called a 360-degree view of the customer. In any event, it is a comprehensive view of the customer (and prospective customer). A database should correlate transaction data, along with location and contact data. Moreover, the database should link together related locations and contacts to enable cross-selling and up-selling.
3. Improve Data Quality
   Due to the diverse nature of business communications, transactions, and data inputs today, the quality of data can suffer. Data quality issues include duplicate

records, incomplete records, inaccurate records and unrelated records. A B2B database can be the platform for continuous and ongoing data quality assessments and improvements, including data cleansing and data standardization.

4. Enhance Existing Data Systems

Often, due to the nature and focus of an internal data management system (e.g., a customer, financial, membership, or agency system), it is difficult to change the structure of the existing internal system or add data from other data sets. A marketing database can include all important data from all sources, as well as be a cross reference to various sources. The database can coordinate with and enhance the existing data management systems with important linked data. This can be done without burdening the existing data system with excessive processing and overhead.

5. Create Accurate and Complete Marketing List Selections and Extracts for Campaigns

With a database built around important data assets, marketing can use the database to create list selects and extracts for various outreach campaigns. The database can also be used for analysis of responses to the outreach campaigns.

6. Manage and integrate External Data into Internal Data Systems

With the myriad of external data sets that are now available, it can be difficult to use those data sets without first reflecting the external data against internal data assets. This is to determine potential overlap and unique records. This is important, for example, when special offers, not being extended to existing customers, are to be made to prospects identified in newly acquired external data sets. The database can be used to manage and integrate external data appropriately.

7. Integrate Data Systems as a Result of Merger or Acquisition

A merger or acquisition will create a need to correlate and integrate data from the data systems of the various pre-merger organizations. The marketing database becomes a key component in understanding the results and benefits of the merger. This includes the extent of the overlap between the two organizations, along with unique customers and revenues from each organization.

Source: Adapted from *Goals of a B2B Database* at http://blog.allthingsdata.com/2014/06/goals-of-a-b2b-database.html

The Impact of Database Applications

The second question to address in your data architecture work is to go back to your strategy and look at what you want to do with the marketing data. Most companies use the marketing data for campaign list selection, as well as analytics. Both applications will have an influence on how you structure the data.

Some applications of the marketing data and how they might impact your data design or architecture are outlined in Exhibit 3.2.

Exhibit 3.2: Marketing Applications and Their Impact on Data Design/Architecture

Marketing Application	Considerations	Impact on Data Design/Architecture
Campaign list selection	• Is the selection primarily driven by company segmentation or individual personas? • What variables are important to the selection? • Do you own all the data required in your systems or are you dependent on other sources?	If the architecture has not been designed to link the data tables properly, list selection maybe performed incorrectly or not at all. For example, for typical list selection, your list of individuals will need to be linked with some key identifier to your table of companies. This is even more important when attempting to link data from outside sources to your internal ones.
Analytics	• Will you be performing propensity to buy algorithms, determining wallet share, or lifetime value? • Do you need to have snapshots of the data at specific times in the selling cycle? • Will you want to link structured (e.g., opportunities or bookings) with unstructured data (e.g., service requests, Tweets)?	Analytics needs greatly impact data design. For example, if you are developing propensity to buy models, you will need several quarters of data to be able to predict the next quarter's performance. If your data strategy and architecture do not accommodate this, you will have a problem. Another example: If sales data flows daily into the database, but you need to compare monthly sales levels, then the database must be designed so the numbers can be transformed for analysis. Yet another implication of design is affected by your need to relate Tweets to campaign measurements. How you tag and make data available have key implications.
Event-triggered marketing	• What events are most important to sales? To marketing? • Who responds to the events? How fast? • Is the automation in place for these triggered events?	Triggered marketing communications get very complicated very fast, building in a tree-like fashion from outbound communication to multiple inbound response options, each generating additional outbound messages. So your database needs to be structured to support this complexity, with, for example, a response table that links back to a promotion history table.
"What-if" analyses	• Who needs to perform "what-if" analyses? • When do they need to do this? • How often do they need to do it?	If the architecture is wrong, getting answers to your marketing questions will be slow, or even impossible for the system to perform. In response to a query it cannot answer, the system may get paralyzed, go into an endless loop, and stop working altogether. Or worse still—deliver the wrong answer to your query.
Market and competitive intelligence	• How do you define your market? • Who are your major competitors? • Which of your customers are also customers of your competitors? • Which of your partners or distributors also sell your competitors' products?	Do you want to use this information in marketing's design of campaigns? If your data should also need to support your marketing strategy, planning for data that includes views of the economy, competitors as well as customers, means structuring your system so as to relate all these different pieces of information. In addition, should you also need to relate this data to Tweets or web logs, then your architecture must be designed upfront to accommodate it.

A Simple Test to Help Your Thinking

Here's an easy way to expand your thinking about the data architecture you will need. Try creating a set of questions you might need to ask of your future marketing database, in the general course of marketing planning. For example:

- How many contacts do I have at a specific customer site in Massachusetts?
- What is the ideal number of touches I should make to inquirers?
- Which products are purchased by which customers?
- How many contacts do I have that have a specific title or do a specific job?
- Which customers can I market to via email? By mail? By telephone? Through social media such as Twitter?

The ability to get answers to questions like this will help you test the system early on, in the design phase.

How Customer Size Impacts Your Data Architecture

One of the key considerations for structuring your data is driven by the size of company that is your customer. The smaller the customer company, the more important the name of the individual (versus simply the title of the contact). Why? Because in smaller companies, individuals tend to play several roles. It's not uncommon for the vice president of finance to be not only the purchasing agent but also the chief technology officer. If you are sending marketing communications to various titles or buying roles in a small company, the mail is likely to all land on the desk of the same person—which is both annoying to the customer and wasteful of your resources.

If you do business only with small companies where you talk to the business owner, no matter what you are selling, then your data design may need to be organized along contact lines.

As you move up the chain by company size and number of employees, the title becomes more important than the name. People move in and out of job roles. Yesterday, Tom was the purchasing agent, but today Mary is the purchasing agent. So you may have better luck addressing your communications to the title rather than the individual. Furthermore, at the enterprise level, there will be multiple titles for the same type of position. For example, assistant buyer, purchasing agent for electronic equipment, and purchasing agent in charge of office furniture may all be in the purchasing department and potential buyers for your goods or services. That's why it's important to capture as many of these titles as possible.

Another area where company size plays a key role is in the issue of "Bill to" versus "Ship to" addresses. In a very small enterprise, you are likely to want to bill, ship, and market to the same address. But in a large enterprise, some sites can receive products—they have a loading dock—but they don't purchase or house any personnel influential in the buying decision. Other sites, filled with accounting people, are perfect for sending a bill, but there's no point in sending them marketing communications. So in such situations, your database should contain an additional table with codes around billing, shipping and marketing activity, associated with each contact.

Understanding Your Customer's Buying Process

As you've been pondering the implications of this discussion, no doubt you have already concluded that understanding your customers and how they buy is critical to building a database that will serve your marketing objectives.

You need to learn what happens at your customer's organization, at the individual contact, at the site, and at the enterprise level.

In today's world, learning how your customer buys may be as simple as mining the data that you already have about them. If you have a company website designed to service your customer, you have an answer to your customer's buying process. In fact, the world of marketing with data is being turned on its head. Instead of always trying to find the right customer for your product, smart marketers are finding that they simply have to ensure that they captivate and hold on to customers who are already coming to them through their web marketing activities.

Let's take a look at how that works.

The marketing funnel so adored by database marketers has been replaced in today's world by a continuous flow of information that pushes the customer and prospect to a website or pulls them into it. This puts pressure on marketers who are used to starting marketing campaigns with a well-understood target audience, enticing them to the company website to download an inspiring article about the latest product, acquiring key marketing data elements such as name, email address and permission to continue the conversation. Armed with this information, marketers can push messages until the prospect turns customer (See Exhibit 3.3).

Exhibit 3.3: Steps to Convert a Prospect into a Customer

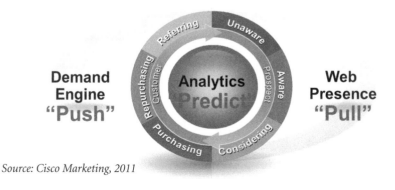

Source: Cisco Marketing, 2011

Designing to capture and use web data requires additional thought and analysis. For example, you may need to know what companies are represented by the individuals who come to your sites. Today, some companies can help you identify the IP (Internet Protocol) addresses for individuals and link those addresses to the servers owned by specific public and private companies. This helps in identifying new contacts who are attracted to your web marketing or who may be just browsing your site.

Today there are a number of different approaches to data for marketing, but here are three:

1. Build a traditional database specific for marketing purposes
2. Enrich and utilize the CRM system installed for sales in your company
3. Build a trigger-oriented web-based system that takes advantage of the velocity and volume of web data

Let's explore the decisions that you must make in order to decide which approach is right for you and how to go about developing each of these.

Deciding on a Data Architecture Approach

Strategy and Architecture

Data for marketing has special uses and can vary greatly from the data normally collected during the course of doing business. Traditionally marketing has needed information about potential customers long before they appear on the forecasts of a sales team. That often creates a need for marketing to develop data sources outside the enterprise business systems that track customer interactions, such as order management or sales automation systems. Many times marketing also requires specific contacts, names of individuals who are not part of the systems data for sales and billing. In addition, marketing communications fall into a different world of privacy concerns than do normal business transactions. This is another reason why marketing often raises the requirement for a data source outside the regular business environments. In these situations, marketing can either become their own IT department and build a database specific to their function or outsource this to a vendor who specializes in building marketing databases. Either way the end result is that marketing ends up with a database that fits their needs and is managed by either an internal or vendor-managed marketing operations team.

Other marketing departments are discovering that the closer marketing is to sales, the more measurable and important marketing becomes. For this reason, marketers are developing closer relationships with CRM systems such as Sales Force.com and insisting that marketing automation tools integrate seamlessly into the sales systems. Managing data from lead identification to sales quote creates a shared responsibility between sales and marketing. This means that often the systems must also be shared or at minimum be tightly integrated. From a data perspective, this means that both marketing and sales share responsibility for quality and usage of the data. The goal is to maintain data quality throughout that process.

And finally, as the Web has become the primary tool for most marketing departments, the use of web data has also expanded. Some companies such as Cisco Systems (see sidebar) develop big data lakes that put both structured and unstructured data into play for marketing.

The advantages and disadvantages of each approach to architecture are presented in Exhibit 3.4.

Exhibit 3.4: Pros and Cons of Different Approaches to Architecture

Architecture	Pros	Cons
Marketing-Owned Data Source	• Control of data quality for marketing-specific purposes (i.e., privacy designations) • No dependence on IT for updates or system changes • Data quality is controlled by marketing	• Non-marketing expense of managing systems and data quality • IT expertise is isolated in marketing organization • Potentially useful corporate data is isolated in a silo in the marketing data mart • Marketing owns data quality
CRM + Marketing	• Puts marketing closer to sales; easier to integrate from lead to quote • If sales organization has an incentive to maintain CRM, data can be highly valuable to marketing	• Marketing data quality may take a secondary role to sales opportunity • Communications efforts must be closely monitored to ensure that marketing messages are guided appropriately and do not jeopardize sales • Multiple data sources can be created if CRM tools are not linked to marketing tools
Big Data Approach	• Can provide unique customer insights from web interactions • Data management is easier	• Requires unique analytical skills • Specialized tools and infrastructure required

Cisco's Novel Approach: A "Gigantic Marketing Lake"

Cisco Systems has come up with an innovative way to gain access to marketing data while sidestepping the whole database "build" challenge. For decades, Cisco had gone after customer and prospect data in the traditional fashion, sourcing data from systems all over the company and assembling it in a relational database for use by marketers, salespeople, and channel partners. They also purchased fresh lists of contacts to populate the database.

After years, and millions of dollars invested, they found that they were gaining no measurable improvement in contactability rates. "We grew the number of contacts in our database from 6 million to 12 million, but our ability to reach customers is worse," says Joseph Puthussery, VP of Cisco's Demand Center. "We learned that list purchasing is fraught with expense, duplication, and quality issues. And just buying contacts and building a database is not the answer."

So the team came up with a new approach: Leave the data in its original place, but pull it in as needed to create customer "virtual profiles" on the fly. For example, when a customer visits the Cisco website, a cookie is set. Say the customer visits again, several times, and eventually registers, providing an email address. At that point, Puthussery's team builds a profile, matching that customer to an account using the IP address, and appending account-level purchase history. Perhaps the forecasting system shows that there is an ongoing deal in process at that account. So this customer's visit becomes part of the account-level behavioral profile, showing the research behavior and adding richness to Cisco's understanding of what's going on in the account relationship.

They call this alternative to a traditional database MODS, or the Marketing Operating Database. It can be compared to a "gigantic marketing lake," says Puthussery.

These virtual profiles are being used to model opportunity. Cisco has ten years of history capturing cookies and recording responses and purchase behavior. So the models can be used to predict future behavior. So far, the models are being used to:

- Identify the best contacts in a prospect list.
- Qualify sales leads.
- Create a "technology interest score," based on the contact's consumption of various content, like data sheets, product pages and configuration guides.
- Find correlations between online and offline behavior. A prospect who has both visited a product page and attended a business event is showing a higher likelihood of purchase.
- Identify more active contacts at an account, more being an indicator of larger deal sizes.

At this point, the MODS is limited to North America, due to the challenge of matching IP addresses matching internationally.

"This means a new mindset," says Puthussery. "It's still hard. We need to get better at analyzing and identifying business opportunities on the spot. We're trying to develop a capability now to score leads automatically and generate the ideal next touch." The team's next step is to make the profiles even more predictive, adding external data from social media, retargeting, and search.

The result: A much faster and cheaper way to scale, to move data around, where infrastructure is not a constraint. The team credits the new approach with higher productivity in the call center and a five times improvement in click-through rates.

Essential Questions to Address

Making the decision as to which kind of marketing data source best fits your organization can be difficult. Here are a few key points to consider:

- Who is your customer?
- What do you need to know about your customer or prospect to market to them effectively?
- What functions—push, pull or analytical—will you be asking the data source to perform?
- How will the data source be maintained? By whom?
- How will you measure the effectiveness of your data source?

Who Is Your Customer?

This important question sets the stage for the data that you need for performing effective marketing campaigns, for reaching the right buyers at the right time. From a data perspective, this question breaks down into several. Are your buyers' organizations—companies, government entities, not-for-profits? Or, are they individual consumers? In other words, do your buyers or customers purchase for themselves or for a larger, corporate-like entity? If your buyers are organizations, is your product or service intended for specific functions within an organization (e.g., accounting, supply chain management, sales)? Or is it more broadly appealing to the entire organization such as education or professional services?

This is an important set of first questions because it helps to identify a Customer Master Record within your data source. The master record should contain the essentials identifying a customer. Other systems such as order management, CRM, and support may add additional transactional information to this record to provide further insight into your customer, but at the heart of your data source is this basic information. Maintaining the quality of this key record is at the key function of your data maintenance as well.

Exhibit 3.5 provides examples of Customer Master Records for different types of customer bases. Note that maintaining a record ID for each organization, or a customer ID in the case of individuals, is important when you want to link your marketing information to sales or order management. It gives you a quick reference for doing so.

Exhibit 3.5: Sample Customer Master Records for Various Customer Bases

Organization

Data Element	Description/Example
Full Organization name	International Business Machines, Inc.
Stock ID or Short Name	IBM
Address 1	12 Road
Address 2	Corporate Building
City	Armonk
State	New York
Zip Code	06000
Record ID[1]	Dun& Bradstreet number, Value Added Tax (VAT) ID or internal, unique number

Government Entity

Data Element	Description/Example
Agency Name	Veterans Administration
Address 1	123 Old Soldier's Lane
Address 2	Department of Purchasing
Branch	Armed Forces
City	Washington
State	District of Columbia
Country	United States
Postal Code	42353
Record ID	Purchasing ID or internal, unique number

Individual within a Company

Data Element	Description/Example
First Name	Mary
Last Name	Porter
Address 1	456 Rue de St. John
Address 2	Floor 3
City	Toronto
Province or State	Ontario
Country	Canada
Postal Code	A3B3C3
Customer ID	Social Security Number or other unique ID
Role	Purchasing Agent
Title	Sr. Director of Strategic Sourcing
Company	Rogers Communications

What Do You Need to Know About Your Customer or Prospect to Market to Them Effectively?

The examples of customer records in Exhibit 3.5 represent the core of the data elements you might need to identify a customer for your products or services. But there are, undoubtedly, other pieces of information that can help you pinpoint customers more effectively. Some of this information may be gleaned from other systems. For example, understanding what customers have purchased in the past may require the order management or bookings source. If you sell a consulting service, it may be important to understand what engagements the customer has had with you in the past.

But there may also be information that your sales organizations or support organizations can add to the basic records of your customers. For example, it may be important to know the financial cycle of the companies you sell to—are they on a calendar cycle or does the financial year go from August 1 to July 31? Does this customer have a support agreement that carries with certain entitlements? Is this individual customer the head of the household?

Making the decision as to which information is most important for your marketing activity helps you to structure an effective data source. This is an important first step.

What Functions—Push, Pull or Analytical—Will You Be Asking the Data Source to Perform?

Marketing today requires that you perform all three of these important actions, but your marketing organization may have specific reasons for employing one or two of these discretely. Let's look at exactly what is meant by each action.

"Push" is a way of describing traditional database marketing actions. You have a message for a specific target market. You produce that message in some form—brochure, letter, email—and send it, or "push" it, to the prospective customer. "Push" strategies are dependent on knowing well your target customers and understanding how to reach them. For example, if you sell medical supplies to ear, nose, and throat doctors, you have honed your target audience to a specific set of individuals who may be reached only via phone. Push strategies are much more pinpointed and often depend heavily on accurate data sources.

"Pull" simply means that you make your messages available to your target customers but do not specifically address the messages to them. For example, if you sell beauty products to salons, you may find that positioning your messages on Yelp or Facebook may reach your market more effectively. From these sites, a buyer at the salon clicks on your message and is "pulled" to your website or order information. In this scenario, you do not require specific information on the potential target, but you do need to know interests and other general information.

"Pull" strategies are not exclusively limited to the Internet and websites. For example, posters or marquees in a shopping mall may draw or pull a customer into a specific store for a specific product or service. Here again, you don't need to know names of individuals, but you do need to know what attracts them. "Pull" strategies may not require the same kinds of data that might be employed in "push" strategies, however, over time, both strategies may accumulate similar information about the customers. How that data is acquired represents the key differences in these strategies.

The "analytical" approach or strategy is highly dependent on understanding customer or prospect behavior. This approach is often deployed in support of both the push and pull strategies and requires a robust data source. Building an analytical marketing data source may be the most difficult. First, an analytical data source contains all your key information about your target market and customer. This data can be about your customer specifically or it could be about the market your customer represents. For example, if you are selling refinery equipment to the oil industry, your analytical data source may contain up-to-date information on the price of oil by country.

An analytical data source for companies who transact primarily on the Internet may consist exclusively of web traffic data that is mined daily for insights about potential customer behaviors. The primary purpose of an analytical data source is to use data to target customers effectively and efficiently.

Deciding which approach fits your business best will make it possible for you to build the right data source.

How Will the Data Source Be Maintained? By Whom?

Building a marketing data source requires up-front thought about its "care and feeding." Data deteriorates rapidly. So thinking ahead about maintenance is a necessity. This also means that you need to think about what resources will be required for this task. Maintaining data is not a skill that most marketers have or want to acquire. If your organization is large enough, it may have the luxury of a marketing operations department that can maintain the data source. But if you are smaller and lack the resources, this is a particularly important decision.

In today's cloud world, there are many options for where to maintain your data source (see sidebar). Cost, accessibility, and data ownership are key considerations when engaging a cloud vendor to help with building your data source. Maintenance, however, can be one of the many benefits. Often maintenance as well as overall management are included with the contract.

In larger organizations, the IT department may be engaged to help in building your marketing data source. This is especially helpful if you need to connect your customer or prospect data to other internal sources such as orders or support records. Soliciting the support and help of the IT technologists can help you build and maintain a solid data source for marketing, one that can grow with your business. But be aware that IT often speaks a different language from marketing. It's helpful to have marketing technologists on your team when designing a data source.

Cloud Computing: What It Means

The "cloud" is everywhere. It probably dominates a lot of the conversations you've had lately with your IT professionals. They talk about the "cloud" as if it were as common as, well, a cloud.

But to businesspeople who haven't spent the last decade trying to understand the changing landscape of information technology, the "cloud" brings with it lots of possibilities and, equally, lots of risks. For those businesses that have decided information and data are key assets and want to manage them better, the "cloud" brings its own special considerations.

Just to level the understanding of "cloud" here's a quick definition. Wikipedia says this: *In common usage, the term "the cloud" is essentially a metaphor for the Internet.* Okay. That's partially right. It does mean that because of the Internet, we have the capability today to distribute computing power.

For example, we know that a desktop PC has the power to (1) compute or process, (2) provide applications such as Microsoft Office or Quick Books and (3) store your data. The "cloud," or the Internet, simply makes it possible for you to put these functions anywhere on the network that you like. That means that you can use the computing power of several server farms that process information faster than your desktop. You can access applications that don't reside on your PC, but on someone else's computer in another state. And you can store your data in large storage facilities—like renting a Public Storage unit for your data.

By distributing the functions that a computer does, you gain speed and agility as well as save costs. You don't have to buy computers for everyone on your staff nor create an IT department to manage them. You can "outsource" these functions to the "cloud." That's the real appeal of cloud computing.

When it comes to data in the cloud and the management and use of it for driving your business, then you have some additional considerations. Here are three questions to ask about data in the cloud:

1. Do I collect and store sensitive data?
   This is one of the first considerations around the "cloud" and data. If you collect and store sensitive data such as name, address, social security or credit card numbers, you need to ensure that your cloud provider has tight security, not only on the systems that store your data, but also on the facilities where the data is stored. It is a fact that the majority of data thefts occur, not from being hacked online, but from having data downloaded onto a thumb drive and walked out the front door. The recent Target data loss happened because the hackers got into a HVAC system that managed a store—not your usual entry point for computer theft. So ensuring that your "cloud" provider has covered all possible routes for data theft is your first consideration.

2. Do I need real-time or near real-time access to the data?
   Some businesses require that data be available instantly, or in real-time, from their applications or from processes that create the data. For example, if you own a catering business that is dependent on knowing the number of orders that have been placed for your services *before* you place your food order, you may need that information in real or near real-time. You can't afford to not have that data available to you in

aggregate form. You need a list of all orders broken down by items required to fulfill the menus and you may need it at a certain time each day or each hour, depending on your business volume.

Because most cloud applications are only as fast as the networks that serve them this can be an important consideration when deciding how fast you need access to your information. Remember, too, that some network providers charge for faster networks so this can become a consideration for expense as well.

3. Am I using data for operations, reporting, or analytics? All? Or any combination? Deciding up front what data you will need from your cloud provider is important. Do you just need a dump of the raw data from the application each day or week so that you can develop your own reports for operations or will you be dependent on the reports provided by the cloud application vendor? Will you have a requirement to delve deeper into the data based on the reports that are provided? Does the vendor allow for this additional data analysis? How will you handle the data analysis environment? Will you need to create your own data warehouse on premises or can the cloud vendor provide this capability?

If you are only storing data with a cloud vendor, what tools can you use to access the data? Will you need additional training or expertise?

Cloud computing is valuable to businesses because it provides flexibility and increased computing power at a reduced cost. But remember, your data is an important part of the overall "cloud" architecture and deserves careful consideration in each environment. Here's a quick chart to help guide your decisions.

Deciding Where to House Your Data

Consideration	Cloud	In-House	Outsourced
Expense	★		Maintenance
	★	Analytics Capa-	bility
	★		Real-time access
★		Sensitive Data	★

Legend:
Better choice = ★

Source: Excerpted from a column originally published in *Latin Business Today*, March 3, 2014. Used with permission.

How Will You Measure the Effectiveness of Your Data Source?

Building an effective data source for marketing can be expensive. So measuring the return on this investment is important no matter how big or small your marketing operation. Financial managers in companies want to see two measurements: 1) increase in orders or revenues and 2) decrease in expenses. Following this line of thinking, try to look at your marketing data source in these ways. Leads generated by marketing should turn into sales, but we know how difficult it is to maintain the lineage from marketing touch of an individual in a company to order placed. In companies with two or three-tier distribution strategies, the visibility to marketing's effects is obscured by the intervening channels. Managing the marketing data in these situations requires close relationships with partners and channels to ensure that data is managed by both parties and good contract negotiations require partners to report customer data beyond orders entered.

When measuring the effectiveness of marketing data, remember that you are not necessarily measuring the overall effectiveness of marketing, but of the data that supports it. In a survey by BlueKai in 2013, 91 percent of marketers agree that data is of primary importance for segmentation and targeting of their marketing efforts.Here are some basic examples of the types of metrics you could consider putting in place to measure your marketing data source:

1. **Measure whether the data used help marketers reach the target.** Was the email deliverable? Was the response rate from the marketing message up to your industry's standard?
2. **Data enrichment for better targeting.** Was the data complete enough to enable marketers to pinpoint the appropriate targets? What percentage of each data record is complete with valid information?
3. **Number of records for driving sufficient response.** Does your data source have the number and quality of records that your marketing team feels are necessary for driving leads and eventually revenue?

Measuring the effectiveness of marketing will depend on how complete and actionable your data sources.

So up to now, you have begun to formulate your data strategy and decide what you need from a marketing data source. If we were building a house, you would have had your initial "dream" session and perhaps identified an architect. Now, it's time to meet with the architect and discuss all the functions and features that you might need.

Efficient Planning for Data Architecture

"Measure twice, cut once," says the wise carpenter. And true, too, when designing for marketing data.Actually building the data source is the least expensive portion of the project. So plan carefully in advance. Thinking things through at the initial design stage saves time and money later.

Begin with a group of interested parties such as the marketers who will use the data source, the IT personnel who will help you build it or outsource it, and the sales and customer service people who can contribute to the data. Here are some important points to remember in gathering this team:

- Include all the channels within marketing that will be using the data—email, direct mail, advertising, events, product marketing, etc.

- Include representatives from your external partners or channels. In the B2B world, engaging your sales channels early in any project helps ensure that they are part of your solution.

- Identify a champion for marketing data. This is a person will own the accountability for marketing data, its use, and maintenance. This person is integral to the architecture planning process.

Here is a step-by-step scenario that you can follow for ensuring that your design session goes well. Start by gaining a consensus of understanding around the tasks that you will undertake:

1. Define what it is that you want to have when the task is complete. Do you need access to a data source? Do you need a database that you can manage and restructure when the business need arises? Do you need rapid access to web data? What role will analytics play?
2. Define how you will use the data. Will its primary use be for email to potential customers? Or, will you primarily depend on a pull strategy that engages the prospect first on the Web and then pulls them into revealing more of their needs as they encounter various portions of your web structures?
3. Locate all the data that you already have available. Look around to your order entry systems and your CRM systems to see what data is already collected. After reviewing what is available in the systems, locate all the data that you think would be helpful to your marketing efforts and record where it is and how best to obtain it on an ongoing basis.
4. Determine if it necessary to move or transform the data from these systems for marketing's use. If the data in your order entry system is incomplete and you require additional attributes to make the most of it for marketing, then you might want to move the order entry data into a marketing data-

base or source. If, however, the data in your CRM system is fairly complete and you value sales having the same data as marketing, you might want to consider keeping the sales and marketing data in the same system.

5. Define the levels of expectation for the use of the marketing data source. [See the sidebar on Expectation Management.] Once you are very clear on what you want from the marketing data source, you and the team should spend time to determine the service level agreements that need to be reached so that everyone's expectations are met. For example, if marketers expect that data will be instantaneously available to them the minute a sales rep enters into the CRM system, then you will need to ensure that there rules in place for the usage of that data and that both sales and marketing understand clearly what *is* and *is not* possible.

6. Define the success metrics that you will use for building the marketing data source. These might be different from the overall metrics that you choose when the data source is complete and working. For example, you may want to make one of your first metrics the identification and completeness of records for 100 percent of the customers who have purchased over $1,000 in the past quarter. This will give you both a glimpse into the effort it will take to secure the appropriate data and a view of the completeness of the data you already have.

7. Identify all the roadblocks that you may have and decide, in advance, how you will handle them. For example, budget is often a key roadblock. If this is true for you, take the time to propose and gain approval for a budget. If you anticipate resistance from the sales teams, align sales management to the project early—make it your first priority.

Managing Expectations in Building Data Architectures

A major pitfall in developing a marketing data source can come from the overblown and inconsistent expectations that the various parties are likely to have about what the database or data is going to do for you. It can be like a blind person describing an elephant.

One useful way to mitigate this outcome is to give design-meeting attendees some experience in how to query a database. Invite participants to write down a dozen or so questions they'd like to have answered by the database. You will quickly find that many of the questions people have in mind cannot be answered by the most beautifully designed data source in the world. For example, they may think the database is going to spit out answers to such questions as "Who is my best customer?" and "How many touches are required to close a sale?" Although the database may ultimately be designed to deliver these answers at nanosecond speed (often another expectation), data sources not structured for these kinds of queries can never yield these answers.

So caution participants that their questions must have the following characteristics:

1. Be a question, not a statement.
2. Quantitative. Avoid words like "why" and "who."
3. Objective. Avoid words like "best."

Here are some examples of how the questions should be built:

What the participant really wants to know	How the question really works for a database	Implications
Did my campaign work?	How many responses did we get to campaign X?	Each activity must have the ability to capture responses and make them available to inquiry.
How much money can we save by converting our communications to digital?	For how many of our customers do we have an email address?	If you have few email addresses for your customer, you have limited opportunity to communicate via digital means.
Which tactics are most effective?	How much revenue did the tactic produce? How much did it cost?	Each tactic must be discrete with results and costs associated to each.

Be prepared: The design phase is likely to be, in turns, painful, contentious, and boring.

If you hear any of the following words, from either potential marketing data vendors, or your IT department, beware:

- "We have a design that fits everybody."
- "I have a design. We'll just put your data into it."
- "We have this 45 percent done."
- "Let's focus on the 80 percent you need now. We'll worry about the other 20 percent later."
- "We'll just customize it."
- "We'll write some code."
- "I can get it done for you really fast."
- "Don't worry. I have most of it built."

These comments are signs that those involved in helping you are not listening to what you require.

The group assembled to help with the design of the marketing data source should be complemented by the ideas and advice of other groups after your initial design sessions. For example, it's often advisable to consult product fulfillment, accounting, legal, and inventory as well as other ancillary groups. Each of these teams may bring information that is very necessary to the design of your data source. For example, legal may advise that each email carry a designation as to whether the customer has given you permission to send unsolicited marketing messages. Accounting may insist on knowing the tax code for each company in the data source. And support may require the contact name of the person who can call the support line. All of these requirements could be represented in the data source.

In data source design as well as with countless other business decisions, the Pareto principle comes into play. Designing a data source that fits 100 percent of your customers may not be advisable when designing for 80% could be just the right requirement. The 80/20 rule serves you well in that most companies generate 80 percent of their revenues from 20 percent of their customers. It's advisable that you begin with a look at exactly who the 80 percent of your customers are, how they buy, what they buy, and how you best communicate with them. Be prepared for some political nightmares. There may be issues of control—for example, who really owns the data? Where should the data be managed? There may be issues of money—for example, where does the funding come from, now and in the future? By concentrating on the key customer group, you at least start with the core to your business operation.

Basic B2B Data Record Architecture

The data architecture of a B2B marketing database is built around the data associated with an organization such as IBM, General Electric, or another corporation. These companies can be public, private, for-profit, or not-for-profit. Each of these designations is important when building a B2B data source. Building begins with a key building block. In consumer data sources, the key building block is an individual consumer. Data sources are built around a person, that person's demographic information, and his or her relationships both to you as a product provider and to the family unit with which they associate.

Unlike a consumer data source, a B2B data source is usually built on a physical location of a business. With the advent of businesses born on the Internet, this description of "business" has changed slightly. But the fact remains that most businesses in the world have to receive goods, invoices, and tax records at some physical location. So in building a B2B data source, starting with physical location is a logical place.

Let's explore what physical location means, however, to building a complete record of companies like Berkshire Hathaway, IBM, and General Electric. We'll also explore how situations change when we move from U.S.-based Fortune 100-like companies to European Union and China-based organizations.

Although "site" or "location" is primary to the description of a business, other local layers make identification of a business more difficult. For example, an organization or enterprise may have multiple sites, and a site may have multiple departments that purchase. Often these departments are unique because they could be separate business entities in the same building. For example, you may sell to a company that houses its U.S. sales organization in the same location as its corporate headquarters. These could be two separate organizations represented in your order management system by two separate, legal contracts.

Managing contacts associated with companies only adds to this complexity.

Most order management systems, for example, keep track of who in purchasing should get receive invoices, but don't track on who actually makes the purchasing decisions. For marketing, this approach is of little value. Marketing needs contacts who make the purchasing decision and often those contacts are kept in the CRM data source closely guarded by sales.

Let's delve into some of the complexity born of identifying the right locations within a company and then tackle the issues around associating the right contact to the right location. You can imagine that this represents a challenge to data source design. Here's a brief explanation of each level from the example of General Electric below:

Global Parent is the highest level within the hierarchy of an organization. This is the headquarters name and location. In the example shown below in Exhibit 3.6, General Electric is the Global Parent.

Subsidiary designates the different businesses within General Electric—GE Capital, GE Energy, and GE Healthcare are all in separate businesses and, as such, operate independently of GE Corporate.

Country designates facilities associated with the subsidiaries that might be located in other countries such as Italy or the U.K. as well as the U.S. But even within those countries you can have different locations.

Exhibit 3.6: Corporate Structure of General Electric

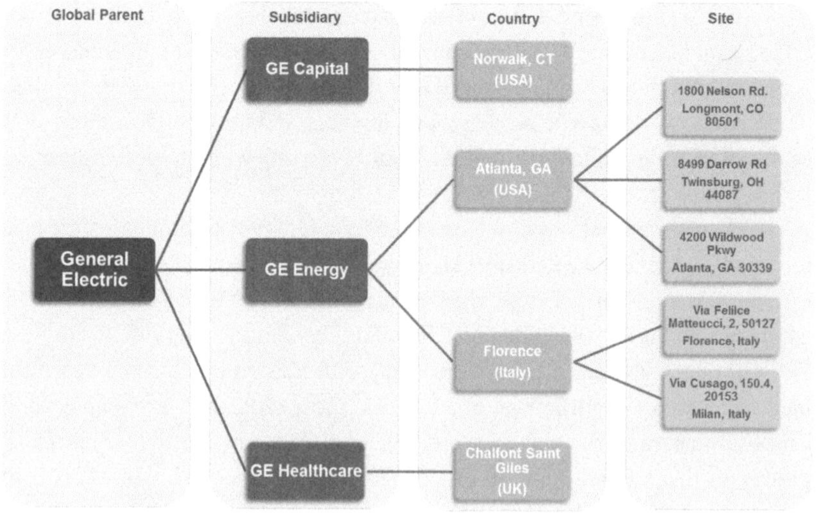

Each of the boxes in the diagram above could and should be a separate record in your data source but with the linkages established so as to be able to associate site to country organization to subsidiary to parent.

In addition to the basic information such as company name and location, there are other data elements that are helpful to the marketer. These pieces of information complete your understanding of the customer but, again, this is only information associated with the organization or company. Exhibit 3.7 below details some of the fields that are helpful to marketers and data source designers.

One of the areas listed in the exhibit is a DUNs number. For most B2B businesses, a D&B number is a requirement especially for communicating financial worthiness. But, D&B also has for the past twenty years marketed a data source called World Base. This database keeps track of all company changes and maintains the data quality of companies worldwide. When companies are acquired, merged or go out of business, D&B records this information and makes it available to its subscribers. In addition to providing company information, D&B also provides a D&B number. This unique number allows you to associate sites of a company to its subsidiary and parent.

The D&B number is extremely helpful in maintaining a data source for marketing, but it is not the only way. Some companies such as Avention provide their own identifiers on records. And, you can, of course, develop your own internal system should you have the time, money and desire. But having a key field to link data sources is a requirement no matter what the number. This aspect is covered in more detail in Chapter 9, "Troubleshooting."

Exhibit 3.7: Sample Database Fields

Key Fields	Examples of Additional Fields Needed for Marketing			
Company, Location	D&B	Product Specific	Market Intelligence	Industry Specific
• Record Identifier • Global Parent Name • Subsidiary Name • Country HQ Name • Site Name **Location** • Street Address • City • State • Postal Code • Country	• DUNS • # of Employees • Segment • Industry Vertical • Standard Industry Codes (SIC)	• # of units • Contract Status • Credit Worthiness **Relationship Type** • Consumer • Re-Seller • Partner • Distributor • Vendor • Systems Integrator	• Total IT spend • Annual Sales Local • Annual Sales in U.S. dollars • Local Stock Exchange Rank • Number of Servers and Desktops • Number of PCs • Total ITC Spend • Hardware Spend • Software Spend • Services Spend	• # of hospital beds • # of doctors associated with clinic • # of agents associated with insurance firm

Now, let's put this information together and show you what a complete data record in a marketing data source could look like (Exhibit 3.8):

Exhibit 3.8: Example of a Complete Data Record

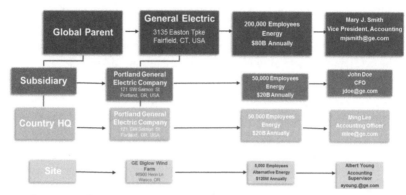

This view takes a company from its parent through to subsidiary within a country and site. At each level, the specifics associated with describing the company could vary. And, of course, the individuals who are important to your marketing efforts are different at each site or level within the company.

Master Data Versus Reference Data

Building a data source for marketing requires two kinds of data often managed by a corporate function. Master data and reference data help you maintain consistency of marketing data with other organizations. Here's a quick review of these kinds of data and how they affect marketing.

Master Data is a single source of business data used across multiple systems, applications and processes. Master data is often a record that acts as the source of truth for various entities across the organization. Product, vendor and company are some of the key master elements managed. Usually the data element contains key values that each department can share. For example, master data for a company should include company name, address and, perhaps, tax ID.

Reference Data is the set of values that are allowed to be used by other attribute fields. For example, "State" as a field in a data source can be completed with any number of possible designations. TX, Tex, Texas—all represent the state of Texas. Reference data, however, limits (for a specific field and particular system) the "state" designation that can be used to complete the field so that "TX" is all that would be allowed. In this case, the state field must *reference* another source, usually a data source specific to information like this. Most enterprise resource planning (ERP) systems have reference data as part of the design of the system, but sometimes you may have to build your own. Other examples of reference data include countries, postal codes, and specific abbreviations by country of address designations such as "St." for street or "Blvd." for boulevard.

The implications of master and reference data in building a marketing data source are important. The primary purpose of both is to create clean, quality data when entering a record. For example, you have probably entered your name and email address several times into a website for the purpose of purchasing a product, entering a sweepstakes, or retrieving information. When you are required to enter your address for product shipment, you may have noticed that the form asked for your ZIP code first and then automatically completed the city and state in your address. The information that this data source is referencing is a table or reference data that contains all the ZIP codes in the U.S. and associates them with the correct city and state. This keeps you from entering mistyped information and it keeps the data source clean for the company whose website you are visiting.

Master data has some of the same benefits from an organization perspective. If you work for a company such as IBM and go to a website to purchase something for your job, you may well be prompted to complete the company field with International Business Machines instead of IBM. In this case, the data source for the website could be referencing the master data that it has set up for companies with whom they do business. This master data could also be sourced from a reference file such as D&B, but the company whose website you are visiting may wish for all designations of your company to be carried as IBM US. In this case, they may prompt you for this name so as to ensure that your record matches others that they have in their systems. Master data is often transformed specifically for the company's use and may tie back to business practices that require particular naming consistencies on contracts and invoices.

Both master data and reference data can play important roles in developing your marketing data source.

The Challenge of Bringing in New Records

As you plan and execute marketing activities, you need to associate those activities with various locations or company sites and with individuals at those locations and sites that can make buying decisions. Your marketing data source needs to make the connection between company, site, and individual. This is a challenge.

Not only do individuals change jobs within companies often, but they also change companies. One of the most rapidly changing pieces of data in the business world is a person record for someone located at a specific company. According to MarketWatch.com, the typical U.S. worker lasts 4.6 years on a job. That may seem like a long time, but when the majority of workers are changing jobs at that rate, it's unrealistic to expect data to remain accurate for long.

Connecting individuals to their companies is important, but here's what usually happens. Someone from marketing attends a trade show or event and brings back hundreds of business cards. Here are a few scenarios that demonstrate the complexity of managing data from this seemingly simple marketing task.

Individual business card data gets entered into your marketing data source:

- Company name and contact data do not match anything in your data system.
  → Result: Good news—new, potential customer with new contact.

- Company name is in your data source but different from existing company name in your data source's master. (See the sidebar on Master Data.)
  - → Result: A new contact, but one not associated with an existing customer company.
- Company name matches existing customer account; contact does not.
  - → Result: Good news—you have a new contact at an existing customer
  - → Result: Possibly your contact exists at another company site or perhaps information on the contact's business card is different from information completed on your company's website. She entered Martha instead of Michelle, her nickname that she uses more casually.

These scenarios just give you a general feeling for how data can generate a myriad of different opportunities to affect quality

Your overall strategy for the marketing data source should help you decide whether the company or the contact is most important to your efforts in building a data source. For example, if your marketing department is most interested in determining which segments of the market would be most beneficial to approach with your product offerings, then closely managing companies, their overall ability to spend, and their industries will be more important to your marketing efforts. However, if you already are very aware of which markets you sell to and want instead to sharpen your return on marketing investments, you might decide to concentrate on the contact, the person who will purchase your product. If like most marketers, your immediate response is both, then you have the challenge of always connecting individuals to companies.

The record layout described in Exhibit 3.9 highlights which portions of a contact record are actually stored as a contact and which portions could be used by other systems and stored separately. Imagine, if you will, how this record would look with 150 contacts associated with one company address.

This record is for a customer who you may know more about than prospects who may have shared only their email address or some other pieces of this data. Linking partial contact records to companies can be accomplished but requires special support from firms that specialize in equating email addresses to certain larger firms. This works extremely well as long as the contact provides an email address that isn't associated with an Internet service provider such as Yahoo, Google, or AOL. There are some firms that can also trace messages back to the IP addresses of companies. This can provide some additional insight, but also doesn't help if Google manages the company's website as well.

With all of these considerations in mind, your next step might be to consider just how to organize your data source—build it yourself internally or get a vendor to build it for you.

Exhibit 3.9: Sample Record Layout

Field Names	Examples	
First Name	Jane	
Last Name	Smith	
Salutation	Ms.	Contact Master data
Title	VP, Strategic Sourcing	
Job Role	Financial analyst	
Job Function	Purchasing	
Relationship	Purchase approver	
Email	janes@abc.com	
Company	ABC Corporation	
Address 1	123 S. Street	Linked to Company Master
Address 2	Suite 100	
City	New York	
State	NY	
D&B #	132110	

Build the Marketing Database In-house or Outsource It?

In business markets, customer information is a critically important asset. The marketing database contains information essential to sales, marketing, customer service, finance, product development—the entire business. But many businesses find that maintaining a marketing database is a task they would prefer to leave to others.

Businesses typically make the decision to outsource the marketing database to an external services provider based on some combination of the following reasons:

- To take advantage of vendor skill and experience across multiple clients
- To shift the risk of technological complexity and obsolescence to the vendor
- To free up the IT department to concentrate on infrastructure concerns
- To free marketing from something that is often considered "not core" to the marketing competency

Deciding on whether to outsource or not is your first decision. Most consulting organizations suggest that you evaluate the task to be outsourced by looking at it as either "core" to your business or "context." Contextual capabilities are those that support the business but could be eliminated without a great disruption. Simply put, is this capability that you want to build essential to running your business or not? Although a basic question, it has great ramifications for marketing and goes to the heart of what your vision is for the marketing organization. This exercise often helps the marketing leaders decide exactly what their value is to the corporation. These questions can only be answered by marketing and executive leadership.

When the database outsourcing decision has been made, you are likely to follow a fairly well-defined series of steps:

1. Needs assessment and clarification of objectives. This may be the most important step. Without a clear understanding of what you are trying to accomplish, you will not be in a position to select the right vendor.
2. Executive sponsorship, buy-in, and budget.
3. Develop a project calendar.
4. Identify a vendor "long list." This is the list of anywhere from a handful to a dozen vendors who will receive your "request for information," or RFI document. Gartner and Forrester have active marketing operations consulting groups who can identify the key providers of this service.
5. Prepare the RFI document. (See Appendix 6 for a detailed outline of a proposed RFI.)
6. Send out the RFI, and receive submissions. Allow at least a week to ten days, for replies to come back. Make sure that you have included a deadline and that you stick to it.
7. Evaluate submissions and determine the vendor "short list." These are the three to five vendors who will participate in the "request for proposal" (RFP) process.
8. Prepare the RFP document. This is a complex but extremely important document. You will benefit from hiring a professional to assist you or turn this over to your strategic outsourcing team.
9. Send out RFP and receive submissions. Allow two to three weeks for replies.
10. Invite prospective vendors to present to you and your selected team of key marketers.
11. Select the final vendor, negotiate, and execute the contract.

Deciding what architecture you need is best done with a professional database architect and there is no ONE right architecture because the needs of companies are different as is the development of the marketing organizations. What fits Cisco today is not what was needed when the company first started. Making decisions about architecture means considering where you are today and where you think your company is going.

Build Your Data Architecture for the Future

Establishing a plan and an architecture for your marketing data source requires forethought and decision making. In this chapter, you have gotten a preview of the considerations and decisions required for setting up the architecture in the right way.

You start where all marketing should start—with the customers and your strategy for reaching, engaging, and selling your products to them. The data you need to deliver at each of these phases should be built into your data source. How you use the data will also help you decide what access you need to the data and when within your marketing process.

At the heart of your marketing data source is a record. Looking at this atomic level, whether it be a company or a contact, gives you a cursory understanding of the complexity that can be part of designing and building a solid, usable marketing data source.

And, then there is the question of how you get started. Do you outsource the entire task? Do you take advantage of the cloud market and engage a vendor whose tools can help? Or, do you build it yourself? All considerations for the architect of your marketing future.

The future looms large when developing a marketing data source. The tendency is to design for what you need today, but because these projects can stretch across quarters and years, it's advisable to consider where you would like to be in two to three years and plan for your marketing needs at that juncture.

CHAPTER 4

Managing Person Data in an Organizational World

Why Bother with Person Data in B2B Marketing?

Business-to-business (B2B) marketing is selling goods and services to businesses—groups of individuals who purchase for a particular enterprise where the end users of the services or products sold may or may not be visible to the seller. Selling goods and services to individuals is the goal of business-to-consumer (B2C) marketing. The main difference is that the individual reached inside an enterprise is usually making a buying decision on behalf of the organization—not for her or himself personally.

But who are we kidding?

B2B marketing is really about reaching the individual buyer, user, recommender, specifier, or influencer within an organization. We can't just market to ABC Corporation and expect that someone inside the company will get the message and respond. We have to reach these individual buyers in some way.

For example, if you sell office supplies, you may need the individual contact information for the administrative assistant who makes the buying decisions for the office and that contact may be sufficient.

If, however, you sell complex machinery for a company's manufacturing line, you may need the names of all the general managers who are involved in the decision—not just the name of the manager at the site where the machinery will be installed.

This means you need to have a contact management system that can help you identify the right person for the business decision that needs to be made and connect that individual to the right office location of their company.

To further complicate the identification of the correct person for the decision, you need to be able to identify the role that the person plays in the decision. Although their title may be Purchasing Agent, the individual you have associated with a particular company may not have the authority to purchase products in the price range of your products or they may not have the authority to purchase for a particular division or location.

In other words, you need to know far more about individuals within a business organization than their names, titles, and email addresses. And managing contacts in a B2B world is as complex as managing households in a B2C world and then some.

In this chapter, we explore the individual contact record—what data you should have on contacts, where this information is best stored, and how it can be managed successfully.

Rise of the Contact in B2B Databases

Marketing organizations have always understood that individuals make buying decisions, but as corporations get larger, more diverse, and begin to decentralize purchasing capabilities, the job of managing contacts responsible for buying your products has also become more cumbersome, complex, and often onerous.

Couple these facts with the reality that some companies whose products appeal to both individuals and corporations (take Microsoft or Autodesk, for example) have difficulty knowing exactly what the individual's contribution is to the purchase. Did he or she buy for themselves, or for several people within their department, or for the entire company? With online sales and corporate credit cards readily available, there is little confusion as to why this is an issue for some companies. And this situation leaves data management professionals confused and frustrated. It also leaves them with more than a few questions, such as:

- How do they ensure that they capture corporate purchases correctly? No matter whether the buy is for one item or fifty, sellers need to know who will be using their products.
- How do they know who deserves to be supported once the purchase is sold? If individuals buy the product but don't use it, then who does it go to and who will be calling for support if anything goes wrong with the product?
- What data do they as sellers need to capture and manage in order to ensure that they fully understand the buying patterns within a company?
- How do they manage contacts so that marketing messages are coordinated, not overwhelming, and actually deliver the right content to the right kind of buyer?

Throw into this already confusing situation new regulations on privacy that require companies to tread carefully around the use of personal data collected—no matter whether it's for B2B selling or B2C.

Legislation around the use of individual information has centered on the concept of first party, second party and third party data. Simply put, this means that if you acquire information on an individual through your own website, CRM system, or other registration capability, you have first party data and can use it as your privacy guidelines state.

If, however, you engage with other marketers, publishers, or your own reseller channel to use data that they might have acquired as first party data, the laws become stricter. This is now second party data, and here you must clearly understand what the individuals' expectations were when the data was acquired. Did they give the publisher or reseller the right to use their information with another party? If not, then you cannot use this information without violating privacy law.

In the world of social media, the real challenge is third party data. These are data assets available for purchase from a data exchange that may have acquired the information from other marketers, publishers, offline data aggregators, or from trolling the Internet. And the data is not always digital. Often times it can be enriched with purchase transactions or mobile phone location information.

For the most part, this information is usually not personally identifiable. For example, you may not know a specific email address. You do, however, know the behaviors of the individual and can create targets from those who act similarly.

Using big data analytics techniques, publishers and data aggregators can provide distilled, targetable segments of individuals. Although this is extremely helpful for consumer marketing, B2B marketers are just becoming aware of the power of this kind of aggregation for their own marketing efforts.

Privacy laws add complexity to the use of contact information in an Internet age, but individuals still make purchasing decisions, and in order to be successful, marketers still need to be able to talk to these individuals.

The Contact—What Do You Need to Know?

Let's start with the basics. A typical contact record in marketing databases today is shown in Exhibit 4.1:

Exhibit 4.1: Typical Contact Record

First name	Jim	Mary	Joe
Last name	Stanford	Smith	Taylor
Email address	jstanford@gmail.com	MSmith@us.ibm.com	jts@hotmail.com
Permission status	Y	Unknown	Y

Although this information doesn't help tremendously, it does give you a touch-point from which to build a more complete record—at least for Jim and Joe. Mary may be a challenge since your first contact with her did not yield a definitive response to your privacy inquiry. Depending on whether your company follows an opt-out or opt-in privacy policy, Mary has not given permission either explicitly or implicitly to your request to market to her.

But let's begin with Jim and Joe who we do have permission to communicate with.

Acquiring contact information for B2B marketing in the digital age is the equivalent to the process of dating in the twentieth century before Tinder and Match.com. You don't ask someone to marry you on the first encounter. You spend time getting to know them. You exchange information. You have valuable information about your products and services. Your contact has valuable information about him or herself.

With each touch, you should acquire additional information or develop processes for acquiring needed data from other sources. For example, the only information you have about Jim and Joe is their email address, which is not helpful for telling you which company they represent. So it might make sense that the next value exchange with these two could be your acquisition of a company name and location.

Notice, we did not say "address." At this point, it may be more important to gain business name and country or state/province. Doing business with international companies or across state lines may be an essential part of your marketing strategy, so understanding this key piece of data is often necessary.

Once you understand business and country or state/province, you can use a myriad of sources to help you fill out information. Exhibit 4.2 shows the records as you acquire new information. The shaded information is provided by the customer. The rest is completed with outside sources.

In follow-up exchanges with your two contacts, you can complete more information by showing them what you have acquired and asking them to help you refine it even further. This is called progressive profiling and is the best practice among B2B companies today.

In B2B marketing, it is important to understand not only the details of the business that we are selling to but the details of the individuals within the company who are making the decisions to purchase or actually using the product. Associating individuals to the right companies and gathering data on each person's role is important to the success of the marketing efforts.

At the heart of progressive profiling is a key tenet: each contact or use of a contact's email should carry some value with it if you expect to receive value in return, such as more information about the contact.

Exhibit 4.2: Contact Record as New Information Is Acquired

First name	Jim	Mary	Joe
Last name	Stanford	Smith	Taylor
Email address	jstanford@gmail.com	MSmith@us.ibm.com	jts@hotmail.com
Permission status	Y	Unknown	Y
Business name	The Gap		Joe Taylor Sales Inc.
State/Province	California		Ontario
Country	U.S.		Canada
Address 1	123 Merry Way		4567 Happy St
Address 2	Bldg 10		Suite 10
City	San Mateo		Toronto
Industry Code	3199		5063
Industry	Retail		Wholesale
Main phone #	415-354-2222		610-323-2351
Number of employees	3000		10
Turnover/Sales	$540M		$3M

However, as you can see, this data is limited. It tells you only the basics and does not help you identify what part Joe and Jim play in making purchasing decisions at their company. For that, you may need to understand Jim and Joe's job function, job type, and title. Each of these is very different.

Job function is the set of tasks or activities performed by a person in this position. For example, Jim may be a **purchaser** and Joe may be a **seller** within their respective companies. These are the functions they perform. Although their titles may be closely related to their job function—Jim is Purchasing Manager and Joe is Vice President of Sales—the two types of data can be extremely different.

Job type can also be a piece of information to help you market better. Type of job could relate to this person's role in buying within the company or it could be a way of helping you normalize or consolidate different types of titles across the world. For example, does this job type make decisions about your product or service or simply influence or recommend? Often a person's title does not help you determine this.

In most marketing databases, job type is a field reserved for the marketing department. Exhibit 4.3 provides some examples of ways we have seen Job Type used.

How individuals make purchasing decisions is important to the marketer and

Exhibit 4.3: Examples of Job Type in a Contact Record

First name	Jim	Mary	Joe
Last name	Stanford	Smith	Taylor
Email address	jstanford@gmail.com	MSmith@us.ibm.com	jts@hotmail.com
Permission status	Y	Unknown	Y
Business name	The Gap		Joe Taylor Sales Inc.
State/Province	California		Ontario
Country	U.S.		Canada
Address 1	123 Merry Way		4567 Happy St
Address 2	Bldg 10		Suite 10
City	San Mateo		Toronto
Industry Code	3199		5063
Industry	Retail		Wholesale
Main phone #	415-354-2222		610-323-2351
Number of employees	3000		10
Turnover/Sales	$540M		$3M
Job Function	Purchasing		Sales
Job Title	SW Purchasing Manager		VP of Sales
Job Type	End user		Decision maker
Job Type	Management		Executive

this aspect of acquiring individual information adds another challenge to data management.

Ever-evolving Buying Behavior Within a Company

Corporations today are, legally speaking, "individuals." In fact, the Merriam-Webster dictionary defines a corporation as "a large business or organization that under the law has the rights and duties of an individual and follows a specific purpose." It is a body authorized to act as a single person although consisting of multiple persons. It is legally endowed with various rights and duties, including the capacity of succession.

This really only highlights what marketers have felt for years—companies have personalities and as a result they buy in certain ways. Understanding a company's buying behavior is the reason we manage individual contacts within a company.

Because individuals make decisions, individuals use products—for the good of the enterprise.

The information that we need in order to understand this behavior is more extensive than name, email address, and phone number, and because it is more extensive, it makes data collection and management more of a challenge.

Just look at the kinds of individual roles that exist within a company—recommenders, influencers, decision makers, and purchasers. Each of these roles may play an important part in the purchase of your product or service.

How you determine the role an individual plays in the buying process is highly dependent on how you mine and use the data you collect. Exhibit 4.4 offers a few recommendations on what data is helpful in determining buying positions within a company.

Once you have mastered the buying cycle for your products or services, you have taken the first step to being able to successfully manage contacts. Knowing who recommends, decides for, purchases, and uses your products and services is essential to marketing success. These roles may be played by one individual within a company or by hundreds. It is marketing's responsibility to determine not only the buying process, but to identify as many of the individuals as possible to make sales more effective and efficient.

Understanding the Interplay Between Contacts in an Organization

Once you understand the buying process that your customers go through when evaluating or making the decision to purchase your product, you are ready to evaluate how to ensure that you get the right contacts engaged.

If your business is like most, you have contact information in a number of systems around your company. Salespeople keep contact lists. Accounts payable keeps contact lists. Support manages a database of contacts. Each of these systems uses different information about the contact but may indeed be using a record that depicts the same person.

Having one system to track, update, and manage contacts is essential. Having one system that allows you to bring information together on one contact is the ultimate goal.

Establish a Person Master

Like a customer or product master that maintains the definitive record of an organization or your products, a person master system maintains the definitive record of individual contacts for your company. This means that it treats all individuals

Exhibit 4.4: Data to Help Determine an Individual's Role in the Buying Process

Role	Definition	Examples	Data Element Indicators	Ways to Acquire
Recommenders	Individuals who may not make the final decision about a product or service BUT who recommend whether the product should be purchased	• Purchasing committee members • Managers of product users • Users	• Title • Job function • Support calls • Role in this purchase	• Online registration forms • Event attendance forms • Partner information
Salespeople Specifiers	In technical situations, this individual ensures that the specifications of a product meet the requirements of the customer environment	• Engineers	• Title • Job function • Role in this purchase	• Salespeople • Online registration forms • Partner information
Influencers	Individuals who do not make the final decision or even recommend one, BUT who have either explicit or implicit power in the buying process	• Executives • Managers • Consultants	• Title • Job function • Relationship to company	• Online registration forms • Event attendance forms • Partner information • Salespeople
Decision Makers	Those individuals who decide to buy a product or service (The test to see if you have a real decision maker is to ask if anyone in the organization can override his/her decision. If the answer is "yes," then you have a recommender, NOT a decision maker.)	• Managers • CXOs	• Title • Job Function	• Salespeople (Salespeople are usually the only ones who can really pinpoint a decision maker, although many forms ask this question.)
Users	Individuals who actually use the product or service that you sell	• Store managers • Administrative assistants	• Job title • Job function • Support calls	• Product registration forms • Event registrations • Online registrations

that you maintain in your data systems as one entity that can be tracked from system to system.

For example, if an employee quits your company and goes to work for one of your resellers, you keep track of this person by simply updating your person master record. It would change the status of employee to partner and maintain all the other information you know about that individual, such as personal phone number or experience.

Most companies maintain contacts within the marketing or sales systems simply because these organizations may have the most frequent use of the information. But wherever you choose to install your person master, it must be accessible to all users and systems that depend on contact information. It allows you to keep this information current and also provides a single source of permission status for areas within the company that want to communicate via email.

Persons can be maintained within your customer master system as well. In fact, one of the best practices within companies today is to maintain a Universal Person Code (UPC) and profile for each key individual buyer or recommender in your database. This allows you to maintain the important connection between individual contacts and the companies for which they work and gives you an ID number to help you in managing the contact data quality. When company information changes, contact information changes with it and all data elements can be managed by the same teams.

Recommendations for Managing Contacts for Marketing

Contact information is vital to any marketing department's success. Many marketing databases consist only of information on individual contacts. B2B databases as we've mentioned are organized for understanding company information as well as individual contacts within the companies.

Contact management, like account information management, requires both acquisition, retention, and development strategies. New contacts must be acquired when entering new markets or for keeping existing markets growing. Additional information on contacts may be required for servicing or renewing customer interactions. Each of these efforts requires careful thought and planning.

Here's a quick list of actions to take for managing contacts for marketing and sales:

- Canvass all internal systems for contacts
- Decide what contact information is most important
- Establish a progressive profiling program, the best-in-class practice of contact information collection

- Establish a robust data cleansing process to manage data decay
- Use data and eliminate non-used and non-useful data

Canvass all internal systems for contacts.

The first task is to ensure that you have appropriate contact information when your service department needs to call the individual at a customer account to check up on their product usage or to have the customer provide a satisfaction report.

Contacts can be gathered from sources such as accounting, purchasing, sales, product development, and legal. Each of these departments maintains contacts for their specific purposes, but may not realize how valuable it is to understand exactly how each of the contacts interacts around your product or service.

If you begin to gather contacts from CRM, you will soon come to realize that the contact information is "thin." In other words, there are few contacts and little information about them. The truth is that most CRM systems today do not act as true CRM systems, but as sales management or forecasting tools for sales. Still, CRM is your first place for gathering contacts because salespeople make it their business to know their customers.

Finance has contact information as well in the fields associated with purchasing and legal. Undoubtedly, finance knows who inside each customer account is actually responsible for processing the paperwork associated with an order. This is an important person to know for the marketing and sales teams as well.

The support organization also collects information on users of your product. This information is extremely helpful to both sales and marketing, especially if support is sold with the product or service. Understanding a customer's level of satisfaction is essential when developing marketing communications messages. Also, contacts maintained by support can be valuable to sales because the best prospect is a customer with a problem you just solved.

In most companies, marketing already has a head start in collecting contact information. It has one of the best uses of the data—messaging product or service availability, features, and pricing. When contact information is collected, marketing most likely performs a segmentation of customers based on the attributes of the individuals or contacts contained in the database. This allows marketing to create models that indicate which individuals will purchase within a given time frame, which will respond to communications, and many other indicators that help marketing market.

Decide what contact information is most important.

In each of the systems owned by support, finance, and marketing, the contact information may be stored differently and have unique attributes. In bringing these contacts together, the first task is to look at what attributes or information about the contact is most important and for what reason.

Ask yourself these questions:

- *Will contacts be used primarily for marketing segmentation, or will you depend on the company information, or both?*
This is fundamental to your marketing efforts in a B2B world. You may have a fair number of contacts that, when associated with companies, do not represent the company base that you need to reach. You may find that your best prospect companies are shy of contacts. This means that any marketing campaign aimed at your company segment may not reach its goals.

- *Will contacts be used only for email marketing? For events? For mailing?*
The answers to these questions will help you determine what information is important for each contact. For email marketing, you need an email address and permission to market to the contact. For events, you may need a telephone number. For mailings, you need complete and accurate addresses. Your marketing plan will help you determine which of these you require. Of course the answer is ALL of them. But if you are just beginning to build a database, you can start with email address and build your contact records as you develop additional marketing tactics.

- *Will sales use the same contact database? If so, what are the expectations for the use of the contact information?*
Answering this question helps you determine whether you require a monitoring system or not. Here's what we mean. In the B2B world, the laws governing privacy are specific only to unsolicited emailed marketing messages, the kind that marketing communications must send to tell prospects and customers about new products, invite them to events, or communicate product news. The laws specifically exclude communications regarding sales transactions between a customer and a company.

This means that customers can be contacted regarding product upgrades, orders, and other situations that are specific to a transaction, such as credit checks. When contact information is combined into one database for sales and marketing, you must be very careful as to how the contacts are used. Marketing cannot simply email all customers because they recently purchased unless the communication is specific to that purchase, such as a "thank you for doing business with us."

Managing the communication flow to these customers and contacts is essential. Sales may also be sensitive to the number of email messages sent to their customers and especially sensitive to their timing. Many an errant and ill-timed marketing message has thwarted an open sales opportunity by announcing a pricing change to a customer who was making a decision on a product at a higher price or inviting the customer to a product demo of the latest product when a sizeable order is in the works for a much older one. Co-ordinating messaging with sales is of utmost importance.

Establish a progressive profiling program, a best-in-class practice of contact information collection.

The process outlined in the section called "The Contact—What Do You Need to Know?" is essentially progressive profiling. This is the process of collecting information about the contact with each website visit or encounter. Remember, we said it's like dating in the twentieth century when you got to know a person a little more with each date.

Progressive profiling today is largely associated with the online marketing world, but in B2B marketing it's just as powerful to ensure that all encounters with a contact add to, correct, or replace the information that you already have.

In addition to progressive profiling, identity stitching has also become very popular in the world of online marketing. Identity stitching is the process of identifying all the different events on a user's path to purchasing your product and "stitching" them together to form a holistic view. Stitching together these events makes it easier to build models for customer interaction and helps marketers understand the effects of their marketing efforts.

But identity stitching is difficult and often anonymous. Users interact with your website, but also a host of other websites before purchasing your product. They use different browsers, clear their web cookies often, or use different computers— the one at work and the one at home.

For these reasons, companies need to have users identify themselves on the company website. By logging in or registering, the users identify themselves. When the user does this, you can then associate all the web traffic that you may have collected to a specific user. Building a contact record in this fashion often gives you valuable information on the user *before* you know who they are.

Establish a robust data cleansing process to manage data decay.

Managing the quality of contacts is by far the most laborious part of building a marketing database. Here's why: People have different ways of representing themselves—even in business-to-business communications. And they change this representation more often than companies change their identities.

Surprised? You shouldn't be, not in today's world of email anonymity. The average person has a minimum of two email addresses—one for business and one for personal use. But guess what—they often use both for business.

What this means to the B2B marketer is you cannot manage your contact database on email addresses alone. And you cannot manage this data without some help from the customer themselves, your resellers or distributors, and your sales organizations.

Here are just a few challenges to managing contact data:

- **Multiple email addresses for one individual.** Because this is so prevalent, most marketers do not try to connect email addresses for one individual. What they do is try to ensure that individuals are associated with the companies they represent no matter what email address they choose to use.

- **ISP masking.** If multiple email addresses weren't enough, you will also be faced with the inability to identify companies for individuals who elect to have Google Gmail, Yahoo, AOL, or any number of other ISPs host their email accounts. Obviously, not everyone works for Google, Yahoo, or AOL, but their IP addresses may give you the impression that they do. Individuals who use their computer from a work location often have IP addresses that originate from their companies. These IP addresses can be captured and associated to the companies they represent. For example, Demand Base and Profound are two companies that specialize in connecting IP addresses to companies.

- **Nicknames.** Not everyone uses the name that their mother insisted on putting on their birth certificate—the legal name that marketers want because it makes our job easier. In fact, the use of nicknames is on the rise, perhaps because it gives Internet users a simple way of distinguishing themselves and maintaining different personas for different kinds of web activities. The use of nicknames, however, creates a data management nightmare. Do you match Joe Smith with Tiny S if they work for the same company and have the same telephone number? Or do you only match Joe and Joseph?

- **Mobile phone usage.** As the use of mobile phones rises, marketers face the decision as to which phone numbers to associate with contact records. Do you collect the company number? Do you collect the direct line number for the contact? Do you collect their personal cell phone number? Do you collect all three?

  For some mobile phone users in the U.S., receiving calls is equal to placing them when it comes to cost. So contacting customers via cell phone, even by texting them, can be viewed as unacceptable. You should acquire permission for either of these outreach mechanisms.

  And with today's practice of retaining cell phone numbers when people move, you don't always know when you are calling a person. Waking up Jennifer at 6 A.M. in California because she has a Connecticut area code number can cost you customers.

- **Change.** We have already seen from previous chapters that company data deteriorates quickly. But individual contact information decays much faster.

This year alone nearly 80 percent of all individuals in business will change something on their business card—their phone number, their title, their address. This constant change requires relentless data management.

With these challenges in front of you, keeping contact information up to date in a B2B marketing database is daunting. The primary issue: how to determine which record survives when new information is presented. Here are some simple rules to consider when developing your own data management process for marketing contacts:

- **Develop a framework that evaluates companies first and associates contacts to companies**. The fact is we often do this exactly in reverse— we acquire contact information from our websites, events, third party lists first and then we try to associate them with the companies they represent. We really need to reverse the order of our work. We should start with which companies are important to our success and associate contacts ONLY with those companies. This also means that we spend less time managing contacts that are not valuable to us. Remember one of the time- proven adages in marketing: "It's not what you do, but what you don't do." Deselecting certain contacts because they represent companies outside your segmentation helps you spend time and money managing the best contacts.
- **Decide what source or sources you will trust the most.** Will you consider that customer-entered information is THE source of truth or will you deem sales entered data THE source? Or will you decide that neither is suitable? No matter which you choose be sure to establish a baseline for accuracy *before* making the decision. Most marketers wrongfully assume that customer-entered information is THE most accurate and for your company, it could be. But before making that decision, actually sample your contact data and spend the time and money to evaluate through direct marketing research whether the information you have is accurate. Once you determine the probability that one source is better than another, set up your data management systems to ensure that data from this source survives when other conflicting information is provided. Here's a secret—you won't get it 100 percent right. If your source is 80 percent accurate, consider yourself lucky and move on. The only constant in the task of data management is change itself.
- **Develop alliances with sales and partners**. B2B marketing benefits greatly from working with sales and channels. Nowhere is this more important than in securing support for managing contact data. Creating a semi-annual review process with sales and partners can help you evaluate whether your selection of "Source of Truth" is still valid. Involving your sales counterparts also helps to minimize friction between organizations on the use of contact

data. In creating this review process, concentrate on keeping it simple and easy to do. Your partners will appreciate it.

• **Set up a data management machine.** Organize a group of individuals who can manage contact data for you. Whether you choose to do this in-house or with an external agency, it's important that one organization have primary responsibility for this effort and that it develops the process and tools for managing this important asset. Refer to Chapter 5 on managing data quality. It will give you some good pointers.

Use data and eliminate non-used and non-useful data.

Maintaining accurate contact information for B2B marketing means constant vigilance regarding data quality, but it also means being very deliberate about what data you acquire and use. It starts with the usage.

Here's a good rule of thumb: Don't acquire data you won't use. Seems obvious, right? Wrong. Marketers are data hoarders—they never seem to know for sure when they might need that particular piece of data. So, they collect a lot of it. And worse still, they store a lot of it because, after all, storage is cheap. What's not cheap is the labor required to manage the growing size of accumulated data in marketing departments. More data means more complexity, more complexity drives labor costs up.

So how do you keep from acquiring a huge number of records? Begin with the end in mind. Start with canvassing all your internal systems for contacts at the beginning of this list and first decide why you need contact information and how you will use it. A plan is a helpful first step.

Then, make sure that you monitor each marketing person's requirements for gathering new data elements. Ask them the same questions about usage and maintainability. Just because one campaign needs to know the T-shirt size of the people they invite to an event does not mean that your marketing database must allot a field for maintaining this information in perpetuity.

Regularly evaluate your entire database for record and field usage. Notice that we recommend evaluating both record and field usage. The record usage tells you whether marketing is really considering this individual as important in the buying process. The field usage tells you whether you are collecting the right information about this contact. These evaluations together give you a very good idea of which information is most important to marketers. Use equals value.

Records and fields that haven't been used in three to six months should be marked for deletion or archived to make room for information that will be used. With marketing data contacts, the best message to marketers is: "Use them or lose them."

A final note: one of the most important fields to maintain in your marketing database is the field that tells you where you acquired the initial contact information. This is important when you start to evaluate your records because it will tell you whether your identification of the "Source of Truth" is serving you. It will also provide insight into which acquisition source is most effective. It helps to have this information close at hand when you negotiate with list or data providers.

B2B marketing is complex and made even more so by having to manage contacts in association with the companies they represent. Putting together a plan for what data is important, organizing a data management system and group, and enlisting support from sales and partners are all ways to help manage the daunting task.

CHAPTER 5

Data Management: Keep It Clean

Everyone in B2B sales and marketing complains about data. It's inevitable. People involved in selling to other businesses are well aware that they need to do a better job of collecting and maintaining accurate and up-to-date information about their customers and prospects.

The 2014 *Marketing Data Benchmark Report* from NetProspex sadly concludes that 84 percent of B2B marketing databases are "barely functional." A 2013 report from Aberdeen shows that only 38 percent of companies, on average, have a "well established process for cleansing" their marketing databases.

But there's hope. The same Aberdeen study says that 64 percent of "best-in-class" companies do pay attention to keeping their databases clean. Fortunately, there are steps you can take to keep your data clean and fresh. Unfortunately, this job often falls to the bottom of the heap, elbowed out by more glamorous needs like campaign planning, research, and strategy.

How Business Data Degrades

Business data is said to degrade at the rate of 3 percent to 6 percent per month. Jobs change, departments are reorganized—numerous forces conspire to make it tough for us to stay in contact with our customers and prospects.

This means a third of your information on business buyers and prospects may be useless by the end of every year. The result? Your communications may be un-deliverable. Your database may give you false intelligence. You are likely to annoy your customers. And you will certainly lose business opportunity.

Consider these vivid examples from D&B about the volatility of U.S. business data:

- A new business opens every minute.
- A new business files for bankruptcy every eight minutes.
- A business closes every three minutes.
- A CEO changes every minute.
- A company name change occurs every two minutes.

To help you think about the business impact of these changes, look at the annual rates of change for a variety of data elements, also from D&B:

- **Business addresses.** In a year, 20.7 percent of the business postal addresses on your file will have changed. So, if you are not keeping on top of it, nearly 21 percent of your business mail may be undeliverable. And it can get worse: If your customer is a new business, the rate of change is higher, at 27.3 percent.
- **Phone numbers.** Phone numbers change at the rate of 18 percent overall, and 22.7 percent among new businesses. No wonder your sales force is always complaining that your data is no good. Then consider the issues associated with maintaining phone numbers that allow for direct access to individuals in the companies you target. Collecting and maintaining mobile numbers is a greater challenge.
- **Company names.** Even the company name is unstable, changing at the rate of 12.4 percent among all companies and a whopping 36.4 percent among new businesses. How are you going to sustain a business relationship when you don't have the current company name?

But it's not only about data churn, it's also about the complexity of the business customer record itself. Leaving aside important database elements like purchase history and promotion history, let's just consider the contact information. In a typical B2B database, you need information about the company, the address elements like postal address, phone and fax, as well as the "firmographics," like industry and company size.

But many companies have multiple places of business, known as "sites," and marketers need to contact multiple people—buyers, influencers, product specifiers and recommenders, purchasing agents, purchase decision makers—at each site. Furthermore, some companies are part of larger enterprises and marketers need to keep track of those "family" connections, like parent company or sister company, because they influence buying behavior. Now you see why B2B database administrators tend to be a very patient lot.

This goes way beyond "four-line," which is the traditional mail order view of a business address. In fact, the U.S. Postal Service recognizes up to eight lines, including the mail stop, the contact name, lines for two types of titles, company name, department name, and the regular two-line address.

The Business Case for Clean Data

The benefits of clean data are fairly easy to demonstrate. At a high level, value comes from:

- Improved response and sales by reaching more contacts.
- Lower costs from less waste trying to reach targets at an incorrect postal address.
- Avoidance of the customer dissatisfaction that may come from being incorrectly addressed.
- Avoidance of fines from regulatory agencies for emailing to the wrong people.
- Avoidance of any poor perception of your company for using bad data.

In financial terms, Reachforce makes a compelling case in its 2014 ebook, *The Cost of Dirty Data*. Beginning with a hypothetical database of 100,000 B2B email contacts, Reachforce assumes each contact cost a dollar to acquire. Thus, the database represents a $100,000 asset value to the firm, in cost alone.

From there, an annual deterioration rate of 24 percent is applied, based on names going bad and duplicates, and another 2 percent is subtracted to account for spam traps. At this point, 74 percent of the email file is deliverable.

And there's more. Accounting for unsubscribes, the cost of storing bad records, and the cost of replacing the bad records, this calculation lowers the deliverable email rate to 49 percent. Reachforce ends up with an estimate of the annual cost of dirty data at over $83,000—on a database of 100,000 names. You probably wouldn't invest in an asset—a building or a piece of equipment, for example—representing that kind of devaluation in just a year's time.

These are all hypothetical calculations, but a vivid reminder of the importance of vigilance when it comes to keeping the data clean. And this doesn't even account for the price of the lost business that comes from the inability to stay in touch with current customers and acquire new ones. The results of a survey of marketing, sales, and business professionals done by Ascend2 (see Exhibit 5.1) shows that data quality—or the lack of it—greatly impacts marketing success.

Exhibit 5.1: Data Quality Is the Top Challenge to Marketing Success

Respondents were asked: "What are the most challenging obstacles to data-driven marketing success?"

Obstacle	Response
Lack of data quality/completeness	54%
Lack of skills and knowledge	35%
Lack of an effective strategy	34%
Inadequate marketing budget	30%
Lack of data-driven decision process	30%
Inadequate marketing technology	26%
Inability to demonstrate ROI	22%
Lack of consensus on importance	21%

Source: *Data-Driven Marketing Research Summary Report*, Ascend2 and Research Partners, 2014

The State of Your Business-to-Business Data Today

Part of the data quality problem faced by business marketers is definitional. While everyone says "My data is a mess," they may mean different things by it. Marketers, for example, may be talking about situations when their direct mail arrives at the target company but doesn't get delivered beyond the mail room. For salespeople, it's when they pick up the phone and discover the customer's direct phone number has changed.

But there are other ways the data may be wrong, or out of date. The business may have moved its offices. Or the customer's title may have changed. Or the data fields may be mixed up; for example, an old purchase order number that's parked in the customer name field. Or the state of Nebraska may be abbreviated NB, while the post office only accepts NE. Or the contact has left the company and you don't know where he or she is. It goes on and on.

Each of these problems is common in business marketing databases and creates enormous waste—of marketing communications investment and of business opportunity—not to mention frustration at all levels. So what can you do about it?

The solutions lies in data hygiene, defined as follows: *Correcting inaccurate fields and standardizing formats and data elements.* There are two general approaches to data hygiene: manual options and automated clean up. Let us look at what each of these can—and cannot—do for you.

Manual Processes

There are two key manual methods involved in data hygiene:

1. Enter clean data in the first place.
2. Institute ongoing updating processes.

The most important is the first: If the data is entered or received incorrectly at the start, you have not only wasted a business opportunity, you have created needless extra expense to go back and correct the information. Bad data is worse than no data at all.

Smart companies are using the following key methods for correct data input:

- **Master source.** Start with a master source that maintains the correct company information for all of your customers and prospects. Allow all applications that create customer views for leads, opportunities, sales, and support to access this information easily. A best practice is to build a look-up capability into each of these systems when it is necessary to create account-level information. The master also ensures that this information is corrected when it moves from system to system so that you can keep your information accurate.

- **IES standards.** Create and maintain a set of processes known as Input Editing Standards (IES). These are the rules for data elements that must be followed at the point of entry. For example, you might standardize all references to the International Business Machines Corporation as IBM. You would require that two-letter state abbreviations conform with USPS standards. And you would require that all titles be spelled out fully. Reference data sets are important for helping in this way. For example, maintain a list of all states with their abbreviations and make sure that this list is always accurate and referenced by those responsible for record inputs. Most companies create an input standards document when they first create a computerized database of customer information. But over the years that document may get lost, outdated, or filed somewhere collecting dust. Your first step is to find that document, review it, refresh it, and put it into use. If you can't find it, then you have to write one.

- **Training.** Train data entry personnel on the IES rules and repeat the training at least quarterly. Training is not just for new employees, it's also needed as an ongoing refresher. A corollary point: Don't expect to pay your key-entry personnel peanuts and get great results. They need substantial training and incentives to do a good job maintaining your data asset.

- **Address-checking software.** Use address-checking software at point of entry to ensure deliverability. Make sure that those developing applications for websites or internal operations use a standard approach to checking entries.

Starting out with clean data is only the beginning. As mentioned, business data tends to degrade at the rate of 3 to 6 percent per month, so you must invest in ongoing maintenance. Here are the best manual methods for data cleanliness:

- Train and motivate employees who have direct customer contact to request updates at each encounter. This includes call center personnel, customer service, salespeople, and distributors. It may be the job of marketing to keep the database clean, but data is a valuable corporate asset and everyone has a stake in its quality.
- Segment your file and conduct outbound confirmation contacts for the highest value accounts. This can be done by mail, email, or telephone. Commit to a certain level of accuracy for these accounts, and inform your sales team regularly on where you stand on this measurement, to bolster their confidence in the marketing data.
- When using first-class mail, request the address correction service provided by the USPS. Put in place a process to update the addresses from the "nixies," meaning the undeliverable mail that is returned to you.
- Invite your customers to help you maintain their information correctly. Make the contact information available on a password-protected website, and ask your customers to key-enter changes as they occur. Offering them a good reason to do so, or perhaps a premium or incentive, will result in higher levels of customer compliance.

The Automated Method

Once you have manual methods underway, send your data out to a service provider for regular clean up. We recommend data cleansing at a third party at least twice a year. Large providers of business data are skilled at matching your file to their databases of standardized, updated records and giving you back the good information. On a per-record basis, automated clean-up is inexpensive and should be combined with an ongoing manual program of data hygiene.

There is quite a bit of misapprehension about the nature of automated data hygiene. Because it involves a matching process against a larger national database, some people confuse it with other data processes. So, before we go into more detail about what it can do, let us be clear about what we *don't* mean by automated data clean up for business marketers.

Sending your names out for clean up is not to be confused with:

- De-duplication, which means identifying records that qualify as duplicates
- Data append, which means adding extra fields like an industry code, years in business, a credit score, or company size

At the same time, it's important to realize that automated data hygiene cannot clean up everything on your database. For example, changes to a person's title or direct phone number are unlikely to be reported with any speed to a national database, so much of the time the vendor will have no fresher title or phone data than you have yourself. Some help has arrived recently with the new services that scrape information from corporate websites, but this data is usually limited to very senior executives. And make sure that your legal department has cleared your use of this kind of harvested data.

And there's another matter to consider: Whose data is correct? If the name you have on your file for a company or a person is different from the name on the national database, how will you decide which one to accept? Most companies give preference to the data that was most recently collected or confirmed with customers.

The national databases maintained by various vendors have only one ultimate standard against which address accuracy can be measured, namely, the USPS. In fact, the only "true" address, street, state, and ZIP code, are those recognized by the postal service. This means you can count on the outside vendors to clean up addresses to the point where they will support mail delivery, but you can't have the same level of confidence in the potential clean up of telephone numbers, fax numbers, email addresses, and job titles. For such elements, verification via outbound contact and/or inbound web-based updating is the only method to ensure accuracy and timeliness.

This may be a disappointment to those who were hoping that they could simply "send our data out for clean up." In fact, the best method for ongoing maintenance of many important data elements used by business marketers is outbound contact and verification. Because this is an expensive and time-consuming process, we recommend that you verify your most valuable accounts first and then decide the benefit of continuing on to your lesser value accounts.

Data Hygiene Best Practices

Business contacts tend to represent a lot of value, so it is both important and potentially profitable to invest in data hygiene. Here are some ways to keep customer and prospect data fresh and up to date.

Standardize and Format Business Addresses

- Standardize your format of business addresses. Refer to Publication 28 from the USPS for examples of recommended field selection and layout of business addresses. It is available for free as a PDF and can be downloaded at: http://pe.usps.gov/cpim/ftp/pubs/Pub28/pub28.pdf.
- Reward good behavior. Good data and data hygiene can mean money to your company, so why not share the wealth?
  —Determine how much data quality costs your company.
  —Determine what your company can save thanks to good data.

—Share the savings with your employees as motivation for help in keeping data clean.

- Include three types of address options for a customer: Ship to, Bill to, and Mail to.
- Add an open-ended field for "delivery instructions" to keep any such instructions from getting into your name and address fields. But remember: Open-ended fields are not to be used for selection or for later marketing efforts. They are only useful if someone is going to actually read and act on the content. Open-ended entries are there because there is some other problem with the database, either in its design or in the user's training on its proper use.
- Keep an eye on your software as it ages. Consider updating your software as new required fields, like email address and LinkedIn URL, enter the business information universe.
- Good address standardization and consistent formatting helps reduce duplicate accounts, allowing both internal and external duplicate identification programs to work more effectively.

Establish Good Data Entry Practices

- Focus on entering the data correctly in the first place. Create a standard operating procedure for data entry, and train your key entry personnel on it.
- Find the Input Editing Standards document that was developed when your system was first created. It's probably buried in a file somewhere in your office. Use these standards to train personnel who do key-entry. Update the document as needed and keep it current.
- If you could not find the original Input Editing Standards document, you must create one from scratch. This is not a trivial task, so you may want to get some professional help. And be sure you have a plan in place to put the document to use.
- Consider naming a small number of data standards specialists who will maintain the standards on an ongoing basis, craft updates as needed, and serve as go-to people for the rest of the data entry personnel.
- Make sure your call center personnel are compensated correctly. If they only receive commission on new orders entered, you are likely to end up with a lot of duplicate records. People will do what they are paid to do. If clean records are important, pay them for accuracy.

File Cleaning and Updating

- Use data cleansing software regularly. Send a sample of your data to hygiene vendors to find out which one does the best job on your file.
- Run your house file through the U.S. Postal Service DSF2 (Delivery Sequence File) protocol, which identifies whether an address is a consumer household or a business. Large database marketing companies like Harte Hanks, Acxiom, or Anchor Computer can help you with this. The process will allow you to sort out residential "3-line"addresses from real business addresses that just happen to be missing a company name. It also identifies potentially undeliverable business addresses. But keep in mind that if you are marketing to SOHO (small office/home office) targets, which are often based at residential addresses, this technique will be of limited value.
- Take regular statistical samples of the data and check it manually, using an outbound phone call. Decide in advance the acceptable incidence of errors in the record. If that error rate is exceeded, then undertake an outbound communications program by phone and email to update the records. You may want to segment the file, investing more in keeping up data about your best customers and less in those who have not bought from you regularly.
- Ask for customer data regularly, and make it very easy for the customer to provide the information. Always ask for the information the same way—no matter where you ask for it.
- Encourage your best customers to maintain their own data on your website. Build a password-protected area for them to use, and explain the value to them in maintaining contact with you, their supplier. You might even consider offering an incentive, whether better terms or a discount.
- Use data analytics to create exception reporting. Have your less-busy call center shifts review the exceptions and clean them up, either using common sense or through outbound contact to verify. If you are facing a large volume of exceptions, segment by customer value and deal with the most valuable first.
- Pay for postal returns (endorsements) and update your files with the returns. This should be done at least once a year, and ideally two to four times a year.
- Conduct an audit of your best customers' mail room processes. This is often extremely revealing. In some larger firms today, mail is not distributed regularly. Some firms even have a standard practice of not distributing obviously commercial mail. Find out what the processes are for your key customers.
- Also evaluate how your target firms deal with email. IT departments today are using all kinds of filters that keep your email messages from reaching the target.

- Learn the pros and cons of the different endorsement options and how they operate within both Standard and First-Class Mail:
  —Address Change Service (ACS)
  —Address Service Requested
  —Return Service Requested
  —Change Service Requested
  —Forwarding Service Requested
- USPS.com has a wealth of good information and tips on addressing options. Find them at:
  —www.usps.com/businessmail101/addressing/specialAddress.htm
  —www.usps.com/directmail/undeliverablemail.htm
  —www.usps.com/business/addressverification/welcome.htm
- Add NCOA as a new address, and mail both old and new addresses. But after mailing the old address once, you may want to suppress additional mail to the old location.
- Send a sample of your data to hygiene vendors to find out which one does the best job on your file.
- Use overtime or off hours (second/third shift) to review suspect records identified by the outside vendor.

Company Classification and Identifying Buyer Roles

- Standard industry codes like SIC and NAICS are extensive, complex, and difficult to use. Decide what value these codes provide and use them only when they make a great difference to your marketing efforts.
- Don't bother asking customers their SIC or NAICS codes. They don't know it. Other options:
  —Provide a menu of industry-level classification options, such as Manufacturing, Distribution, Retail, etc.
  —Append the data via an outside supplier.
- Number of employees can be just as important as SIC, and can be obtained by third-party data append, or directly from customers, especially if you provide check off boxes and ranges. But keep in mind that number of employees is tricky. You must decide whether you want the number of employees at each location or the number of employees for the entire business, no matter how many locations. Again, this data element should be important to your marketing strategy, otherwise don't collect it.
- Buyer role is very subjective. The best way to gather it is to use drop-down menus. Include an open-ended field they can write in if their role does not appear. Keep in mind that open-ended fields will not allow the data within

to be used for selection, but they can be used to spot high-frequency titles, which you can then later add to the functional drop-down menu.

- Use separate fields for actual title and functional title. While this approach is ideal, most companies have just one field allotted.
- Invite customers to self-classify online whether they are business, consumer, government or education, so your name and address screens can be tailored to make sense.

Handling New Customer Data

- Make it very easy for the customer to provide their contact information. Always ask for the information the same way—no matter where you ask for it.
- Train new reps on your input standards. Give all reps refresher courses every ninety days. Send out frequent reminders and updates to the reps.
- If you need to verify before shipping, use a service such as QAS, Group 1 or Firstlogic, to identify suspect addresses and send them to customer service for review. Ideally, this process can be set up to be interactive so the customer service rep can make fixes on the spot.
- Consider conducting a human review of all Internet-based orders from new customers.
- Confirm email address by sending an order confirmation or a newsletter. If it bounces, then verify the address by outbound phone.
- Improve email capture rates by requesting that the email be typed in twice.
- Some vendors, like QAS, offer software that lets the customer review a suspect address in real-time. It can pop up a message saying something like "Please look over your address and make sure it's correct." Or it can identify the actual problem and offer valid alternate choices.
- Use input edits to either prompt the customer on problems or to kick out orders for manual review.
- Here are some characteristics that make an address suspect:
  —ZIP does not agree with city/state
  —Address does not exist with ZIP
  —Missing/wrong directional on the street
  —Building number does not exist within the street

Capturing and Maintaining Customer Data Supplied by Field Sales and Business Partners

- Create automatic look-up tables that include a listing of the existing companies that occur within your files. This way, instead of creating new company records, salespeople or business partners can first choose from pull-down menu items listing names of companies you are already doing business with.

- Also create standardized lists for such fields as function and level in your database values. This encourages your teams to choose from a pre-defined list and improves consistency, quality, and accuracy.

- Develop logic-based programs. For example, you can automatically populate the city and state fields based on ZIP code, or you can generate an error message if an area code doesn't match an address.

- Sometimes the toughest problem with data from salespeople is getting their cooperation in the first place. Salespeople should be selling, not diverting their attention to administrative functions. So you need to devise a data capture method that does not interfere with their work. Ideal is an automated feed from their contact management system. If you can provide value by updating their data, they are more likely to cooperate with you.

- The biggest issue in data that comes from third parties is that of duplicate records. Small differences in the company name, address, or phone number can cause them to look like new and unique records, resulting in wasted duplicate outbound contacts—not to mention embarrassment and customer frustration. One solution for duplicate records is technology that matches the duplicate entity and retains the unique elements in a master record. This can save you from mistakenly purging a valid but apparently duplicate record.

- Tie together companies that have a business relationship, similar to house-holding in the consumer world. This "family linkage" will reduce the incidence of duplicates, allow more efficient selling, and help identify business opportunity in your accounts.

- Sometimes people will look for any way to just fill in a data field, so set up programs to reject common field fillers, like all 7's in a phone field, or all X's in the company field. It's also helpful to maintain a file of "not so nice" words that when matched can let you eliminate the record.

- Do not permit illogical key entries. For example, a phone number field should not accept characters, and a title field should not accept all numbers.

- For actual order entry, it's well-nigh impossible to get your salespeople and business partners to learn and follow your data entry standards. Instead, pass the orders to trained customer service reps for key entry.

- If you do decide to have salespeople or business partners enter orders, use interactive editing tools to flag obvious errors or duplicate records. Or put in place a post-entry screening process to review orders before they are shipped and billed. Recognizing or paying sales and partners for quality data entry is the best way to ensure quality data.

Determining Duplicates

Figuring out whether records refer to the same person or company—a process known as de-duplication, or merge/purge, is a source of great aggravation for B2B marketers. Given the complexity of the B2B customer record, there are few effective solutions to the problem.

The best approach is to determine in advance whether you want to determine duplicates based on the contact, the site, or the enterprise. For example, the following records are all for the same person, but the data can come to you in several formats:

Bernice Grossman	Bernice Grossman	DMRS Group Inc	B. Grossman
DMRS Group Inc	304 Park Avenue South	304 Park Avenue South	DMRS Group Inc.
304 Park Avenue South	New York, NY 10010	New York, NY 1001	304 Park Ave S
New York, NY 10010	New York, NY 10010		

Say you are the kind of company that is marketing to certain sites and you have chosen the site level as the basic element of your marketing database. In campaigning, you are likely to communicate—by direct mail, for example—with a variety of the contacts you have at the site. Plus, you might enhance your coverage of the site with mail addressed to certain additional titles or functions at the site, to try to reach contacts who are important to the buying process but whose actual names you don't happen to have.

In this situation, your de-duplication process is best done at the site level. You would identify that unique postal address as a match, and then you would look for the same last and first name at that address. An identical name appearing at another address would never qualify as a duplicate.

If, on the other hand, your database architecture is based on the contact, your de-duplication process would give equal weight to the name and the address. You would consider the following records to be duplicates:

John Smith   John Smith
ACME Company   ACME Company
123 Industrial Blvd.   P.O. Box 123

Enterprise-level de-duplication decisions are usually done via a commercially available identification code like a DUNs number, ABI code, or A-T number. Each enterprise is identified with a unique indentifying code. New records are given an enterprise-level code, and then matched against the records in your marketing database.

No matter what approach you use to keep data accurate and complete, the investment is worth it. It helps you reach customers effectively and efficiently, as well as helping you maintain a good working relationship with sales and business partners.

CHAPTER 6

How Business Marketers Use Their Customer Information

Gathering data in any form can be an overwhelming task for marketers who may not be technologists as well. But once gathered, making use of the data requires additional skill and capability. This chapter deals with making use of the data you've collected and managed, either within your own databases or via a cloud application.

For traditional marketers, analyzing the market for where the opportunity lies can be a crucial first step. Analyzing the market for where you can best serve it is one of the first uses of your data. This analysis leads to identification of your best targets. In B2B, targets often begin with the identification of companies appropriate for purchasing your product.

For example, if you are lucky enough to have some market research about your product, you have the beginnings of an understanding of your market opportunity. What's trickier is translating that opportunity into actual companies that need your product and actual people within that company who can make the decision to purchase it. This chapter gives you some guidance as to what data may be used for what purposes in your marketing environment.

Data provides market understanding, measures market response, and can help move a lead to an opportunity for sales. Data provides insight throughout this process. Exhibit 6.1 outlines some of the different types of data and the analyses that can be used at each step in the marketing process.

The list in Exhibit 6.1 represents only a small portion of all the ways data can be used to inform marketing actions. In fact, here are some very specific ways to use data that are explored throughout this chapter:

Exhibit 6.1: Examples of Types of Data and Data Analyses

Process Step	Types of Data	Types of Analysis	Outputs	Examples
Market to Demand	Survey data to research a specific area	Market intelligence	Primary research studies	Descriptive view of market your product serves, such as personnel directors in SMB companies
			Pricing analyses	Direction on pricing for your product or service
		Segmentation	Similar groups that share like preferences and/or attitudes	Personas of groups that are evangelists for your product or service—first movers
				Analysis of your existing customer sets to find which customers are most profitable
				Analysis of customers to understand how they budget for your products and how much of that budget they have spent (share of wallet)
Demand to Lead	Customer purchase data	Campaign planning	Existing customer retention	Reward program for customers who are regular purchasers
			Development of most profitable accounts	Offer of additional products and services to existing accounts
			New customer acquisition	Analysis of non-customer accounts that are similar to existing customers (look-alike analysis)
	Response data	Campaign analysis	Target segment response	Analysis of who responded with view of how often they passed along the information and to whom
			Target behaviors	Tracking of targets behavior on your website
	Sales data	Lead analysis	Sales leads	Hot/cold analysis of individuals who fit sales's requirements for purchasers within a given time frame

Process Step	Types of Data	Types of Analysis	Outputs	Examples
Lead to Opportunity	Purchase data	Propensity to …	MPriority score on each lead indicating a specific next action	Customer list with prioritized score indicating customer's likelihood of purchasing your product within a given time frame
		Market basket analysis	Analysis of what can or should be offered to a customer	List for each lead of products often purchased at the same time or within a given time frame of each other (e.g., support at time of product purchase)
	Partner data Channel purchases	Channel analysis	Analysis of which channel can best act on the lead	Distribution of lead to appropriate channel

- Support sales and communications channels with data about customer behavior.
- Model and predict customer behavior.
- Query and perform "what-ifs" to stimulate marketing ideas and actions.
- Profile customers to gain insight into their needs creating what are called "personas."
- Segment customers for differentiated treatment.
- Simulate and test audience response to new product introductions.
- Identify prospects, score them for sales potential, and nurture a relationship with them until they are ready to buy.
- Select customers and prospects for promotional campaigns.
- Measure campaign performance.
- Track marketing tests and experiments.
- Build and sustain customer relationships by using specific information about customers.
- Track and manage the entire customer experience.

The uses of your data depend entirely on what you want to accomplish, on the marketing strategy your company has put in place. This is especially important to guide not only the use of the data, but the acquisition and maintenance of it as well. Using data acquired from market analysis, customer and partner interactions, as well as from internal business processes, makes it possible for marketers to paint accurate, helpful pictures of their customers, their needs, and their behaviors.

The Unified Theory of Database Marketing
by Ruth P. Stevens

Database marketing is all of a sudden the new holy grail. What with CRM, data warehouses, one-to-one marketing, data mining—a number of techniques are capturing management time, attention and bucks, and they are all built around customer information. So now we have new opportunity to pick up some of the powerful approaches that database marketing has been developing over the last fifty years and apply them to our Web businesses, to generate substantial value.

That said, there is a general misconception abroad about what database marketing can do. I'll never forget the comments of a very senior but very uninformed sales VP at a company I was associated with several years back. My job at that company was to help apply database marketing to an old line business that had lots of data but little clue of how to put it to work.

This sales exec, who was extremely influential, indeed powerful, was in a position to be a valuable supporter of the project. But to hear him talk about database marketing was to cringe. Here's the kind of thing that came from his mouth: "This stuff will let us find blue-eyed one-armed paperhangers who graduated from Yale, and then we'll be all set."

Yikes! What's a database marketer to do? The spirit is willing but the flesh is weak. I know that somewhere, deep inside, he "got" what database marketing is generally about, but he had no clue as to the art of the possible.

So I am inclined to lay out a few principles of what database marketing can do and can't do. What database marketing is really about. And why it's so powerful.

The first thing we have to keep in mind is data availability. My sales VP's confusion was that he didn't understand that marketers only have a very limited amount of information about customers and prospects to work with. We may have our customers' transaction history, some demographics we've gathered or rented, and, if we were smart, our promotion history.

Then, database marketing boils down to three major marketing applications: profiling for look-alikes, segmenting, and predictive modeling.

Profiling for look-alikes. Profiling usually supports customer acquisition. This application analyzes current customers or, better yet, our best customers, and identifies their characteristics. This is called a "profile," and might be generated by a cluster-type analysis (CHAID or CART) or a multi-variate regression analysis, where various characteristics are identified as having either positive or negative correlations.

Once we know that about our customer, or our ideal customer, we can then apply the model to vast universes of unwashed prospects, select the closest matches, and then communicate with them. In theory, and usually in practice, these modeled "look-alikes" will be much more likely to become good customers for us than the great unwashed universe as a whole. Profiling uses analytics to identify strong prospects, saving vast amounts of money that might be wasted on promoting to the uninterested.

This approach can also be used in reverse, profiling unprofitable customers, for example, and using those characteristics to suppress, or avoid doing business with, undesirable new customers.

Segmenting, and treating the segments differently. This application is primarily used for customer retention marketing. The idea here is that not all customers are of equal value, or have similar preferences or buying patterns. So a smart marketer will analyze the customer base regularly, divide the base into groups, and set up programs, policies, and processes that allow them to be treated differently, to increase the likelihood that they'll buy more, and stay longer, or whatever is the marketing objective.

The classic segmentation analytic is RFM, where the customer base is regularly grouped based on the recency, frequency, and monetary value of their transactions with the marketer. RFM is easy to perform with the kind of data most sales operations have lying around, and it is extremely powerful at identifying individual customers by value.

There are hundreds of other ways to segment, too, depending on the needs of the business. Segment by purchase channel preference, or by sales coverage, or by prior purchases. By geography, language, or demographic characteristics. The only requirement is that the segment needs to be real, meaning people in one segment are truly different from another, and that the segment is useful, meaning that there is some real business value to be had by grouping people this way.

Predictive modeling. Some may argue that this application is nothing more than another type of profiling. I wouldn't disagree. But I call it out because it is such an important contributor of value to the whole notion of database marketing.

Predictive modeling is used to identify the likeliest people among a customer or a prospect universe to respond to any given marketing campaign or offer. It considers not only the characteristics, but the purchase or response propensities of the buyers. It's perfect for up-selling and cross-selling.

Predictive models may sound a bit like voodoo, but they are based on a simple concept quite like the one used in profiling: finding look-alikes. First, we identify the people who did buy that product, say, or who bought through that channel, or who bought at that certain point in their relationship with us. We identify their characteristics, which include not just who they are, but also when, where, and what they tend to buy. And then we apply those characteristics to the rest of the population, looking for the likeliest prospects for the campaign or program.

So that, my friends, is that. If you happen to have data about one-armed paperhangers, who knows, it might be predictive of future behavior. The point is, database marketing is very straightforward, it makes a lot of sense, it's a powerful marketing technique, and it deserves to be better understood.

Uses of Data in B2B

Customer behaviors are essential to marketers today. The Internet has provided unlimited ways to guide, position, and engage with customers and potential customers. But when web data is combined with traditional data obtained from trade show events, telemarketing, sales representatives, or data suppliers, the richness of the information about customers grows.

Bernice Grossman and Ruth P. Stevens conducted a survey that showed what marketers were really doing almost ten years ago. Marketers haven't changed much. With the push to big data, these percentages will only have increased (see Exhibit 6.2).

There are essentially four basic uses for marketing data in the B2B world: targeting, testing, tracking, and trending. Each of these requires different view of the data, sometimes the same set of data from a different angle, sometimes enriched data that provides more insight. Let's look at each of these areas separately.

Exhibit 6.2: How B2B Marketers Use Their Databases

Uses of Marketing Databases	Response Percent	Response Count
Marketing to prospects	80.11%	145
Campaign target selection	70.72%	128
Contact or inquiry management	61.33%	111
Query	60.22%	109
Export data (e.g., to your mail house, or email vendor, or to a co-op database)	57.46%	104
Campaign response tracking and analysis	44.75%	81
Import data (e.g., from in-house sources, like operating system, sales force automation system, or from your website)	44.20%	80
Customer profiling	42.54%	77
Capture data about end-users	36.46%	66
Perform data hygiene/record deduplication	31.49%	57
Segmentation for product development purposes	29.28%	53
Identify multi-buyers	28.73%	52
Data append or enhancement from 3rd party supplier, like D&B, InfoUSA or Experian	28.18%	51
Campaign strategy planning	27.07%	49
Identify unique buyers at a site	18.78%	34
Lifetime value (LTV) analysis	14.92%	27
RFM	13.26%	24
Modeling to predict campaign response	13.26%	24
Modeling to predict sales or purchase	12.15%	22
Predictive modeling using regression	9.94%	18
Predictive modeling via cluster analysis	8.29%	15
Modeling for winback or reactivation	8.29%	15
Predictive modeling using tree algorithms like CHAID or CART	7.18%	13
Modeling to predict defection	6.63%	12
Other (please specify)	4.42%	8

Source: Bernice Grossman and Ruth P. Stevens, "What B2B Marketers are REALLY Doing with Their Databases," September 2007

Targeting

The first task of any marketer is to determine who needs or wants the product or service being sold. In today's world this targeting is more passive and seductive than it is active and invasive, but all good targeting begins with segmentation using data to profile the best targets.

Segmentation

Segmentation is a way of dividing a broad target market into groups who have common priorities, needs, and purchasing patterns for the product being marketed. With these groups identified, you can use similar approaches to reach, engage, and sell them.

As a B2B marketer, you segment before targeting because it helps:

- Manage the cost of marketing communications—you don't market to businesses that won't buy.
- Manage the cost of product development—you don't develop products that have little appeal.
- Sales be more efficient, thereby lowering the cost of sales.
- Increase profitability of products and services offered.

Although is highly advisable to segment your market before you target it, market segmentation in the B2B world is as much an art as a science. It can begin with broad marketing surveys that provide views of potential customers' needs and priorities. In fact, which of these descriptions would you consider a market segment?

1. Large companies over 1,000 employees.
2. Small companies whose number of PCs is greater than or equal to the number of employees.
3. Medium-sized companies that buy only particular products from you.
4. Business decision makers who make recommendations for specific purchases.
5. Accounts covered by the sales teams.

The answer is all or none depending on what you hope to accomplish. To be an effective target, your market segmentation must be:

1. Identifiable and measurable.
2. Large enough to be profitable.
3. Reachable.
4. Responsive or likely to respond to your messaging.
5. Unlikely to change too quickly.

The challenges that B2B presents to segmentation are numerous, primarily because market segmentation was originally designed for the consumer market, to reach individuals. Like most market research, it is difficult to find one person in a company to interview who can act for an entire organization. It is also difficult to understand how an entire organization responds when you can only see individual purchase behaviors. Companies are complex entities, not holistic in behavior or attitudes.

Exhibit 6.3 illustrates the traditional way that B2B marketers look at segments:

Exhibit 6.3. Traditional View of B2B Segments

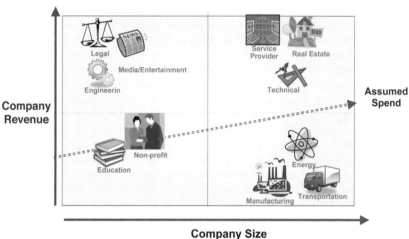

A more effective way to segment the market requires a deeper understanding of buying patterns as well as attitudes. Take a look at this segmentation, shown in Exhibit 6.4, for a high technology company's small and medium business markets.

Segmentation provides the savvy B2B marketer with targets that are most likely to purchase and are easily reachable. This makes targeting more effective because segmentation supports:

- Creation of discrete, definable clusters
- Research that can generate more in-depth information on buyer attitudes and opinions based on pre-defined groups
- Creation of unique segments that can be targeted with specific products via the specific communications channel required by the segment

Segmentation can also be used to group like individuals. Although B2B marketing usually concentrates on groupings of companies first, grouping individuals can also be extremely helpful. Developing "personas" for individual buyers is a form

Exhibit 6.4: Variant on B2B Market Segmentation

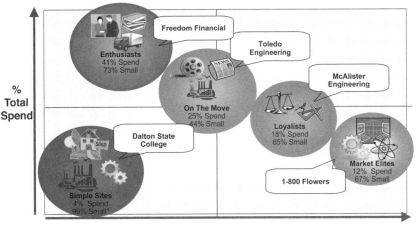

Market Sophistication

of segmentation. Personas in B2B are usually managed as groups of different types of buyers. For example, the buyers of computing products might have traits associated with technical innovation or cost, such as those illustrated in Exhibit 6.5.

Today, the majority of buyers research and evaluate potential purchases by visiting the Web *before* they visit a physical store or make an inquiry about the product. These web behaviors as well as other information about buyers can be captured and used in your targeting efforts.

Exhibit 6.5: Personas

Innovative Techie
Looks for latest in technology
Needs technical validation
IT department title

Cost-Sensitive Purchaser
Responsible for budget
Look for total cost of ownership
Purchasing department title

Business-Minded Technologist
Needs best technology at reasonable $
Evaluates based on support
Business department title

While on the website, the potential buyer may provide you with information about their interests or information that helps you identify them with a specific company. Coupling this information with any data acquired from other marketing efforts such as events, telemarketing or direct advertising only enriches your understanding of the buyer.

Targeting begins with your own customer data in your own accounts receivable data. Here you begin to gain a clear understanding of who your product is for and why the buyer would want or need it. Segmenting your own customers helps you understand who your best customers are, who might need some additional customer care, and who you might want to encourage to seek other vendor relationships. This information makes it possible for you to target and attract the best customers for your product and services and not waste money or time doing so.

With segments identified, you can now begin to apply different techniques to help you target companies and individuals within the most important segments. Here, marketing analytics can help with your targeting through model building.

Analytical Models

Building analytical models may require specialized skills from your marketing staff and a statistical understanding. With that capability available, there are several kinds of models that can be used specifically for targeting. Here are some examples along with the kind of data that you need to make these models really work for you:

1. **Look-alike models** are those that identify potential customers who look very similar to those who have already purchased your product or service. For example, if your product sells well to medium-sized businesses in the manufacturing sector in Iowa, you might want to extend your targets to medium-sized manufacturers in Indiana or Ohio. These models can be as simple as making some key correlations between traits of a customer and potential customer or so sophisticated that they evaluate the budget potential as well as growth of potential customers.

   The data needed for these models should be rich in describing your customers. For example when identifying customers for hospital supplies, you may need the following data: size of customer described by number of beds at the hospital, number of doctors associated with the hospital, area of expertise (cancer center, burn center, or trauma center), etc.

   Notice that the data collected for this industry is different from what you might need for wholesale distributors or manufacturing plants. The more unique the data is to your customer base, the easier it is to find look-alike customers *if* you can find the same data on organizations that you have not sold.

   Working with a good data broker or marketing service provider can help you identify the key elements. Here's a story that illustrates the power of a good data source.

Jon Lambert, the late chairman of Acton, shared this story from a Japanese client who distributes electrical components to the manufacturing industry. The client's database was matched against the Acton database of Japanese companies in hopes of identifying look-alikes on the larger database that would be productive prospects for the distributor. Acton was disappointed to be able to identify only 649 records. But after a few months of working those names, the client joyously reported that they had generated 100 orders, and over $1 million in sales. Truly, in B2B, it's all about quality over quantity.

2. **Propensity models** are statistical equations that identify which of your customers or potential customers may have the inclination to purchase your product or service. The more sophisticated of these models will identify not only the customers with these tendencies but will also indicate when they will buy and how much they will spend.

   Data required for propensity models often includes the same kind of customer descriptors identified for look-alike models as well as purchasing history—three to four quarters—of your customers. Here is where you can get caught. If your products and services are new to the market, you might not have a purchase history.

   When purchase history is lacking, it might be wise to develop propensity models for stages of the marketing process. For example, a "propensity to respond" model can help you identify the potential customers who are most apt to be responsive to your marketing message. These models are built on response data from your various marketing campaigns and should be more available than purchase data if the product is new.

3. **Cross-sell/Up-sell models** identify which of your customers would be open to purchasing additional or newer products (up-sell) or would buy other products related to the purchases they have already made (cross-sell).

   Data to support these models must come from your own purchase data, but it's also helpful to include any data that describes customer support, such as customer inquiries or calls to your product hotlines. Often, marketers forget that the best time to sell a customer on a new product or an additional service is when the customer calls or contacts you with a problem. Capturing this data and making it available to your analysts developing models can help provide more accuracy and pinpoint targeting.

Testing

The best way to make sure that you have identified and are targeting the right customers or potential customers is to test your message in the market. B2B marketers often find it difficult to conduct traditional testing—for good reason. For one thing, most B2B campaigns are complicated, with multiple touches and long sales cycles. Simple split testing won't answer your most important questions, like which touch is essential and which is fluff.

Furthermore, B2B campaigns target multiple contacts in single company accounts, so testing can raise thorny policy issues and cause dissatisfaction not only among customers but also with the sales force. It's not easy when a sales rep comes screaming into your office complaining that your offer test has created confusion in her territory.

But the major reason why DM testing is tough in B2B is the size of the typical target universe. When the entire prospective audience is smaller than 10,000 accounts—a not uncommon situation—test-and-rollout strategies are likely to be pointless.

So, how do you take advantage of the power of testing when universes are too small to support traditional split methods? Let's look at four types of work-arounds.

1. **Eliminate outliers.**

   When you cannot test to a sample and roll out to the whole, you are in effect campaigning to the whole every time. So what can you do to improve the odds of going out to the target with your best shot? Use pre-testing to eliminate the least-powerful offers and creative approaches.

   Some of the pre-testing techniques that work for B2B marketers include:

   - Using email and phone to pilot offer and creative ideas, and then apply those results to other media, like the mail
   - Focus groups, whose opinions can eliminate the least promising ideas while also providing deeper insight into the motivating factors behind respondent behavior
   - Online surveys via low-cost tools like Zoomerang and Survey-Monkey

   These efforts help to hone in on the population that will best respond to your message.

2. **Take manageable risks.**

   When you can't do pure testing, with statistically projectable samples to provide reliable predictions of campaign results, one alternative is to adjust your expectations, accept an increased amount of risk, and then seek ways to mitigate that risk.

Here are some approaches that can work:

- Lower the confidence level required for your tests. Mark Klein, CEO of Loyalty Builders LLC, points out that reducing your expected confidence level from the traditional 90 to 95 percent to something in the 60 percent range can make dramatically smaller test quantities productive, or at least directional. "This kind of testing, while more prone to error, still improves your chances of hitting a winner with a small target universe, which is the whole point," says Klein.
- Campaign sequentially. When you are running campaigns to the same audience over time, the results will mirror what you'd get from a split test. There is some risk, since you are introducing time as a variable. But, says Andrew Drefahl, director of customer insight and technology at Hunter Business Group, "Rapid iteration becomes a learning process. You learn by failure, developing rules of thumb that you can then apply to other campaign situations."
- Make reasonable assumptions. For example, take what works in one medium, like the phone, and make the assumption that it will also work in the mail.

The Math Behind Reducing Confidence Level Requirements

Bill Vorias, a mathematician with Loyalty Builders, offers a hypothetical example of how a lowered confidence level requirement can work. With a universe of 2,000 email addresses, say you send two different emails to two equal segments of 1,000 each, and you produce responses of 7 percent and 10 percent, respectively. So your question becomes: Is the 10 percent side of the split a true winner, or just a random error? According to Vorias's math, 72 percent of the time this result represents a significant difference. Not 95 percent, but not bad. To get to 90 percent confidence in this situation you'd need a sample size of roughly 1,700 for each group, or 3,400 for the campaign. Or, looking at it from the other direction, if you only have 2,500 email addresses to play with, you'd have to be satisfied with an 80 percent confidence that the difference is meaningful. For anyone who wants to reproduce these numbers, Vorias says you need to know that this was at an alpha level of 0.05 and it was a one-sided (versus two-sided) test.

3. **Get the most out of what you have.**
Even if you don't have a universe large enough, some tools are available for taking advantage of what little you have.

- The **"Power Test,"** pioneered by The Hacker Group and now in wide use by such skilled DMers as The Kern Organization, provides a methodology for generating a control direct-mail package from scratch using only 50,000 names. Essentially, the Power Test suspends the need for each test cell to be statistically projectable on its own, but lets you read results in aggregate across several lists. This way, with only two test runs of 25,000 each, a control package can be culled from two offers, three creatives and five or more test lists. A very neat technique indeed.
- The **enterprise-wide control group.** As advocated by Richard N. Tooker, author of *The Business of Database Marketing*, a company can set up a single control group for multiple campaigns over time by establishing an ongoing, standard control group made up of, say, 5 percent of the customer base. The purpose of the corporate control group, which receives no marketing communications at all, is to assess the value of the direct marketing program as a whole. But it may also be used as a benchmark for particular campaigns, if the campaign goes to the entire balance of the universe. Tooker cautions that if the campaign is going out to a smaller segment, the portion of the corporate control group that is comparable may quickly become too small to be valid.
- **Test at the contact level, but read results at the site level.** Andrew Drefahl, founding partner at Experience Design Works, LLC, suggests a neat way to enhance the size of your campaign universe by contacting as deeply as possible into an account, but then measuring campaign success in aggregate, by how well the account as a whole accepted your value proposition. Drefahl recommends using the phone to measure this acceptance, or "uptake," since it allows you to probe on the whos and whys of the response. "Using the phone is critical to the test and learn approach, which is often the only way to open doors in a small B2B audience," he says.
- **Steal from your competitors.** Jim Obermayer, founder of the Sales Lead Management Association, suggests that B2B marketers take a page from DM creative directors, who have learned over decades the value of the "swipe file," which stores competitive control ads based on how often they see the piece in the market. "If

your competition has figured out what's working, why not reap some benefit from the other guy's investment," says Obermayer.

- **Offer the hottest premium**. Businesspeople respond well to free stuff, and new tchotchkes are coming on the market all the time. If you build a strong relationship with an ad specialties vendor, you can be first in line to use the hot new item. "Remember those fans a few years back, where the brand name was spelled out in the air via electrodes?" says Obermayer. "Everyone had to have one. There's no staying power in this strategy, but you will certainly be giving the market your best shot."
- **Use your house file as your testing medium**. As Stephen R. Lett, president of Lett Direct, points out, "The higher response rate from your house file enables reliable testing with a smaller universe. You can then take these results and apply them to your prospecting campaigns. It's not perfect, but it's better than no testing at all."
- **Run an A/B split test in print.** Trade pubs often have a circulation large enough to permit valid split testing—offer, headline, or copy platform, for example. The results can then be applied to other media.
- **Swing for the fences**. With small universe sizes, you don't have the luxury of testing nuances. So test the changes that will have the most impact, advises Lee Marc Stein, the veteran copywriter.

4. **Leverage the Internet**

Internet media offer B2B marketers several brilliant new options for improving their campaign results.

- **Pre-test using email and banner ads**. A/B splits in Internet media do little to enhance the size of your universe, but what they do provide is speed and convenience, making testing cheap and easy. So take abundant advantage of split testing in headlines, offers, subject lines, and other variables that can then be applied to your campaigns in other media.

  As multi-variant testing takes off, the dear old A/B split is losing favor with statisticians. "Split testing is simply wasteful," says Mark Klein. "It misses the interactions among variables, it takes too much time to read results, and most important, it doesn't give you the chance to try out all the possible variables that might have been powerful and effective in your campaign."

- **Website-based multi-variant optimization.** Thanks to free tools like the Website Optimizer in Google Analytics, marketers can set up multi-variant tests on critical web pages like registration forms, order forms, and landing pages—anywhere that a response is requested.

The Three Rules of B2B Testing

The small universe problem is not unique to B2B markets, but there are some principles that reflect the unique realities of the complex sales environment of business marketing:

- Keep your sales force in the loop. There's nothing worse than alienating your sales channel by testing into their territories and taking them by surprise.
- Upsize, don't downsize. You'll get more bang for the buck by testing more powerful creative and offers than you will by seeking cost savings. For example, Lee Marc Stein suggests testing your way from envelope mail to a dimensional package, or move from a #10 to a #14 mail piece.
- Do it, don't duck it. There are plenty of obstacles to testing in B2B environments, but the payoff can be dramatic if you make the effort.

Tracking

With the advent of the Internet, tracking for database marketing campaigns changed drastically. Where once we would check our mailboxes, we now have different checkpoints and much more detail about where our messages go and how long it takes the recipient to open the email and then to respond to it or to trash it. Tools today can provide all this information.

The great volume of information on customer behavior information has coined a new term for marketers—the customer journey. Understanding this journey is made easier by being able to track customer interactions across a myriad of marketing tactics. In fact, the world of marketing is moving:

From:	To:
Lead generation	Presenting choices
Lead qualification	Acquiring customer information
Transaction based	Interaction based
Interruption model	Engagement model
Measuring number of leads	Measuring customer lifetime value
Marketer control	Customer control
One-time sales proposition	Lifetime relationship
Leaning back waiting for customer	Leaning forward to meet customer
Push marketing	Pull marketing
Command and control	Communication and collaboration
Customer satisfaction	Total customer experience

These requirements of the marketing process put more pressure on our marketing systems to track our customer interactions and be prepared to react to them.

Tracking is by definition the reporting that you put in place to provide information about the path your message takes once you have introduced it into the market. In today's world, most of this information can be obtained from the data collected via your web tools.

Your marketing database, if constructed effectively, can also help with the analysis of how offline tactics support the customer throughout their journey. When information about emails is combined with data about visitors to your websites, or to other websites related to yours, you get a much more complete picture of your buyers' journey in search of information to facilitate a purchase.

And don't forget that one of the most powerful uses of your marketing database is simple query. Having the ability to query your database to determine what actions your customer is taking at each stage in their buying cycle is extremely valuable. Or querying the database asking "what-if" questions, such as "What if we delivered this message to this customer type at this time, what might happen to the customer journey?"

Exhibit 6.6 provides a framework that can be used to help you plot your customer's journey. The tactics on the left side illustrate the different ways messages can be conveyed to your customer while the stages across the top represent, in general terms, the different phases of a customer life cycle. Your marketing database should help you determine:

1. Which tactics are most effective at engaging the customer at each step in the journey from awareness to bonding.

Exhibit 6.6: Customer Journey Life Cycle

Customer Journey Life Cycle

	Awareness	Discover	Purchase	Use	Bond
Website		●			
E-commerce site			●		
Call Center			●	●	
Web Forums		○		○	○
Social Sites (Facebook, Twitter, LinkedIn)	●	○			
Mobile Ads					
Email	○			○	
Mail					○
Trade shows/Events	○				●
Reseller			○		

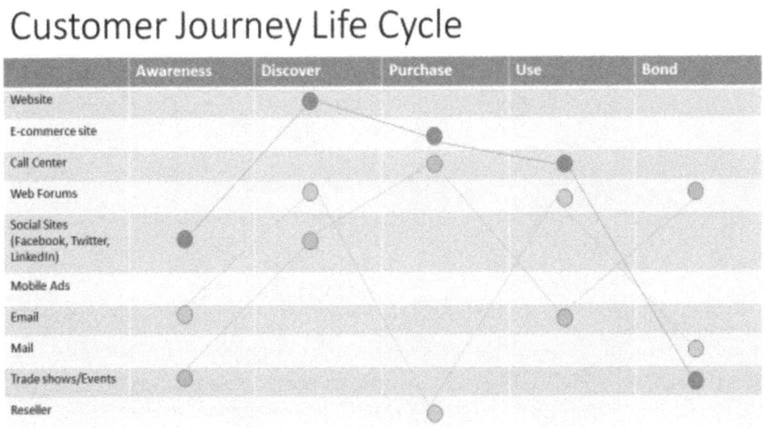

2. Which tactics are most appropriate for which stages of the customer journey. Do trade shows speed up the customer's discovery phase? Do emails generate visits to websites for further discovery or purchase?
3. What channel is most appropriate and cost effective for supporting the customer, for example, web forums or call centers?
4. What part does your company website play most effectively in the customer journey? Was it designed for that purpose?

Throughout the journey, you can engage any number of tools to advance your understanding of the customer's progress on the way to purchase. Companies such as 6Sense have developed analytics to help predict how customers will move through a specific journey.

What you immediately see in Exhibit 6.7 is that different tactics require different tracking mechanisms. For example, here's that same list of tactics with associated tracking measurements:

Exhibit 6.7: Tracking Measurements

Marketing Tactic	Tracking Measurements
Website	# of visits # unique visitors
E-commerce Site	# of purchases # of carts abandoned
Call Center	# of inbound calls # of outbound calls Avg mins per call
Web Forums	# of visitors to website coming from web forums # of website visitors going to forums
Social Sites (Facebook, Twitter, LinkedIn)	# of website visitors logging in with Facebook, Twitter, or LinkedIn IDs
Mobile Ads	# of responses to mobile ads
Email	# of emails opened # of responses or click-throughs
Mail	# of responses # of non-deliverable
Trade shows/Events	# of visitors/attendees
Reseller	# of customers sold by reseller # of leads referred to reseller

Applying Numbers to One Part of the Journey—Email

The majority of companies today employ email marketing tactics. In fact, it is estimated that over two billion emails a day are sent in the U.S. alone. Because email is relatively inexpensive, most companies often use this tactic as their primary or only means of communicating their marketing messages. This puts a huge burden on email to perform—to make customers aware and move them to discover more about your product or to actually buy. That's why tracking an email is very important.

For email marketing, tracking is essential for two parts of the process—when you send out the email and when you receive a response. The data captured can provide you with valuable information:

Data captured:	What it tells you:
Bounce backs	How many emails actually made it to the recipients' email box
Open notices	How many of the emails received by the recipients were actually opened
Responses from targets	How many of the messages opened were responded to by the recipients
Responses from non-targets	How many of the messages opened were responded to by others who were not the initial targets of your message

Remember that responses to emails need to be measured from where they are directed to land. For example, you might have directed your target to "Just click on this link to . . ." In this case, the "click" might direct to a website where the target customer or prospect completes a form that provides you with more information about who is responding. Both the data you collect via your web form as well as the click on the website that collects the information are important to your understanding of the message's attractiveness and your campaign's effectiveness.

In recent years, companies have also experimented with capturing information about where responders go *after* they have been to your site. This is especially helpful if you have a partner organization that participates with you in messaging to a joint target or if you have purchased ads on specific sites. The use of "cookies" on your site will also enable you to determine who visits your site more than once and where they go afterward as well.

For example, you might have launched an email campaign that directs your target to your web form but also contains a pop-up ad or a reference to another site that provides additional information. Data collected from these other sites should provide numbers of hits redirected from your site. This data, when combined with the data collected from your web form, can be very helpful in determining the extent of your target's interest in your product or service and adds richness to your understanding of the buyer's journey.

Just remember that this kind of tracking can be seen as invasive by some visitors. Make sure that you have thoroughly vetted your privacy policy with your legal team. The mandate for ensuring privacy is to ensure that visitors to your website always know what you are collecting and how you will use it.

Privacy Basics
by Theresa Kushner

In the late last century, then-CEO of Sun Microsystems Scott McNealy, made an outrageous comment during a product launch. "You have zero privacy anyway. Get over it," he declared. Well over a decade later, Sun Microsystems is an entry in microcomputer history and online privacy rests precariously close to the "zero" that McNealy prophesized.

Today, millions of businesses collect data that describe customers personally. With each click, online shoppers and users give away a piece of their privacy. In exchange for that privacy, they receive product and service discounts, online messages about the newest products from manufacturers and various other kinds of alerts, from national disasters to celebrity malfeasance.

As a business owner, you benefit from collecting that data. Personal information is either explicitly given via credit card purchases or market research surveys, or implicitly derived from tracking customer interactions on the Web. Both kinds of data play an important role. Here are five key things to remember when collecting and using personal customer information.

1. **Notice and Choice.** In the United States, you have a legal obligation to give your customers notice and choice. This simply means that you must *notify* them on your website that you are collecting data and what you will do with the data you collect. You must then offer customers a *choice* to either allow the use of personal data or not.

2. **Don't collect what you will not use.** Today's customers are savvy enough to know what data is really essential in transacting business with you. So don't ask questions that are too personal or that won't provide them with what they feel is an equal exchange—their information for something of value that you have. For example, the local bakery who gives away cupcakes on your birthday can easily collect birth dates (just day and month, please). But the cleaners might have a difficult time extracting the same information.

3. **Use what you collect—for good, not evil.** If the data is important to your business strategy, then it's important to collect and use to further your customer relationships. For example, if your business is highly dependent on repeat customers, then understanding "why" customers keep coming back is essential. This one piece of information can be collected through tracking surveys on your online site, through email, or in-store surveys. Just make sure that when you collect the information, you use it. Asking customers for their birth dates and then never using that data creates a breach in the exchange and makes customers less likely to give you additional information.

4. **Keep the promises you make to your customers.** The privacy statement on your website is your promise to customers about how you will use the data you collect. If you plan to sell or share their information with other companies, tell them. If you promise not to sell or share it,

don't. Remember that Facebook's greatest issue with privacy was when it failed to respect the users' privacy wishes. That failure means that for the next twenty years Facebook must undergo regular privacy audits—the price of a broken promise to its customers.

5. **Stay on top of the privacy laws.** January 28 is International Data Privacy Day (http://en.wikipedia.org/wiki/Data_Privacy_Day) and your opportunity to learn more about how to ensure data privacy for both you and your customers. By ensuring that you are current with the laws, you protect your business. If you do business internationally, it behooves you to secure legal representation that understands the intricacies of privacy laws in other countries.

By taking these simple steps, you can help ensure that customers continue to feel that giving up some of their privacy results in value to them as consumers. Remember, it takes on average twelve to eighteen months of regular transactions to gain a customer's loyalty to your business, but usually only one transaction to lose it.

Source: *Latin Business Today*, January 5, 2012. Used with permission.

Trending—Tracking Over Time

Just go to Google and type in "trending" and you can find out at any time what is trending in popularity on Google—whether Oprah Winfrey or Bill Gates is more popular on the Internet or whether the Dog is outdoing the Cat in number of inquiries. Trending tells you who is popular on television, in the movies, or in politics. It is the new NEWS! Because trending is so popular, marketing has also developed an obsession with trending.

Trending, by definition, is the change or development in a general direction. For example, the economy is trending downward. But the more modern definition of trending is the subject of many posts on a social media website within a relatively short period of time. We've all heard the phrase, "Look what's trending on Twitter." The only difference in these two definitions is the amount of time usually associated with the "trend."

If tracking provides you with the knowledge of where targets go in search of information, trending provides you information about that same set of activities over time, short or long. And allows you to see each step your web visitors take. Although trending is primarily associated with web activity, you can also develop trends for your offline activity as well.

Since web marketing is the result of numerous messages sent to your targets, trending is important for providing insight into how your messages persist over time in their effectiveness: (1) as the customers continue on their journeys and (2) as your messages deploy across the calendar—before and after specific offers, through seasonal purchasing, during certain times of the day or week.

Trending data often provides insight into your campaign that point-in-time reports cannot.

For example, having just launched an email campaign designed to capture interest in your latest product to be available six weeks from now, you may be extremely interested to know how the responses to your email messages accumulate over those six weeks. Does response escalate as the time nears or does it wane over that same period?

One of the decisions you might need to make when evaluating the need for trending data is whether you want to trend responses for specific email messages or for all messages against a specific target set of buyers. Both of these approaches are valid, but have very different informational values.

Watching the trend of responses to a specific message tells you how well the message is being received by your target. You can also evaluate these responses against other messages to the same target. Or you may want to evaluate the responses to one email compared to another email message to the same target. This could be an in-market A/B test to evaluate response to two messages to the same target.

The A/B test strategy might be expanded to include the capture and evaluation of data from all messages deployed against a specific target. Holding the target constant and trending information from all marketing activities produces insights into the accumulated effectiveness of all your messages.

Some of the more innovative ways to take advantage of the information gleaned from tracking customer behavior is being managed by companies like 6Sense, a company that bills itself as a predictive intelligence engine for marketing and sales. With their ability to keep track of customers throughout the buying cycle, they were able to produce for BlueJeans, a cloud-based video conferencing service, the following results:

- Nine hundred new accounts likely to buy.
- Four times lift in opens over average.
- One-third the sales efforts to create an open opportunity.
- One in ten touches to open versus average of one in thirty-three.

Trending data produces insights into the endurance of your messaging over time and can help to provide you with insights as to the accumulated effects of that messaging over time.

Data collected from your marketing actions serves one very important purpose—it helps you improve. Feeding your insights from tracking and trending back to your targeting and testing efforts provides the learning environment so necessary for excellent marketing results.

Measuring Marketing

The primary reasons we target, test, track and trend our marketing activities are to:

1. Ensure that we are getting our message across to the right buyers
2. Show return on our marketing investments (ROMI)

Earlier in this chapter, we listed measurements used in tracking web visitors. These metrics, like others for offline marketing, measure the operational success of your marketing activities and are designed to help you be as efficient as possible in driving marketing tactics.

But measuring effectiveness of marketing is the ultimate goal. How much marketing contributes to your company's overall revenue is of particular attention to chief marketing officers today. It's the subject of many books and countless articles, but it's still elusive, especially in companies that depend on a one- or two-tier distribution. How do you truly measure who or what specific tactic influenced the prospect to buy?

In a document promoting Hubspot (http://offers.hubspot.com), six marketing metrics are identified as those important to your CMO. They are basic but important:

1. Cost of acquiring a customer
2. Marketing's percent of spend in acquiring a customer
3. The ratio of lifetime value of the customer to the cost of acquisition
4. Time to payback for customer acquisition
5. Percent of new customer business driven by marketing activities
6. Percent of customers marketing influenced during the sales cycle.

As you can see, most of these metrics concentrate on marketing's role in customer acquisition, but marketing plays a part in customer development and retention as well, even though these metrics may be harder to generate and even harder for your sales teams to believe.

Above all, metrics help to validate the many uses of marketing and give you a data-based approach to marketing overall.

CHAPTER 7

Managing Marketing Data in a Global World

As the world becomes more connected, marketers can no longer stay isolated within the borders of one country. The Internet has given us the capability to reach and do business with people in remote places, places that have different customs, have different ways of doing business, and speak different languages. It happens that those languages as well as cultural differences in commerce pose interesting challenges for database marketers. And it starts with the increased awareness of data as a business driver.

Value of Data on the Rise

Managing data across the globe means more than just how addresses differ. We must first consider the value of data and its importance to commerce. Here opinions worldwide vary greatly and are rapidly changing. Increased competition, increased awareness of privacy, and the proliferation of Internet commerce all contribute to data being more and more valuable to businesses worldwide.

Increased Competition

The world of commerce is increasingly an international arena. By 2017, commerce on the Internet will have almost doubled. In 2012, Forrester predicted a $1 trillion market for the U.S. alone, but the continuing rise of China may dwarf that estimate by 2020.

Increasingly, e-commerce is becoming a business-to-business opportunity as consumers begin to use the same buying patterns for their business as they do for their personal shopping. The Internet is the first place for information, no matter whether the purchase is B2B or B2C.

All of this adds up to increased competition for B2B companies that must now strive to understand the "consumer" of their products and services and how to position their wares, often within existing distribution channels. Nowhere is competition highlighted more than in Asia where the rise in commerce is the greatest.

Recently Korean technology companies, which for years have been focused on business-to-consumer marketplaces, have begun to turn to B2B marketing. According to PYMNTS, an online resource for companies focused on e-commerce, major Asian tech companies, struggling to keep their profits strong, are turning away from B2C transactions and focusing on B2B.

"The business-to-consumer segment is very volatile and highly competitive, so Samsung is now focusing on the B2B segment as it believes being a solutions provider means stability," an official told the *Korean Times*.

The article in the *Korean Times* also highlighted LG Electronics and its move to invest more in its B2B side. LG Electronics, according to Korean investment analysts, has shifted to selling air conditioners, for example, to businesses as well as to individuals.

Competing with China's burgeoning consumer market puts not only Asian firms but all international organizations at a competitive disadvantage. Although shifting business to B2B markets may mean changing business strategies, the profit margins in these areas can be significant.

Competition drives the increase in the use and interest in B2B data for marketing into these new areas of the business. As a result, more and more companies are trying to learn how to effectively market to individuals in a business setting and they are attempting to use data to reach their potential markets.

Rise of E-commerce in B2B

According to a recent survey by Ardent Partners, 55 percent of supply managers agree that business e-commerce networks will become a major trading partner platform.

In the mid-1990s when the dot.com crash was creating the economic bubble, the idea of networks connecting buyers and sellers in a business-to-business environment was born with giants in the technology world, such as IBM, that had the infrastructure to look at this way of doing business. When the bubble burst in the early 2000s, the implementations for these networks dwindled.

Today, the idea is seeing a resurgence. According to the Ardent survey of supply chain managers, 75 percent agree that B2B networks are beneficial to buyers and sellers and 54 percent say that networks are a key source of new business suppliers, and furthermore, that these networks could increase by more than 40 percent over the next few years.

B2B companies that use e-commerce as part of their channel strategy see buyer networks as important. Companies that sell parts to their partners, such as IBM, or that sell to businesses, like Staples, see buyer networks as extremely important.

This rise in the use of e-commerce in B2B puts significant pressure on the use of data, especially data for vendors and partners within a B2B ecosphere and especially when suppliers and vendors are worldwide. The Internet knows no boundaries in this environment.

The value of data in a world becoming more and more homogenous from a business perspective will only become more important. But as businesses grow in emerging countries such as Africa, Latin America and Asia, how B2B marketers capture data, manage it, and use it will differentiate the winners from the losers in an increasingly connected marketplace.

Increased Awareness of Privacy

While competition and the rise of e-commerce in B2B are prominent factors in shaping B2B use of data, the increased awareness of data privacy has put marketers on the defensive as they strive to understand what is permissible in markets worldwide. This trend makes it necessary for marketers to collect and manage data differently.

The European Union has been one of the most prominent forces in shaping the use of data. Under EU law, personal data can only be gathered under strict conditions. And, people and organizations collecting and managing the data are required by the EU to protect it from misuse and to respect the rights of the data owners.

To this end, the EU not only has strict laws about data collection and use but also around its deletion. The EU is the first governmental body to enact a law governing an individual's "right to be forgotten." This particular law puts stress on database marketers because it means you may be compelled to eliminate an individual from all data sources in your company.

In 2012, the EU commission on data privacy issued new guidelines. For international marketers, it's a must read. The guidelines can be found at: http://ec.europa.eu/justice/newsroom/data-protection/news/120125_en.htm.

Initially, B2B marketers thought they were safe from privacy laws that appeared to protect consumers only. The laws were written to deter SPAM and to ensure protection of an individual's personally identifiable information. They were not always as clear when it came to messaging to individuals in the context of a business- to-business buyer relationship.

Companies had the power to stop unwanted email through the use of SPAM filters and laws never restricted the use of email when conducting a B2B transaction.

But with the advent of tracking mechanisms on company websites such as cookies, beacons, and flash cookies, privacy issues for business-to-business marketing became somewhat more complicated.

Tracking Mechanisms Defined

Web cookie—A small piece of data sent from a website and stored in a user's web browser while the user is browsing that specific website.

Web beacon—A transparent graphic image, usually extremely small, that is placed on a site or in an email. Web beacons allow the site to record the simple actions of the user opening the page that contains the beacon. Web beacons work with web cookies to display information on the visitor or user specifically. In other words, when you open a page, the web beacon consults the cookie and determines what might be of interest to you as a result of viewing your interaction on the website.

Flash cookie—A collection of cookie-like data that a website running Adobe Flash can place on the visitor's or user's hard drive. Like regular cookies, Flash cookies contain information about when you visited the site and may also contain tracking and settings information.

Web tracking and the use of data to understand your viewing preferences can be troublesome for some marketers. If in doubt about your own website and its use of these new capabilities, remember that the laws stress that transparency to the user is of the utmost importance. Often any issue arising from web tracking can be mitigated by ensuring that your viewers know what you are collecting and how it is being used. Your privacy policy should make that very clear and be simple enough for your viewers to understand.

In addition to web data, some countries also restrict the use of data for telemarketing purposes. In fact, the infamous Do Not Call (DNC) lists, introduced in countries such as the United States, have created some confusion for B2B marketers.

In the United States, B2B marketing is subject to far less regulation than telemarketing to consumers. However, some rules still apply. For example, calling a business cell phone may fall under some federal or state cell phone restrictions. When purchasing lists for telemarketing, you often don't know whether the phone is a business phone or a personal cell. The Federal Communications Commission (FCC) recently passed new cell phone rules that are not consumer specific and therefore can apply to B2B calls.

Since Europe sets the standard in these areas, it's recommended that you track

Germany, the most protective of the EU countries. In Germany, B2B telemarketing is allowed but under the following guidelines:

- Telemarketing is not allowed unless:
  —The telemarketer has prior consent from the businessperson
  —There is an existing contractual relationship
  —The telemarketer presumes the interest of the businessperson called
- Once the call is answered, the agent must state:
  —His or her name
  —The client's name
  —The purpose of the call (It is unlawful to be deceptive about the real purpose of the call.)

Data for an Increasingly Connected World

Managing data for organizations that do business internationally has a different set of issues than are found when managing data within the United States only. But as we've seen, the Internet is driving the increase of international commerce and the data we collect and manage is and can create challenges for the B2B database manager.

Sheila Donovan, President and Founder of Global DM Solutions, manages an international direct marketing agency and knows well the field of international data. Here is Sheila's overview of how to manage international data gleaned from years of helping marketers do exactly that.

Managing a Global Address Database
by Sheila Donovan, Global DM Solutions

It is a global market. You can try to hide from it or you can thrive in it. In order to thrive in it, you must understand that address data is the new currency of global business. Whether you use postal mail, ship packages, or use geocoding systems, correct address data is vital to the success of your business. The United Nations currently recognizes 193 countries and most people will agree that this number reflects a geopolitical view of the world. However, most logistics professionals agree that there are over 250 countries and territories worldwide. For example, Bermuda is a British Overseas Territory under the jurisdiction of the United Kingdom and not recognized as a nation by the United Nations. From a logistics point of view, if you needed to send a letter or ship a package to someone in Bermuda, you would not send it via the United Kingdom.

Understanding global address data management goes well beyond a simple study of geography and geopolitics. Accommodating international addresses can require database modifications, especially for American databases.

The American addressing system is sophisticated and highly automated. Decades of refinement have resulted in a well-documented, data-driven system and a well-trained population of consumers. Americans are trained to know their ZIP code and the majority of people could properly enter their address into a form. Address data quality professionals know the format for capturing most U.S. addresses is two to three address lines (depending on the nature of your business), city, state, and ZIP code fields plus company and department if you handle business addresses. Finding the correct ZIP code for a given address is just a mouse click away.

When examining foreign address formats, it is important to understand what comprises a correct address. The good news is that developed nations such as Australia, Canada, France, Germany, and the United Kingdom have sophisticated addressing systems. Like the United States, these postal administrations developed standards for addressing and documented them quite well. All of these nations offer work share programs that enable large-volume mailers to earn postal discounts for complying with addressing and presort standards. For any of these nations, structuring an address and identifying unnecessary data in an address block is relatively easy because of the wealth of available documentation, data sets, and software programs available.

This is not to say that handling data for these nations in a U.S.-centric structure is not without challenges. A typical United Kingdom address can occupy six address lines. The postal code in Germany is placed before the city name and the province is not used.

For developing nations, addressing standards, or lack thereof, makes address data management an even greater challenge. In developing nations, people often used landmarks when describing their address. For example, in Latin American nations it is common to see "directional" phrases like "Circa Iglesias," meaning "near the church." In India, the directional phrase "Opposite" is frequently abbreviated as "Opp." and is used to describe a location, such as "Opp. Patel Café."

It is important to understand that "directional" addresses can be quite lengthy and can exceed thirty-five characters. While the directional elements may appear odd to a non-native and might not be a documented standard of the official postal administration of the nation, these phrases hold great meaning to the delivery person. It is best to maintain these elements in the address block in order to ensure accurate delivery.

Learning some world geography is extremely helpful for managers of global address data. Being able to dissect an address requires that you understand what it contains. For example, New York is both a city and a state, just as Oklahoma is a city and a state. This is common knowledge amongst database managers in America. However, the United States is not the only country where a place name spans multiple geographic elements. In Brazil, São Paolo is a city and a province and in Japan, Tokyo is a both city and a prefecture (state).

Do not remove redundant data in international data before you understand its function. This information is critical for address accuracy as well as mail and parcel delivery.

Understand that address characteristics vary around the world. Learning the address formats for your top markets will greatly assist you to identify address elements accurately. Below are some useful tips that will help you get you started.

Postal codes are alphanumeric in some nations:

- Postal codes are positioned before the city name in many countries and below the city name in other countries.
- House numbers are positioned after the street name in many countries.

- Apartment numbers are often found with the house number and separated by a slash (/).

Today, the vast majority of international address data is captured via the Web. Keep in mind that people around the world use native keyboards and type native characters into web pages. Many character sets around the globe use diacritics, which is a lengthy subject unto itself. Briefly described, diacritics are the marks above or below alphabetic letters that give indications about pronunciations. Some examples of letters containing diacritics are é, o, Å, ā, and Ô.

Munich, one of Germany's largest cities, serves as a good example of the use of diacritics and how language influences spelling. To an American, the place name is Munich; to a German, it is München. In order to preserve the diacritic character found in the German version of this place name, you must use the correct encoding system. Like diacritics, encoding systems are complex and lengthy subjects. The simplest solution is to use the Unicode encoding system, which has become the standard for handling global data sets.

Be advised that most web applications these days are Unicode compliant, so sometimes this requirement is overlooked in the master database application. Keep your eye on the ball and make sure that your master database is Unicode compliant as well.

Use the globally friendly term postal code instead of ZIP code on your data capture forms. Although widely used around the world, ZIP code is predominantly an American term and can confuse citizens of many nations.

Be generous when designing your global address record layout. Give your global customers and prospects the ability to completely enter their address data. Do not force foreign visitors to cram their addresses into a restrictive U.S. structure. Increase the number and length of the address lines you maintain. Your address database should have:

- Address lines (at least two, preferably three)—Minimum of 40 characters
- City—Minimum of 50 characters
- Province—Minimum of 30 characters
- Postal Code (alphanumeric)—Minimum of 15 characters
- Country name—50 characters

Once you've built your database, take care of it. Maintaining a global database is an ongoing process. Be sure to constantly examine delivery issues and troubleshoot the source of the problem. Stay abreast of trends in your top markets by visiting the official postal administration of each nation.

If you begin to feel overwhelmed, think about this. Almost 95 percent of the world's consumers live outside the United States and 70 percent of the world's purchasing power is outside the United States. Growing global is certainly worth the effort.

Considerations When Managing Global Data

Once you have mastered data for addresses worldwide, it's time to tackle some of the other challenges posed by international businesses. Here are questions to ask that will help you manage data effectively in an increasingly connected world.

What Are the Most Important Countries for My Business?

Regardless of what industry you are in, your business strategy has probably already decided which countries are most profitable for your products. For example, if you are in the oil equipment manufacturing business, you probably want to make sure that you have ways to conduct business in the Middle East, Brazil, and parts of Canada. Likewise, if you are selling products that can only be sold in the U.S. because of intellectual property reasons or because you don't have the capability to sell outside the U.S., then making decisions about international data in your marketing database may be an easier one.

However, it is important to design your database with both today and tomorrow's requirements. To illustrate this, let's look at a small catalog distributor of fine jewelry. After you have cleared the way to sell in another country—set up international operating divisions, secured banking relationships, established a presence—you also need to decide exactly how and who will market within that country. Will you be taking orders within the country in native language? Will your website be localized for people within the country and feed data back to your U.S. location or keep it in country? The answers to these questions have an effect on what data is collected in your marketing database.

Although you may be comfortable moving only to one country today, tomorrow your business may require that you move to other areas of the world. Setting up a marketing database that includes today's requirements as well as tomorrow's helps you move quickly. However, try to get a future view with some specificity.

For example, knowing that you will be moving into Russia in the near future may require more effort on the part of those building your marketing database than knowing that you will be only required to market in Europe. The Cyrillic alphabet of Russia provides different challenges than the Roman alphabet, complete with diacritical marks, in use by the majority of the countries in Europe. Launching businesses in Israel where native language is written right to left also represents additional challenges.

Again, this is a strategic decision. Understanding the value that you will derive from moving into another country will help you make that decision. What is often not considered is the operational effort required to make an impact on the market in another country.

Which Languages Are Most Important for Doing Business in These Countries?

Even if you decide that you only want to sell in English-speaking countries, such as Canada, you need to be aware that other countries describe the data about their businesses differently and often in a variety of languages. It is not possible, for example, to sell in Canada without making all of your sales and marketing materials available in two languages—English and French.

Although Canada requires that both languages be available on all products, there are some countries, and even some regions of the U.S., that may require different language use just because it is appropriate for the market. For example, marketing in Florida and Texas often creates an advantage for firms who translate marketing messages into both English and Spanish.

Other parts of the world may recognize English as the "official" language of business, but require that to reach markets messaging must be in local dialect. In fact, English is often the second or non-official language of businesspeople. But don't let that fool you. Marketing in native language is often required to reach your intended audience.

Look at these countries. India's official languages are both Hindi and English but the regions speak over fifteen different languages. Belgium's actual official languages are Dutch, French, and German, but the majority of Belgians speak English as well.

As we become a more diversified world, the requirement to market in languages spoken by the majority of your intended market is both a market differentiator and a necessity.

How Will I Use the Data?

Phil Maitino, Chief Technology Officer at Melissa Data, had a very simple way of helping marketing managers determine how to best approach international data. He questions them by asking, "Do you want your customers to think you are marketing locally or not?"

That is the question!

When your goal is to acquire, retain, or grow customers within a specific country, you need to reach them so that they will be receptive to your message. Sometimes in B2B marketing, however, U.S. companies assume that most companies in other countries speak English. Although that is true for the major markets in the world, the emerging markets are often where you need to market the most.

Here are a few questions you can ask yourself when developing a local database for marketing in a specific country:

1. Is this country ready to receive leads from marketing? Are sales and partner channels in place and working?
2. Are all products market ready?
3. Are major marketing materials translated for this market?
4. Is the website in local language for this country?

If you are ready, then dive in and use the data to generate leads, gain market share, and present a face to your market that says, "We understand how to reach you where you do business."

How Will Data Be Acquired in These Countries?

Acquiring data outside the United States is a challenge. First of all, you need to be familiar with the culture and how data is viewed in a business context. Any number of market research organizations can provide you a view.

Here's an example of information provided by one such organization in the Middle East.

ictQatar, the Supreme Council of Information and Communication Technology in Qatar, published a report on May 25, 2014 (http://www.slideshare.net/ictQATAR/research-report-35091356) that presented their findings about the attitudes toward the Internet in the Middle East and Northern Africa. They found that the people in these regions were not concerned about data collection but were against data repurposing. In other words, they felt comfortable providing information for a specific purpose, but did not like the idea of the information being used for something different. These kinds of insights can help you tremendously as you start to build a marketing database, either through marketing activities like events or online through your company website.

There are various ways to go about securing data for your marketing database. Here are a few that you should consider:

1. Purchasing local data from a reputable firm. D&B, Corporate 360, or Global DM Solutions offer data both in English and in native languages.
2. Telemarketing or cold calling. This tactic, although effective for increasing your database, has some significant drawbacks: (a) you need a list of phone numbers to start with, (b) telemarketing can be expensive, and (c) in some countries, cold calling—calling a company without a reason (gathering information is often not considered a viable reason) is prohibited by law.
3. Crowdsourcing. In recent years, the Internet has provided a new means to acquire data worldwide. Crowdsourcing is the process of obtaining services, ideas, or content such as data by soliciting contributions from a large, dispersed group of people, usually from an online community. The pre-

mier companies in this space provide you with tools and services to teach you how to make simple data acquisition from the Web. Then, you train their representatives, who are paid on the amount of data they find, correct, or enrich. It is a fairly inexpensive way to get a good start on a database in countries where you may not have a presence.

Translate or Transliterate?

If you do not want or cannot manage technically data in your marketing database in native language, you may face the issue of whether you want the data translated or transliterated. Here are definitions of both of these means of handling international data:

- Translate—To express the sense of words or text in another language. This means that you express the intent of the words from one language to another.
- Transliterate—To write or print a letter or word using the closest corresponding letters of a different alphabet or language.

Here's an example of exactly how this plays out in your database. In Japan, the name Mitsubishi is represented in Kanji as:

The red diamonds in the logo are very significant. If the word "Mitsubishi" were translated, you would be looking for this Japanese company in your database as "Three Diamonds." Instead, the Kanji has been transliterated to Mitsubishi, an English character representation.

Although Phil Maitino of Melissa Data says he abhors transliteration, there are places where it might be beneficial. AddressDoctor, a division of Informatica, has experts with detailed knowledge on transliteration, but even Frank Hellenthal, Head of Product Management for the company, says that transliteration should only be used with specific content. AddressDoctor has a centralized language capability that transliterates to English and back again but only for very specific cases, such as harmonizing data for analytical purposes.

Both methods have their value, but you need to consult experts when making these decisions. What you decide affects your marketing system and could affect your internal operating systems as well. It's wise to make this decision carefully.

How Are My Systems Set Up to Manage Data?

One of the key decisions you make when setting up a marketing database is whether you want the database to be able to handle a language other than English. This decision should be one made along with the architecture (see Chapter 3). If you want to manage international data, the database you decide on must be capable of handling Unicode.

Unicode, according to Wikipedia, "is a computing standard for the consistent encoding, representation and handling of text expressed in most of the world's writing systems." The latest version of the Universal Character set (Unicode) has over 110,000 characters covering 100 written languages and multiple symbol sets. In addition to defining character sets, the Unicode also recommends how to manage these characters in data files.

As Sheila Donovan mentioned in the sidebar on page 132, remember that your marketing database may feed or receive feeds from other systems, such as your web forms. Ensuring consistency across all these databases is important and Unicode helps you manage that flow of data.

Who Will Manage Data in These Countries?

When managing different languages, it is a best practice to have people who understand the data being entered into your database manage the database. This can represent some interesting issues when it comes to data quality, so it's better to think about this ahead of actually starting to build your database.

Your primary considerations are whether you have a local resource to help with data management. Usually if you have a marketing organization within a country, you can secure resources to help support your database there or you can use your local agency to help you with this support.

For most companies based in the U.S. and managing international marketing departments, the only issue arising from local database management is ensuring that data can be normalized across the world when managing global reporting or analyses. This is something that needs to be considered when developing the architecture of your overall marketing database design. You may need to set up databases in each country that feed only specific data to a U.S.-based marketing analytics database used for reporting and analyses. In this case, the data stored and managed in-country would be used primarily for tactics within the country.

If cost is a consideration and you simply cannot afford to manage databases in France, Germany, Japan and Australia, then consider centralizing your data management activities in regional centers that speak a variety of languages from that region. For example, it is common in Europe to put data management services in the Netherlands because of the variety of European languages spoken. The same holds for Singapore in Asia Pacific.

Test Your Resolve

After fully examining your reasoning and the considerations for setting up an international database, you may be ready to dive right in. A best practice is to start with one country and test your resolve at making a market impact. If your company is U.S.-based, try managing French information for Canada or Spanish information for Mexico. Wade in slowly and see if you have what it takes to really market effectively.

To get started, here's some practical advice on addresses and other information that you may need to round out your marketing database.

Diving into International Address Data

At the heart of managing a B2B database for international marketing is how to represent addresses from different countries in a standard set of fields. The idea of organized cities and towns in which roads have names and numbers is fairly standard worldwide except for some areas of China. For the most part, there are some conventions that are observed throughout the world. We usually name a city, town, or village. Those places are often located in regions, states, or provinces. The more modern use of postal codes, or ZIP codes as used in the United States, designates many of these regions by number or by an alphanumeric postal code. The Universal Postal Union (UPU) provides address information in a standard format for a host of countries. Here's an example of the location information available:

- Address lines—Usually from one to four
- Locality—Name of town, city, or village
- Region—Name of state, province
- Postal code/ZIP code
- Country

Note that it often takes more than one address line to designate a physical location. Those lines can be used for any of several pieces of information, such as:

- Street number—Often numeric or alphanumeric because it could carry an additional character.
- Street name.
- Location or building name—In the U.K., house or buildings are identified by name, not number.
- Street type (Road, Highway, Circle, etc.)—There are more than 250 English language street types, not to mention other languages' translations, such as Strasse or Rue.
- Street direction—North, East, South, and West, plus combinations such as Northwest, etc.
- Location or dwelling type—These provide additional information such as Suite, Post Office Box, Floor, or Mail Stop.
- Locality—Name of the city, town, or municipality. In some regions of the world, neighborhoods or villages are listed before the actual city or town.

- Governing areas—Such as states in the U.S., provinces in Canada, counties in the U.K., federal districts in Mexico.
- Postal code or ZIP code
- Country—Although this seems easy to designate, remember that countries, like people and businesses, change. Managing a table of legitimate countries is important.

When designing your databases, you may have to choose how many lines to include. If you are managing international data, choose three to four. Commas are often used in fields to designate additional information and avoid use of another address line. However, remember that in many countries the order of these fields can vary.

Address formats for most countries in the world can be found at: http://www.bitboost.com/ref/international-address-formats.html#Formats. The following general format is quite common:

1. Address *inside* the country you are mailing to
2. Of the place you are mailing to
3. Name of country you are mailing to

Of the fields listed above, not all are necessary to start your marketing efforts. Notice that individual name has been left off the list. For more detail on managing individuals or contacts, read Chapter 4.

For basic business, you will require at least the name of the company, a means of contacting someone at the company (phone, email, and address) and location. The location drives, for most countries in the world, taxation laws, and even triggers for U.S. companies laws against selling some goods to certain countries. This list of countries is called the Denied Parties List and should be consulted by your data management team.

Location is also important even if all you have in a company record is the company name and a phone number. Calling a company in California at 8 A.M. in New York is an exercise in futility. Knowing that the phone is located in California is helpful. Not all phones today carry area code designations that are indicative of location. This is especially true of cell phones. If your marketing database does not indicate mobile versus landline, you need to be cognizant of this *before* launching worldwide, or even nationwide, telemarketing efforts.

To give you an idea of the different types of address information collected by country, Exhibit 7.1 illustrates addresses from Brazil, Germany, Japan and Russia, taken from data available from Dun & Bradstreet (D&B). D&B's World Base offering picks from each local data supplier those fields that are consistent with other

Exhibit 7.1: Information Differences between Local Data Files and World Base

Local DB	Brazil	Germany	Japan	Russia
DUNS #	897410478	315034264	690564737	366167232
Company Name	Banco do Brasil S/A.	DEUTSCHE BANK AKTIENGESELLSCHAFT	トヨタ自動車（株）	ООО МО "НОВАЯ БОЛЬНИЦА"
Address 1	St. SBS - Quadra 01 - Bloco C -	Taunusanlage 12	愛知県豊田市トヨタ町1	УЛ. ЗАВОДСКАЯ, Д.29
Address 2	Lote 32 - 24Åº andar			'29
City	BrasÅlia	Frankfurt am Main		Екатеринбург
State/Province	DF	Hessen		

WorldBase	Brazil	Germany	Japan	Russia
DUNS #	897410478	315034264	690564737	366167232
Company Name	Banco do Brasil S/A.	DEUTSCHE BANK AG	Toyota Motor Corporation	NOVAYA BOLNITSA, OOO MO
Address 1	St. SBS - Quadra 01 - Bloco C	Taunusanlage 12		29 Ul.Zavodskaya
Address 2	Lote 32 - 24º andar			
City	BRASILIA	Frankfurt am Main	TOYOTA	Ekaterinburg
State/Province	DF	Hessen	AICHI	

Dun & Bradstreet, Nov. 2014

Source: Dun & Bradstreet, November 2014

countries. The World Base database provides a consolidated worldview of the data, but local files in each country provide additional information for each company.

Exhibit 7.1 shows the difference between data in local files versus information in the harmonized World Base. In addition, this illustration shows some of the different information collected at the local level that is not possible to harmonize across countries.

The range of addressing standardizations varies greatly by country. Some countries, like the U.S. and most Western European countries, have well defined standards. Emerging countries in Africa, Latin American, and Asia have less defined standards.

But even with standards spelled out, the same information across countries can vary. For example, German address information usually has no state or province associated with it. The address will carry a city and a postal code. The first digit in the postal code indicates the province. Canada follows a similar style by using the first letter in the postal code to indicate the province or state. But unlike Canada and the U.S., postal codes in Germany come *before* the city, not after it.

Understanding the nuances of address information and how it is used locally is an important part of building a marketing database.

Beyond Address Data

Beyond address information, you may also want to ensure that you have information specific to the way organizations do business in each country where you market. For example, it might be more important for you understand the VAT (Value Added Tax) ID of a company in the U.K. than it is for a company in the U.S. That information may not be collected in all countries where you market. Exhibit 7.2 provides an example of the different kinds of data that is available in India.

Exhibit 7.2: Data Elements Available in India

Category	Typical Data Elements
Firmographic	D&B® D-U-N-S® Number, Entity Name, Trade styles (up to 5), Entity Address, Telephone Number, Fax Number, Generic Email ID, Website, Employees, SIC, Line of Business, etc.
Registration Details	Registration Number, Incorporation Date, Legal Structure, Registered Office Address, Former Business Name, etc.
Banks, Registered Charges, Operations, etc.	Bank Name, Bank Address, Charge Date, Charge Number, Amount Secured, Chargee, Capacity and Production Output, Import and/or Export Indicator, Import Origins and/or Export Destinations, Suppliers' and Customers' Names, Location Ownership (Owns/Rents), etc.
CEO, Directors, or Executive Details	CEO, Directors', and Executives' Names, Title, Qualifications, Experience, etc.
Financials	Income Statement Date, Balance Sheet Statement Date, Audit Indicator, Consolidated Indicator, Revenue, Net Profit, Net Worth, Other Income Statement Items, Other Balance Sheet Items, Statement Currency Code, Nine Types of Ratios (Growth, Solvency, Efficiency, Profitability, etc.)
Linkages	Headquarters, Parent, Domestic Ultimate, Global Ultimate, Branches, Subsidiaries, Affiliates: D&B® D-U-N-S® Number, Name, Address, etc.
Risk, Payment, and Other Information	D&B Rating, OOB Indicator, History Indicator, Payment Experience Date, Payment Experience Type, High Credit, Now Owes, Past Due, Default or Other Adverse Information, etc.

Not all of these elements are available in other countries, however.

In Germany, for example it is often difficult to acquire from outside sources the names of individuals within the company because of privacy reasons, although information about the business is readily available.

In Africa, phone numbers, especially mobile phone numbers, are highly valued as the primary means to reach a business. But mobile phone numbers are not systematically collected throughout the world and in some countries, such as the U.S., mobile phones numbers are only used to reach individuals within a company—not the business itself.

In Russia and other states that once belonged to the USSR, collecting data is difficult and often looked on suspiciously by the businesses asked to provide it. In addition, there are few centralized organizations collecting and managing data sources.

In all data collection the main goal is to collect data relevant to your business and to reaching your customers. The Golden Rule in collecting or acquiring data in any country is "Don't acquire what you will not use."

Checklist for Getting Started

Marketing's first purpose when entering a new country is usually to support sales acquisition of accounts. This requires finding data specific to the country and then enriching it to provide sales with account-level information. That enrichment can then be used to provide those same sales teams with a rudimentary segmentation of the customers they should reach. And ultimately, local marketing databases can provide reports on the effectiveness of the sales and marketing efforts.

So now that you've made the decision to go international and you've tested your resolve in making an impact, here's a final checklist.

Enlist Local Support

Sales organizations are usually the first to enter a country. They are your first local support. Engage the sales team early. Determine what they need to make quota this quarter and help them. In return, you should request that sales help you to build the marketing database with the companies and contacts that they have. This is often possible through a CRM system, but nothing is better than enlisting sales management to help with this effort.

Although this seems like a logical first step, many companies enter markets without thinking about the synergy that should exist between sales and marketing. Marketing is often *not* considered until sales has been established within a country. This puts the marketing team in a "catch up" mode and gives local marketing organizations a bad name with sales.

Besides the sales teams, marketing may need to engage local support for building and maintaining a database. Engaging other sources in the country is very beneficial. Here are some types of businesses to consult:

1. Local marketing agencies
2. Local database marketing firms
3. International firms with local offices
4. Trade associations
5. Chambers of commerce
6. Your own partners or channels

Build the Database

Building a local marketing database with the help of local support is often the first task in supporting marketing tactics. But, if your company is international, there could be other considerations. For example, does the information within your local country need to flow back to or from your corporate systems? Are orders taken locally in local language or do transactions flow through electronic data interchange (EDI) systems back to corporate?

These questions can help you decide exactly how you may need to construct the data in your local marketing database. Take this scenario for example:

Your sales team needs leads for a new product introduction. The best targets for this product are customers who purchased a similar product two years ago from your only international distributor at the time. The distributor is willing to help you by providing the customer list, but it is all in English because the orders were managed in your U.S.-based headquarters. However, the new customers you want to acquire must be addressed in local language.

Immediately you face the issue of translation and how to ensure that the data you use from your distributor can be managed in local language with local addressing considerations. Transforming data from and to headquarters databases is an essential task. Deciding how to do it is a primary concern because how you manage this transition makes it possible for you to link accounts from your local environment to a worldwide view. This is especially important if you deal with global companies who may have branches in your local market.

Building a local marketing database cannot be accomplished in a vacuum without considering other corporate systems.

Use and Refine the Data

Local marketing databases need to be used. Building them for a one-time purpose does not return value to the marketing organization overall. Build them for multiple uses and use them.

Test, use, and refine. That's the way to find out if you've made the right choices in acquiring data for your marketing database. Often the first uses of a local marketing database are for events or telephone solicitations. Both of these activities can be performed with limited data—company name, address, and telephone number. Each of these activities should be formulated in such a way as to enrich the data as well as use it.

For example, if the data is used for telemarketing, then part of the telemarketing script should be to acquire contacts, titles, and additional information about the company contacted, such as type of business, number of employees, or other data that would be helpful to your specific industry. If the data is used to invite companies to events, make sure that you carefully delete from your database all returned mail and record attendees against invited companies to enrich your database further.

Ensuring that your database is kept up to date and actually represents your market as best possible is the ultimate goal of a marketing database no matter from what area of the world your company originates. Managing an international marketing database is a challenge that will only grow as the world of B2B marketing becomes increasingly more global.

CHAPTER 8

Managing Data on a Shoestring: Marketing Databases for Small Businesses

Gone are the days of knowing all of your customers by name, their children, their birthdays and anniversaries, not to mention their idiosyncrasies around the use of your product. If your business is successful, you have too many customers to know that level of detail about each one. However, with today's technologies you can have this information and more at your fingertips, for less money than you might think.

This chapter is a quick guide for small businesses that need to know how they can manage data to their advantage and gain an edge over their larger competition.

Importance of Data

Recognizing that data is important and will be important to your business can give you an edge over your competition.

To get you thinking about the use of data, let's check in at a hypothetical small manufacturing company in upstate Vermont. The company has been in business for over a decade and has always gained new customers by word of mouth. The president and owner of the company prides himself on growing the business by keeping his customers happy and returning.

It's Monday morning and the president, Clive Aiken, has just seen last week's sales figures—down significantly over the previous year. Despite the addition of new machinery and equipment to process orders, the figures have fallen by 20 percent. Clive calls his sales manager, Bill Maven, to have a conversation.

Clive: *Bill, what's happening out there? I see from last week's tally that we're not doing well in the Midwest or the South. I thought you had this under control.*

Bill: *Clive, you know that that new company in North Carolina is eating our lunch. They have started calling on all of our customers with new pricing for the process that we have recently revitalized.*

Clive: *Well, what do our customers say?*

Bill: *Our customers? Uh, it's been hard to get in touch with all of them. I've been going back through accounts receivable records to find the names of the purchasing agents for our largest accounts. You know, we've always called on the VPs of Product Marketing. Those are the names that we have in our rolodexes. We don't really know the purchasing guys and neither do the VPs we call on.*

Clive: *Looks like we need to know them. So how can I help you?*

Bill: *I need help with securing this data. Any chance you can free up resources for a week or two?*

This scenario plays out across the world in small to medium-sized businesses every day. Clive and Bill are not alone. In today's fast-moving, competitive environment having data about your customers and their business environment can help you in a myriad of ways.

You Can Grow Faster

Knowing who your best customers are, what industry they come from, and how they are best reached helps you to position your resources appropriately for growth. For example, you don't open a new sales office in Tennessee if you know that there is little opportunity for your product or service in the area or that your competition owns 75 percent of the market in that state.

And you don't market your product for healthcare if you are aware that 60 percent of your best customers come from the agricultural industry. Marketing with data is as much about what you don't do as it is about what you do.

Growing a business needs customers, the right locations, and good management. Data helps with all of these. By helping you navigate the market, you can position all of these resources for faster growth.

You Can Manage Ups and Downs Better

Over the last decade, the economy has been on a roller coaster. Those ups and downs have created havoc for small businesses—the lifeblood of American industry. But data can actually help businesses manage through turbulent times and provide some stability in an otherwise rocky business environment.

Knowing who your best customers are and what their businesses are doing helps you navigate the economic shifts. For example, simple credit ratings shifts for the customers you deal with can provide insight into what may be happening with your customer. Also, analyzing number of days outstanding from your payment records can give you an indication of how your business is progressing as well as give you an indication of your customer's financial status.

These numbers, whether managed overall for your entire customer base or individually for each customer, are good indicators of how well your business does and also help provide leading indicators for enabling you to navigate rough, or even boom, times.

You Develop an Asset

The last few decades have seen a rise in the number of businesses who put data at the heart of their business plans. For high tech companies such as Google, Facebook and Amazon, data is their reason for being.

But even your business can collect and manage data that gives you a competitive edge. Take for example a company that can penetrate an account more deeply than its competitors, because the database is filled with more contacts than the sales team has acquired from its day-to-day relationships. An account record appended with additional names of key influencers and additional departments or divisions, supplemented by marketing communications to identify additional opportunity in the account, is a corporate asset of great value.

Using data to understand your market means understanding your customer as well as your competitors and their customers.

Seven Steps to Getting the Most from Your Business Data

Let's look at seven strategies a small business can use to gain leverage from its marketing database.

Evaluate Your Top Customers

If your business is small enough, you know who your customers are. Usually in B2B small businesses, you can count your best customers on your fingers and toes. But that doesn't mean that you know all you need to know about them. Successful small businesses survive because they usually can respond faster to a market demand than larger companies. But they have to know how the market is changing and make moves to position themselves to where the market is going.

Let's go back to Clive and Bill for a look at what happened when they evaluated their top customers.

> Bill: *Clive, I just finished going through the accounts receivable records yesterday. Thanks for that intern by the way. He was very helpful. But what I found was more than just the names of the purchasing agents. Jim, that's the intern, found some other interesting facts.*
>
> Clive: *Really? So share.*
>
> Bill: *Well, one thing he noticed is that our top customers have been ordering about 5 percent less each quarter over the past year. And they are paying slower.*
>
> Clive: *What do you think is going on?*
>
> Bill: *I don't really know, but it gives me a good reason for calling all of them and asking a few questions.*

Not only did digging through their existing customer data give Clive and Bill a clue as to their decrease in sales, it also gave Bill a "reason to call" the customers and have in-depth conversations. Feeding that information back to the marketing team can help reposition products, drive pricing changes, or simply give the customer the feeling that someone is paying attention.

Separate Your Accounts Receivables from Customer Information

Although the accounts receivable data was valuable to Clive and Bill, it's important to know that this data is best when complemented by additional information about your customers. Separating key elements out of the financial systems into a marketing analytics database gives you insights into your customers' buying habits.

For example, one of the best pieces of information for your marketing database that can be pulled from your accounts receivable is the number of days outstanding for invoices. Using this information can make it possible for you to determine your best customers, your struggling customers, or just those with different business practices.

The power of knowing which customers are best for you helps you to identify others that might be good as well. This process is usually referred to as "look-alike" marketing. Look-alike modeling for marketing purposes has primarily been used in targeted advertising, using the wealth of data available to online advertisers. But small businesses can employ the concept to gain a competitive advantage.

Once you've identified in your financial systems which customers are your best, you can begin to look for the elements that make a "best" customer in data available either in your own marketing data or from external data sources. For example, if you know that your best customers are those with a credit ranking between A and Z, then you can very easily judge all new customers or newly identified prospects against this criteria. It's always better to acquire customers who look like your best customers.

Accounts receivables and order information are also important to tell you who exactly is purchasing your product—not the company, but the individual who may be signing off on the purchase of your product. Often times this name is not in your sales information, but is still extremely important for sales to know. Making sure that the purchaser's name and contact information is available to sales and marketing can help in the sales process. As purchasers become more and more important in the buying process, this data grows in importance as well.

Decide What Information Is Important to Know and What You Have

Not all data is important to helping you sell more or attract the best customers. Some information is available just because you need it to fulfill orders or manage customer support.

Before you begin evaluating the data, however, it's advisable to think strategically about what information is important to your sales and growth. Start with your sales managers to determine what information they know about customers that is not usually available in any system. For an example, let's check back in on Bill as he has coffee with the marketing manager, Pat.

Pat: *Bill, Clive has asked me to help you grow the business outside our home state. So to start, I thought you and I might have a conversation about your best customers.*

Bill: *OK, Pat. Thanks for the help. What do you need to know?*

Pat: *For starters, describe for me a typical sales cycle. How do you get started? What are the stages of the sale? How do you know if a customer will actually buy or not? How do you forecast when the sale will come in?*

Bill: *Wow! I've never thought about sales in such specific terms. I just do it. How about I tell you how I landed GKF Manufacturing? That's our largest customer upstate.*

Pat: *That would be great.*

Bill: *OK. I met the president of GKF Manufacturing when I was playing golf at the regional golf club last Wednesday. He's got a wicked handicap, by the way. We struck up a conversation and he happened to mention what his firm did. I could tell immediately that there might be opportunity there.*

Pat: *Wait a minute, Bill. Describe for me specifically what it was that caught your attention.*

Bill knows what makes a good customer prospect, but like most great salespeople is an unconscious competent. He's been doing it so well for so long that he has to stop to think about how he knows what he knows. This kind of in-depth interview of your top salespeople can yield all kinds of information that can be translated to data elements that can be captured in your marketing database. Exhibit 8.1 provides a quick list of the kinds of information you might get.

As you can see, some of the information can be captured from external data sources such as lists of chamber of commerce members, but other data may need to be acquired from salespeople themselves, such as personal hobbies of their key decision makers. In small to medium-sized businesses the connection between sales and marketing is essential to make the development of marketing data effective.

Once you know what is important to collect, evaluating each piece of data that you already have can help you determine just how valuable it really is. This act of evaluation is usually performed via a data audit of some kind. According to Techopedia, "A data audit refers to the auditing of data to assess its quality or utility for a specific purpose."

A data audit begins with rounding up all the data sources that you have inside your company and those that you have access to outside as well. Besides your financial systems, you should also try to gather data from sales personnel, support logs, lists from events, or even holiday lists maintained by your executives. Your next step is to evaluate each of these lists and their data elements against the criteria that you glean from your understanding of who is your best customer. If you have the data, you keep it and make sure that you actively maintain it. If you don't have the data you need, you might have to acquire it.

Exhibit 8.1: Data Elements That May Be Uncovered by Interviewing Sales Staff

Comments on Best Customers	Data to Capture
Decision maker is self-made	Affiliation with chamber of commerce or local civic clubs
Decision maker plays golf	Personal hobby information
Company has 200+ employees using our competitor's products	Number of employees at company location
Company has a purchasing process	Name of purchasing agent
Buys XYZ product from competitor	Competitor product owned
Company located outside the city because they need space for manufacturing	Metropolitan Statistical Areas
Company has warehouse facilities	Real estate holdings

Take the example of Bill's customer who is an avid golf player. Most likely, your CRM system doesn't capture "hobby." But if this is a really important factor for your business, then you might figure out a way to make it part of the information captured on your customer record. Other information, such as real estate holdings, can be acquired via state and local sources.

But for every data element that is important to marketing, there are probably several more that are unimportant but extremely necessary for order processing or support. Select and set aside in your marketing database the data elements that are most useful to marketing. Those are the ones that you will concentrate on maintaining and using to attract, retain, and develop customers.

Establish a Way to Acquire, Maintain, and Retire Data

Once you've determined which data elements are necessary for identifying the "best" customers for your business, your next job as a marketer is to acquire, maintain, and retire data.

Let's start with retire first. Although it seems odd that we should start with which data we don't need, this is actually a good starting point. If you have a marketing database today, chances are that you have a good number of records that were acquired over a year ago, have never really yield any revenue for your company, and have not responded to most of your marketing messages.

In short, you probably have about 20 percent of your data that is not useful. Getting rid of this data is important because it helps you to concentrate your database marketing efforts on the most useful records.

The second task is to bolster the records you do have or provide some maintenance to them. This is where the data audit comes in. A good data audit will profile your data and let you know simple things such as:

- How many records you have
- How many of the records are complete
- Whether the data in the fields is valid—state fields have actual states in them
- Whether the fields are consistently formed—U.S. phone numbers are represented as (xxx) xxx-xxxx or email addresses are xxxx@xxx.xxx

With a data audit in hand, you can concentrate on completing fields that need additional information and cleaning up those that have errors.

Finally, your comparison of what you need to identify the best customers and what you have already on hand may provide a list of data elements that you don't have. That's where acquisition plays a key role. Interestingly, most marketers go to acquiring data *first*. But without knowing what is really needed and what you already have makes acquiring data an expensive first step.

Because acquiring data is expensive, making sure that you acquire the right data is essential. When you have already determined what you need, you simply identify either an outside list, a list broker, or a data provider who can help you fill in the gaps. There are some hints about who to engage with these tasks later in this chapter. Chapter 2 also delves deeper into data sources useful to acquisition.

Let Your Customers Know What You Are Doing With Their Data

A lot of what we do today on the Web can be tracked, and is tracked, by major advertising and consumer companies wanting a few vital seconds of your interest. When a company like Facebook or Google can surmise from tracking data that you are a native Texan living in California and might be interested in beekeeping, then they can provide information from various advertisers who consider that niche a valuable part of their market. To ordinary people, that's often just creepy.

B2B marketing is no different. Individuals who make the decisions to purchase your product for their companies need to know how their individual data is being used. Making sure that they know you are collecting data is important.

For businesses, privacy laws have been less robust than for individuals. Most laws governing privacy concentrate on respecting the privacy of the person. But even businesses have limits for privacy-invading email practices. Businesses can be cited for violations of privacy acts if they send unsolicited advertising-oriented emails in violation of the CAN-SPAM Act.

The law applies to B2B communications such as an email to former customers announcing a new product line. Each separate email found in violation of the law carries a $16,000 penalty. As a business owner, you must ensure that your emails to other businesses and to individuals within those businesses comply. The Federal Trade Commission (FTC) categorizes email messages that contain these kinds of information:

1. **Commercial**—Any message whose primary purpose is to market a product or service.
2. **Transactional**—Any communication that facilitates an already agreed upon transaction or helps manage an ongoing transaction.
3. **Other**—Any communication that falls outside transactional or commercial. Holiday greetings fall into this category as long as you don't sneak in a comment about next year's line of products.

---

*The **CAN-SPAM Act,** a law that sets the rules for commercial email, establishes requirements for commercial messages, gives recipients the right to have you stop emailing them, and spells out tough penalties for violations.*

Federal Trade Commission, "CAN-SPAM Act: A Compliance Guide for Business," (bus61-can-spam-act-compliance-guide-business.pdf).

This is why letting your customers know what you are doing with their information is so important. If, for example, you collect information about a business's credit rating and the business is a sole proprietorship, you are actually collecting extremely sensitive information. Letting your customer know what your intentions are with this data helps you strengthen your relationship with your customer.

Engaging a privacy professional to help evaluate your privacy practices and notices to your customers is always a wise move for smaller business owners even in the B2B world.

Use Your Customer Data

"Use it or lose it." This quote from Henry Ford was about money, but it could just as well apply to data. Since data deteriorates rapidly (see Chapter 5), you need to know what you will do with the data *before* you capture it.

In smaller businesses, using data for sales and marketing may not seem as important as using data to manage transactions. But let's look at some very practical first uses of a sales and marketing database.

1. **Get to know your best customers better.** Armed with information on which customers spend the most with you and what they buy, your sales and marketing teams can be more effective at developing programs that keep your customers spending. To ensure that you keep your best customers, try looking at support records—how many times they call the various departments that support them. Don't forget that calls to accounts receivable often indicate more customer dissatisfaction than calls to your product support lines.

2. **Keep in touch and generate referrals.** The Net Promoter Score (NPS) was developed by Fred Reichheld of Bain and Company. It is simply a management tool that helps businesses gauge the loyalty of their customers. NPS was established to help companies better understand how customer satisfaction affects the bottom line. One of the key questions on an NPS survey is whether the customer will refer you their friends, associates, and other businesses. In B2B, this referral is extremely important to the continued

growth of most businesses— large or small. Your data about which customers provide referrals helps you know who your key customers are. Maintaining data on who provides referrals and who was referred should be part of your sales and marketing database.

3. **Identify problem areas before they become disasters**. Data can help you determine where you might have problems in the future and you don't have to have an army of statisticians to tell you that.

For example, monitoring your customer purchasing patterns—who buys what and when—can give you indications about how much additional staff you might require for next quarter or next year. You probably already do this. But monitoring this same data can also tell you what products to combine because customer usually buy them together, what products to promote, and which customers have not purchased your full product line. Both sales and marketing can use this information in planning sales calls and marketing promotions.

Perhaps one of the best places to monitor your data is with your support organization. Often sales and marketing data is considered pre-sales information and, therefore, not usually combined with support or transactional data because that is post-sales information. But wise sales and marketing organizations know that the best place to sell someone something is when they complain or have a question. If you satisfy their questions or interests, your support team can be turned into a sales team at that point of interaction.

It's not enough to use the data once and forget about it. Using it regularly keeps it clean because as you learn new things, you update records. Remember that businesses change names and locations, undergo mergers and acquisitions, and go out of business. All of these changes surface when you use your data.

Evaluate Your Progress Every Quarter, Just as You Do Financials

Most good businesspeople know that measuring your business is a requirement. Where and what you measure, however, are important and highly dependent on what data you collect. All solid businesses measure revenue and growth, but here are some other measurement questions that you may or may not have considered:

1. How many customers will refer us to their networks?
2. How much do our customers spend with us? Over what period of time?
3. How are our customers responding to us? Through social media? Through our support organizations?

4. Which products are our bestsellers?
5. Which products drag additional product or services sales, either along with the purchase or a short time after the purchase?
6. What is our return on sales and marketing investment for each product?

In addition to providing you a view of the health of your business, looking at data for these areas also drives a closer look at the data itself. Here are some questions that often arise when you start analyzing customer information:

1. Why are we acquiring it? How was it acquired and who has access to it?
2. Where is this data kept? Inside or outside the company?
3. How often is it refreshed?
4. How complete is this data set? Who owns enrichment of this data set?
5. How do you ensure accuracy of this data?

Executives who ask these kinds of questions when presented with information are those who truly see the value of data and its use not only in managing the business but growing it as well.

Measuring Data Critical to Your Business:
An Anecdote from a Sales and Marketing Company

Larry Kaul operates a professional services company that helps other companies improve their sales performance. Kaul describes his clients as mostly marketing companies, management consultants, and IT-managed services firms. Kaul found what he calls "surprising and valuable insights" when looking at data over the past year for fifteen of his clients. He began looking at data when engaged as a consultant for another company whose practices were not so successful. The data Kaul concentrated on was sales call information that helped him determine the best way to manage his business.

Remember, Kaul's product is a service that helps other businesses drive sales. Here are some of his findings when looking at data that was important to his "product."

- There is no correlation between number of prospect meetings and sales results!
  —We deliver from ten to forty interested prospects ("interested" equates to meeting request, meeting completion, keep-in touch request, or opportunity created) for each sales campaigns (within a two-month window) and deliver one to two closed deals in three to four months. (True for 70 percent of the clients).
  —FINDING: The number of meetings completed has no correlation to the number of closed deals. This piece of data completely contradicts the value proposition and business model for the entire lead generation industry that charges for meetings scheduled.
- Analyzing responses to sales calls, emails, and leads generated surprising findings for Kaul:
  —70 percent of his pipeline leads come from responses to the emails.

—30 percent come from sales calls.

—80 percent of the pipeline leads had contact with sales. Sales had left a voice mail or chased the lead to schedule time. Cold calls with a voice mail message left for an unreached contact really mattered.

Kaul also found that CEOs are more likely to respond to cold outbound emails than lower-level managers. This also contradicts the conventional wisdom that CEOs won't respond to cold outreach.

Most importantly for Kaul, looking at data changed how his firm thinks about the definition of a result. It changed his whole business model.

It's no longer a meeting scheduled, but now 100 percent focused on revenue closed. Their approach to campaign strategy and the services they provide to clients changed. Their new website talks about "revenue focused sales" rather than lead generation to drive a high volume of qualified meetings.

To Kaul, it's a "subtle but profound difference. Knowing rather than having an opinion that I'm not a lead-generation but a revenue-generation sales company matters to me."

Source: Larry Kaul of Kaul Sales Partners, Chicago, Illinois

What If You Need Help?

So you've looked at your business, examined the data you collect and determined that you have some holes. Where do you start to get a better view of what data you need and how to use it?

Look Inside First

You may be a large enough business to have someone internally who can get you started. Someone in your marketing or sales department may already have a good start in understanding your customers and the data you need to grow your business. Don't overlook the financial department. Often those who look at the accounts receivable information on a daily basis know very well which customers are buying and which ones are having trouble. Take advantage of their tribal knowledge.

Complement Internal Resources

Even if you do have an internal resource, you could still take advantage of an outside resource when beginning this task. Bringing in someone who knows data and how to use it for businesses like yours helps you get a different viewpoint and may uncover key aspects overlooked by internal resources. But don't outsource the strategy. Make sure that you have a clear reason for starting on the journey of data management and usage.

What Problem Are You Trying to Solve?

Whether you look inside your company or go outside for an expert opinion, your first task is to gain clarity on what problem you are trying to solve. This sounds easy, but it's not. Data can help you identify issues and it can help you solve them. Understanding where it's best applied is something only you can decide. Here are three scenarios that could describe your situation. Which resonates with you?

Data, data everywhere but not a fact in sight.

Many businesses have data in several organizations. Marketing has data for emailing product launch information. Sales has data for calling on key personnel within their accounts. And, no surprise, it sits on every salesperson's individual contact management system.

To complete this picture, support has data gleaned from supporting accounts or used for renewing support contracts. Finance has business worthiness data. R&D has market opportunity data and often product usage data.

So if you have this much data, what's the problem? The question is, can you use this information to make business decisions?

Often these data sets are distributed and locked into organizational silos. Bringing them together to answer questions for the overall business can be a daunting, and sometimes very technical, task.

Another important consideration when looking at data silos is to get absolute clarity on what problem you think you are solving when the data comes together. Not only does this clarity of purpose help you determine which silos to integrate, but it also helps you realize value quicker because you have identified a problem that really needs solving.

Here are some reasons for bringing together different data sets across your organization:

- **Sales with Marketing:** Why are sales lagging? Is marketing generating enough leads that are well qualified?
- **Finance with Support:** Why are support costs going through the roof? Which products are generating the support demand? What is the current cost per support call?
- **Financial Pricing with Product Installations:** How is pricing affecting the sales of our latest product line? How are our partners affecting the adoption of the new product?

Securing resources to help you with this problem is perhaps *the* most common issue faced by growing businesses today. Identifying the problem you want to solve goes a long way to helping convince management to provide the resource.

Data, but so what?

If you are one of the lucky companies that has your data centralized or accessible by various silos, then your biggest issue might be what to do with the data. Many companies have a "so what?" attitude toward this asset, not realizing just exactly how valuable it could be.

In this case, you need to show value with the data. That could be through some of the metrics you already manage for your company—such as sales analysis or support performance—or it could be by piloting a specific deep dive on an issue that hasn't been easy to solve.

For example, a software company that has high order volumes at the end of quarter, may want to analyze what the propensity of each order is to book in a timely manner. In other words, how long will it take the order to traverse the system and what variables will keep it from not booking on time?

Another example of using data to answer the "so what?" question is evaluating orders for support. Since time is money, how long does it take to respond to a support request? Which support orders are causing the greatest delays in response? Simple questions that data can help answer.

Data crisis.

You never let a serious crisis go to waste. And what I mean by that it's an opportunity to do things you think you could not do before.

Rahm Emanuel's quote about the 2008 financial crisis can easily be applied to any crisis you might face with data. Often a data crisis is the event that makes management pay closer attention to this asset, just as a fire or theft often generates renewed interest in insurance policies and practices or a natural disaster in emergency preparedness.

Most often today, a data crisis involves a breach of security in some fashion. Although this kind of crisis is often reflective of poor or insubstantial IT practices, it does shine a harsh light on the data itself and how it is managed within your company. This "light" can be used to help you begin to explain the value of managing, protecting, and gaining value from your company's data.

But the best plan of action is *not* to experience the crisis yourself but to use the crises of your competitors or other organizations to jump-start a data review. Start with customer information and make sure that you know what data you do have and how you are using it. That will help to uncover any potential issues such as lack of permissions for email marketing, duplicated data across systems, problems with junk characters, or inaccuracies, etc.

With a solid data audit in hand, you can begin to size up your opportunity for improvement and to zero in on the areas that, with improvement, can be the most productive for your organization.

What Type of Resource Do You Need?

Securing the right resource to help you make the case for data, or help you with the tasks associated with showing value, can be a daunting task.

After you have examined carefully where you stand with your data, you have a much clearer vision of who or what type of resource can best help you achieve your goals.

Exhibit 8.2 provides a quick guide to help you select the right resources for your particular stage of data needs along with potential costs associated with this support. These are generalizations and can always be bettered through negotiation and scope of the project, but should give you a feel for the resources available and what you might expect to pay for them.

Exhibit 8.2: Data Resources and Their Associated Costs

Data Stage	Deliverable Expected	Expense Guideline	Type of Resource
0	Data strategy for overall data program	$$$	Consulting firm specializing in strategy development or advertising
		$$	Independent consultant
		$	Workshop with internal teams and facilitator
1	Data audit to assess baseline and describe fit gap	$$$	Database marketing consulting firm Department within an advertising or direct marketing firm
		$$	Database vendor Internal resources
		$	Internal subject matter experts
2	Data pilot to prove capability	$$$	Analytics consulting firm Analytics department within advertising or direct marketing agency
		$$	Independent analytics consultant
		$	In-house capability
3	Ongoing data management	$$$	Outsourced data management organization Direct marketing firm
		$$	Internal data management team
		$	Low-cost location data management team

Each type of resource is described below. A list of questions you should ask before engaging a resource to support your data goals is also given.

Consulting firm specializing in strategy development.

Management consulting firms are rapidly learning that data is at the heart of some of the business issues that plague a company. Because they recognize the need to have a solid strategy for data management and usage as part of the overall company strategy, many of the high-end management consulting firms have areas of expertise that can easily provide you with a data strategy that supports your company's overall strategy. In fact, if you are working with a consulting firm on company strategy, you might consider approaching them on how they could help you with a data strategy in support of that initiative. Here are some key questions to ask consulting firms when approaching them to help you:

1. What expertise do they have in developing data strategies for firms?
2. Who on their team is qualified for this assignment?
3. How do they approach building a strategy? How do they see a data strategy linking to the company's overall efforts?
4. What expertise do they have in your industry? With companies your size?
5. How do they manage an engagement for data strategy development? On an hourly basis? Set fee? By phase?
6. What is their overall philosophy about helping to implement a strategy once delivered?

Independent consultant.

Independent consultants are those individuals who have an expertise and are not associated with a larger consulting firm. They may have at one time been part of a larger consultancy or a major company. The best of these consultants have developed an expertise specific to data and specific to your industry. Locating them is often the challenging part. Start by doing your research. Here are some questions you need to have answered before hiring them:

1. Why is this consultant considered an expert in your field?
2. What kinds of work has he/she done that is verifiable? Published papers? Blogs or articles?
3. What do those who have used his/her services say about the engagement? Was it strategy only or did the consultant recommend and support implementation? What expertise did the consultant exhibit in both stages?
4. How was the engagement priced? Competitively? Flat fee? Hourly?
5. Did the consultant work alone or bring in others to support the engagement?
6. What in the consultant's background can be helpful to your situation?

Database vendor.

Engaging a database vendor may mean selecting a database or a marketing automation tool that is specific to your environment. This part of the industry has exploded in the last few years and is highly competitive. Some of the more successful database applications used in the marketing environment have been gobbled up by larger computing or software firms as they discovered the need to put data at the center of their marketing operations landscape.

There are a host of firms that specialize in databases, some specific to marketing. These vendors differ from database marketing consultancies because their primary goal is to sell a software product or database. Here are a few questions to ask when engaging a database vendor for supporting your marketing efforts:

1. What services do you offer for helping with designing the overall database environment? Are those services separate from the overall implementation services?
2. What kinds of database audits have you done previously for companies in my industry or size?
3. What references do you have in my industry or with my size company?
4. How is your offering implemented? On premise? In the cloud?
5. How are your services billed for implementation? Fixed fee? Hourly? Part of the cost of the database?
6. Who will help with the implementation? Are they experts internal to your company or consultants?

Database marketing consulting firm.

There are firms that specialize in database marketing that can be engaged to help you with everything from strategy through to implementation. In fact, some of the firms today act as hosted environments for all of your marketing data and because of this are often confused with database vendors. The primary difference is that these firms do not sell one type of database. Instead, they will implement whatever system your business requires or deliver the capability you need without the concern for the actual technical installation. Here are few questions you should be prepared to ask this type vendor:

1. How does your service differ from a totally outsourced capability?
2. In what areas of database marketing do you specialize—sales to marketing connections, marketing web, lead generation, etc.
3. Who would be responsible for my installation? (When working with any consulting firm, it's important to find out exactly who will be assigned to your task.)
4. How do you charge? Set fee? Hourly?
5. What references do you have within my industry? With my size company?

Advertising or direct marketing agency.

Advertising agencies over the past few decades have increasingly developed expertise in database marketing, especially those agencies that consider the entire gamut of marketing communications part of their service delivery. Most agencies today now see that helping to guide and promote the customer through a buying journey is the new face of advertising. But agencies specialize, for the most part, in putting to use the data that you have or that they can buy to engage the customer. Few of them will actually engage with you to develop a strategy around data and its use. But some of them will. Here are a few questions to ask of your advertising or direct marketing agency to see if they are up to the task:

1. How are you positioned to support the strategy and implementation of a database marketing design for my company?
2. How would you approach the problem?
3. What department or individuals within your firm have this expertise?
4. What references do you have from companies our size and in our industry?
5. How would you bid or price this task? As part of your regular advertising fee structure? By the task? Hourly?

Analytics consulting agency or analytics consultant.

The rise in big data has seen a host of analytics consultancies pop on the scene. Many of these were founded by individuals with expertise in statistics that have learned to apply their craft to marketing situations. The agencies vary in size and often specialize in particular statistical problems such as pricing, propensity, or product analytics.

Some analytics consultants may have been associated with larger firms and broken away, while others collaborate with a host of individuals to do a particular task and give the overall perception of an agency.

Engaging an analytics consultancy or an analytics consultant can be tricky, especially if you have not yet established your strategy or made your data ready for analysis. Hiring this type firm to do these tasks is not cost effective.

Here are a few questions to ask of any analytics resource:

1. What is your area of expertise? How are you qualified for marketing analytics?
2. What references do you have? In this industry? With companies our size?
3. What was the outcome of the analytics provided in previous engagements? How were these outcomes measured?
4. How do you approach the situation if the data is not complete or available for the type of analytics you are recommending?
5. How do you charge? By the task? Hourly?

6. Will you share your statistical models? For example, will you tell us which variables are most predictive? Or are your models proprietary?

7. Do you augment our data with any other data? How do you acquire it?

Outsourcing—Do You or Don't You?

Each of the different resources listed above can be engaged at different times for different portions of your data journey. However, you might also consider whether you want to outsource the entire operation. This simply means that you give to an outside vendor the entire task, or pieces, of the setup, management, and extraction of value from your marketing database.

Before you consider this option, evaluate whether this is best for your particular situation.

Outsourcing is a great option if you understand fully what you gain versus what you give up. It's also best when you fully understand what specific tasks will be outsourced. To get to that point, you need a good data strategy that articulates the specific requirements of your data asset.

For example, if your strategy is to use data to help you solve different problems across the business, then it may not be a good move to outsource all of your data tasks. Instead, you might consider only outsourcing the actual management of the data and retain the analytics capability. From a marketing perspective, you might outsource contact management, but retain market analysis and lead management.

The best reason to outsource is to gain a skill or expertise that you do not have available on staff today. However, outsourcing is often looked at as a low cost option, and it can be—if managed effectively. Managing a resource outside your firm may be an expertise that you don't have today inside your firm. Make sure that you have that skill available and that it can be deployed to this task. Just remember that the skill you are looking for is not one associated with the database task being outsourced but with the ability to manage an outsourced vendor. This requires both management skill and solid knowledge of what needs to be accomplished.

Here are a few questions you will need to ask of your team before outsourcing:

1. Why would we consider outsourcing? Cost? Expertise?

2. What parts of the database management and usage tasks are we outsourcing?

3. Who will be responsible for the success of the outsource engagement?

4. How will we measure the success of the engagement?

5. What limitations do we have if we decide to bring it in-house again?

6. How quickly can this capability be implemented?

No matter which resource you select, remember that the responsibility for what you want accomplished rests squarely with you. Having your goal clearly articulated prior to engaging any resource is imperative to a successful engagement.

Offshore or Onshore?

Deciding what you need to do and who will help you accomplish the tasks associated with managing data for marketing can be complicated by where you would like these tasks accomplished.

In the past decade, U.S.-based firms have learned about how to manage cost by sending some of their more mundane and repetitive tasks to workers in India, China, Eastern Europe, Costa Rica, and Indonesia. The attractions for these areas are skilled workers, tax-friendly corporate environments, and the ability to manage resources around the clock. In fact, larger corporations have put major centers in at least three areas of the globe in order to manage customer service and other corporate activities twenty-four hours a day, seven days a week.

Data management is one of the key areas of a business often outsourced simply because the tasks are often repetitive and skills can be developed quickly with native resources. A prime location for offshore outsourcing is India's Bangalore region. Bangalore hosts a large number of multinational corporations drawn there because of the high-tech and engineering skills of Indian students. India boasts one of the most progressive, dynamic environments for technology in the world.

Many consulting firms or database marketing agencies you might wish to engage may outsource to other parts of the world their support of routine database tasks. And more and more, highly analytical tasks are also being outsourced to India and China specifically, as these countries start to surpass the U.S. in mathematics, engineering, and other sciences.

As you might be able to imagine, offshoring does mitigate costs, but make sure that you are ready for all the costs associated with this balance to your bottom line. For example, managing teams in India may require that your U.S.-based team adjust their working hours to accommodate some overlap between teams. This is especially true even if management resources are the only ones affected. For half the year, India is 9.5 to 12.5 hours ahead of the U.S. (During daylight savings time, the U.S. gains an hour and lessens the gap.) This means that holding a staff meeting with India in the winter from your location on the East Coast may necessitate a time slot around 6 A.M. or 8 P.M. Neither of these choices may be optimal for your teams.

Engaging a database marketing vendor who has already built these relationships in other countries is often a good option and something that should be considered when looking to engage a resource. The vendor or agency can often become the go-between for your management team and the resources performing the work.

But, make sure you fully understand the trade-offs in cost, skill, and communications capabilities before you agree to offshore this resource.

How Do You Find a Qualified Database Marketing Resource?

Finding a qualified database marketing consultant is not difficult, but it does take time. Like any purchase, you need to have a clear understanding of what you are trying to accomplish, how much you can afford to spend, and what value you are expecting in return. You will need to engage a resource that helps you at the appropriate stage in your data maturity and one that can successfully see you through to the subsequent stages.

But how to find such a person or organization? Like all purchase decisions we make today, the first stop should be the Internet, but there are other ways to begin your search as well. Here's a quick list of ways to find a qualified database marketing consultancy or consultant:

1. Ask your friends. Once you've toured the Internet and found some direction for the kind of resource you seek, your next step is to engage with others in your particular situation. Chances are that if you are in a marketing organization, you have contacts in marketing who work for other firms. Start by asking them who they have engaged or, if they haven't, if they would be interested in working with you to find a resource. This assumes that your friend is not a competitor.
2. Look at organizations supporting database marketers. The Direct Marketing Association (DMA) is the organization "advancing and protecting responsible data-driven marketing." The DMA (http://thedma.org) has chapters in most large cities and can be counted on to deliver expertise at least twice a year via their conferences. Sign up to go to at least one before you make a choice for someone to help you with your journey.
3. Launch a request for information on LinkedIn or some other web-based organization that can provide you access to companies in your vertical market. This is a good way get a lot of people providing you information, but it might also be overwhelming. So, again, be clear on what you are looking for and make sure that your request is clear as well.

In today's highly networked world, it will not take you long to locate a resource that can help you.

No matter at what stage you find yourself—getting started or improving your database— you now have the tools to continue on your journey.

CHAPTER 9

Troubleshooting:
Thorny Problems and Solutions

Business-to-business marketers are plagued by data problems. Business data is complex and fast-changing. Customers transact with us through a variety of channels, and often provide us with conflicting information. Our legacy databases are not as robust as we need. It's a never-ending battle.

In this chapter, we identify 27 of the thorniest data problems facing B2B marketers, and offer solutions that are practical, straightforward and realistic. Our special thanks to Bernice Grossman for her contribution in preparing this material.

Thorny Problem #1:   Matching and De-duplication
How do I match and de-duplicate customer records effectively?

Solution: Three approaches to consider:

1. Establish—and enforce—data-governing rules to improve data entry, which will keep your matching problems under some semblance of control.
2. Find a solid software vendor with a tool specifically designed to parse, cleanse, and otherwise do the matching for you. Test a few vendors to find the one that works best with your data. Most of these tools require some tuning to ensure that the matches they provide work well in your environment. Engaging a subject matter expert from the software vendor is recommended.
3. Write a custom matching algorithm. As a place to start, ask several match/merge companies to show you examples of the results of their algorithm against your data.

Thorny Problem #2:   The Record of Truth
When data elements conflict in my house file, how do I decide which is the "truth"?

Solution: The short answer is by date. The most recent data is the one you should default to.

But also keep in mind when importing data to enhance your records that appended data will always have its limitations and is best viewed as directional, versus real, "truth." Be careful not to build targeting or segmentation processes that are primarily dependent on appended data.

You could consider conducting an audit to validate the quality of your various append sources. (This is usually done by telephone, and it's not cheap.) Then you can add a score to each appended element, based on its source, to manage the risk of relying on any particular element.

Thorny Problem #3:   Bad Data Entry
Data entered by our salespeople ends up as mush. They don't follow the rules, or there are no rules. That may be okay for the rep, but it's not okay for the company.

Solution: Here's the best practice: Create a centralized data input group. Train and motivate them well. Give them objective rules to follow. Develop a simple method for testing the accuracy from this group as an ongoing practice. If this group cannot follow the rules, then the rules should be re-evaluated.

Then, develop a very simple process by which reps pass their data to this group. Dedicate particular group members to certain reps, so the input person builds experience about the rep's behavior and communication style. The bonus: these two parties will team, build a valuable relationship, work together well, and improve data quality.

Consider enabling the data input group with a real-time interface with a database services provider to prompt the standard company name and address. This can be an expensive, but very helpful, tool.

And remember, it's not just sales that needs this kind of teaming. Order management is an organization that can also challenge your data standards. Embrace them as well.

Thorny Problem #4:   Multiple Addresses
Which corporate address should I put in my database? There's the legal address and the financial (banking) address, which may be different. Or there may be a street address and a P.O. box address. Equifax and D&B often supply the financial address. The address to receive proxies is different from the address to receive advertising mail. How should I sort all this out?

Solution: As a marketer, your concern is delivery. You care about a bill-to and a ship-to. Focus on the address where mail and packages are delivered. These are the addresses that have the highest probability of being CASS certified.

Thorny Problem #5:   Attribution

Measuring the impact of each touch in our omni-channel world is driving us nuts. Any ideas?

Solution: The attribution problem has heated up recently, fueled by the rise of digital marketing. But it's really nothing new. The traditional attribution methods of assigning the credit have long been either the first touch (the inquiry source medium) or the last touch (the channel through which the lead was either qualified and handed off to sales or converted to a sale). Marketers are in general agreement today as to the deficiencies of either of these traditional methods.

Digital marketers are experimenting with various approaches to the attribution problem, like weighting touches based on stage or role in the buying process, or by the type of touch—attending a two-hour seminar being weighted more heavily than a content download. An excellent discussion of this thorny problem can be found in *The Definitive Guide to Marketing Metrics and Analytics* (definitive-guide-to-marketing-metrics-marketing-analytics.pdf) produced by Marketo's VP of Marketing, Jon Miller.

Thorny Problem #6:   Unstructured Data

How should I handle unstructured data, like social media content. All of this "big data" stuff is getting bigger, and meaner, every day.

Solution: We recognize that social media content may offer valuable insights into customer needs and issues. But marketers first must think through how they will use the information to drive business results. First, you must develop a use case. Then, you must develop a way to attribute the information to a record. For example, collecting multiple cookies to find an email address or other identifier, to allow the match. There may be situations where you want to track sentiment without attributing it to a particular customer but to a group, like large companies versus small. In either case, we suggest that you test the value of the data before you put a lot of time and money into capturing it in your marketing database. Big data, although unstructured, must be "tamed" or consolidated and provided structure so that it can be associated in some way to other structured data to be entirely useful.

Thorny Problem #7:   Out-of-Control Job Titles

Job titles are increasingly inconsistent—and proliferating. Categories like Marketing Manager *and* Financial Analyst *don't seem to work anymore.*

Solution: Several companies offer job title standardization services, called something like title mapping, title translation, or title beautification. A resource like that is a good first step.

Then, consider sending an outbound email, perhaps with a follow-up phone call, positioned as a "contact verification" message. Invite the target to indicate his or her functional job title, from a list.

After that, you will be left with a relatively smaller list of remaining titles. At that point, you need to decide on a default for the rest of them. For example, anything that sounds like IT will go in an IT functional bucket. And, depending on how often you query your customers, you can always gather answers to this question over time.

Then, you are faced with the remaining issue, which is far more difficult, namely the crazy new titles that some people are using these days. We've seen bizarre titles like Chief Instigating Officer and Marketing Diva. With these, you have two options:

1. Force aberrant titles into your standards, by hand, using your best guess. Use a default code for anything you can't really figure out.
2. Leave them as they are and link them to a table of standardized job functions. But maintain the self-reported wacky title, too, so you can still address the person the way he or she wants to be addressed.

You might also consider using forced drop-down menus for job function and job title, at the point of key entry. One of the ways that some companies approach this is to create a job-type category that allows the respondents to specify what the title means to them. This helps normalize differences across countries, where titles can vary dramatically. In Germany, for example, the title "director" is a very high level, C-suite job role, and very different from the U.S.

Thorny Problem #8:   Real-time Data
Is real-time updating really necessary? If so, how should I do it most efficiently?

Solution: There is certainly value, but the necessity of real-time data acquisition in B2B is highly debatable, unless you are a bank or an airline. Should you decide it's important for your company, you'll need the help of an expert. We suggest getting three competitive bids.

Thorny Problem #9:   Contact History Migration
How should I handle job changes? When an employee leaves and goes to another company, does his or her history with my company go along?

Solution: We are going to assume—a big assumption—that you actually know the person has gone to a new company. It's more likely that you will not know. This is why it's a good idea to do periodic de-duplications by functional title to get a sense of new names that have popped up at the companies in your database.

When you know that there is a job change and you have the new information, you must move the contact to the new company in your database. It's a good idea to send along behavioral data like communications preferences. You might also add a LinkedIn profile URL to the record. If you believe the prior behavioral data is important, then take it as a duplicate and put it in a separate field, not attributing it to the new company record.

The purchase history belongs with the original company, and should stay there. Indicate in the company record that the individual has left.

As a general rule, in marketing databases, never overwrite. Keep everything date stamped.

Thorny Problem #10:   Identifying Website Visitors
How do I find out the names of individuals who visit my website?

Solution: There are two ways to de-anonymize the website visit. First, add a registration invitation to your site. This could be an email sign-up or a piece of gated content, like a white paper or research report, in exchange for providing important data elements like name, title, company name, address, phone and email.

Second, use the IP address to identify the company from which the visitor arrived. This can be done by hand, using Google Analytics, or more easily by using any number of services that enable IP address look-up. Marketing automation systems are increasingly baking this option into their tools.

But the IP address method will still not get you the name of the visitor. You can infer the visitor's interests and, possibly, role by looking at the time spent on various pages. And you can drop a cookie and retarget the visitor with text or banner ads later.

Thorny Problem #11:   Data Capture by Sales Reps
We want our salespeople to be selling, and to keep administrative tasks to a minimum. But these people are also the closest resources to our customers. How can we motivate them to capture important data about the customers and prospects they are interacting with?

Solution: Boil down the mission to just one or two key data points that reps are asked to collect and report. Job title, buying role, and email address might be among the most likely to change, and the most important to keep current. Train and reward the reps—very publically—for consistent reporting on the selected elements.

Thorny Problem #12:   Web-form Data Holes
In an effort to improve web-form response rates, we are asking for only name and email address. What's the best way to create a company record in this situation?

Solution: We recommend that you consider hiring a service that will fill in the company record on the spot, as a start. Or send the file out to a third-party compiler to append the records you need.

Another way is to parse the email address. Take the letters after the @ and before the .com. For example, if the email is formatted as firstname.lastname@hp.com, the meaningful letters are hp. Search for other emails with these letters in this position in your file and build a business rule that every email with these letters shall be assigned that company name. If you have a standard record on your file, import it.

If the email address is a generic one, like gmail.com or yahoo.com, you're out of luck. Email the prospect and ask for more data. You could also consider preventing email addresses other than those from company domains from being accepted on the web form. But keep in mind that there is some evidence that individuals filling out web forms with personal email addresses tend to be more responsive over time.

Thorny Problem #13:   International Data
We need to get our international customer data under control. Where should we start?

Solution: First, add country name as a required field in your web forms and other response vehicles, so that future data collection will be set. Use a drop-down menu to improve capture of a standardized country name. Prevent the record from moving forward until the country is specified.

Then, look at what parts of the world you do business in. Estimate how many countries, and how many customer records in each country, so you can see how big an issue this is.

Next, figure out which records in the database are non-U.S. This will take some effort. Many databases don't have a non-domestic indicator. Do an audit, by eye-balling, of the city, state code, country fields, and email addresses in your file. There is no easy way around it.

Country names are increasingly important as laws change. Consider Canada's onerous new email law, which requires proven opt in before emailing. You can't assume that those email addresses ending with .ca are the only Canadian emails on your file. One suggestion is to update your web forms with a message like "If you are in Canada, opt in here."

Thorny Problem #14:   Data Priorities
I don't know which of my data elements is the most important. In other words, which fields have the most impact on sales results?

Solution: Start by looking at what data you capture. If you only capture name and address, product purchase, dollars spent and date, then you'll find that they are all important.

From there, the question gets more and more complicated with the amount of data you keep. Eventually, the best way to find out is to model your data. Using multi-variate regression, let sales be the dependent variable, and let the other elements sort themselves as the independent variables. You will have your answer fast. But there are two caveats:

1. A model costs real money to build. You'll need to budget north of $20,000 for this exercise.
2. Models have a shelf life. You'll want to re-do the model at least annually.

The plus side? You'll know which data elements are most important to maintain and keep fresh. And, if you find some elements with negative correlations to sales, you may be able to use these fields as a negative predictor—a suppression factor—for saving money on fruitless campaign targets.

Thorny Problem #15:   Missing Data
I don't have access to important data elements. Where can I acquire them?

Solution: Start digging. There are plenty of unusual sources of data out there. You just need to get creative in how you search for it. Look for highly targeted, industry-specific compilers, for example:

- MCH provides lists of government, school and institutional contacts.
- HG Data and the Computer Intelligence Technology Database are sources of installed technology information.
- Judy Diamond Associates compiles directories of insurance and health benefits administrators.
- The Public Safety Information Bureau offers data in law enforcement and public health.
- Look for private databases that aren't normally available for rent, like industry and professional associations.
- Make deals with trade magazines in your industry. Controlled-circulation publications, especially, tend to have very rich data on their readers.
- Enlist your distributors or resellers. They may be willing to provide data to an aggregated database that doesn't specify which reseller provided the information.

Thorny Problem #16:   Product Taxonomies
Developing comprehensive product taxonomies is a nightmare in my company. Products have multiple purposes, there are scads of SKUs, and new products are being introduced all the time.

Solution: Get very friendly with your new product development group. They are likely to have the taxonomies that make sense for the firm, and they also have a bead on what new products are in the pipeline. Set up both formal and informal links between marketing and the new product team. Try quarterly information-sharing meetings, supplemented by occasional brown-bag lunches. Educate them on the value of the marketing database so that they are motivated to keep the information exchange going.

Enlisting the aid of the finance group, who must account for product profitability, is also recommended as a way to bring sanity to out-of-control SKUs. Finance shares your interest in getting a simplified view of products.

Thorny Problem #17: Fields Too Small
My database was set up in a different era. With today's requirements for foreign words, long words, NAICS, ZIP+4, Internet addresses, and other new data elements, my files just can't accommodate the data I need to maintain.

Solution: Bite the bullet. The old marketing database architectures that allow only thirty characters in data fields are no longer adequate. The only solution is to modernize. Whether your database is in-house or managed outside, it's time to get it upgraded, with either a complete redesign or an entirely new platform.

Thorny Problem #18: White Mail
We have an ever-growing level of orders and inquiries that come in without source codes.

Solution: Take comfort. This is a problem that plagues all marketers—even catalogers—today. There are some things you can do:

1. Motivate your customers to use your source codes. Give them incentives. Make it easy for them to find and use the code.
2. Motivate—and reward—your order-taking personnel.
3. Use data matchback. Just be sure you budget for it. Depending on your key code structure, you may match at the site level and/or the contact level. If you use a multi-part key structure, you may be able to track at the site level even if the contact that responds is different from the one you originally targeted.

Thorny Problem #19: Job Changes
We can't track our customers when they change companies.

Solution: We feel your pain. This is a problem that plagues every B2B marketer. D&B is now assigning numbers to individual contacts to help with this. Ultimately, what we need is some kind of New Movers file for business marketers. But until that happens, here are some steps you can take:

1. Train your customers. Whenever you talk to them, remind them to keep you informed. Fortunately, business relationships tend to last over time, so a happy customer is naturally motivated to stay in touch. But you have to request: "If you change jobs, please let us know." Make it easy for them, with such techniques as a web-based COA form.

2. Get together with other marketers in your industry vertical and share data. This is a perfect example of the benefits of sharing. Everyone is better off.

Thorny Problem #20:   Missing Email Addresses
Our rates of email address coverage are disappointingly low.

Solution: Here is where we business marketers can learn from our consumer counterparts. First, get very proactive about asking for email addresses directly from your customers. Make it easy, give them an incentive, and ask them at every touchpoint. This is not a one-time project, but an ongoing effort. Second, you may want to explore some of the opt-in email append services provided by reputable sources.

Thorny Problem #21:   Email vs. Postal Addresses
We have such a mixture of address data. Some of our records have complete email and postal addresses and others have only email. So we are, in effect, maintaining two databases, instead of one integrated database.

Solution: First, be proactive in motivating your customers to give you both addresses. (See Solution #20, above.) But, beyond that, you must force the situation in your database. The solution is to develop two sets of de-duplication rules in the same database. Namely, set up separate rules for:

1. Records with both postal and email.
2. Records with only email.

Thorny Problem #22:   Competitive Data
We need to know what competitive products and solutions our customers are using today. Where can we get this kind of information for our database?

Solution: In some industries, this data is compiled and available for sale. The CI Technology Database from Harte Hanks and data from HG Data are good examples in the tech sector. Elsewhere, however, you must compile this information first-hand. Begin with your sales team, which is very likely to have gathered much of this already—although you'll have to organize and standardize it. Then, look at techniques like Internet research, perhaps by an intern. Finally, some trade publications will allow you to "buy" questions in a reader survey, which is typically a less expensive method than primary data collection, although it won't give you full coverage.

Thorny Problem #23:   Purchase Intent Data
We need to know what products our customers are considering for purchase. Is this kind of data available?

Solution: A start-up called 6Sense gathers inferred intent data at the account level from multiple sources. Alternatively, there are reasonably inexpensive ways to compile it yourself. Here are some steps to take:

1. Survey your customers, using an incentive. Use low-cost media, like inserts in ongoing communications, or web-based survey tools.

2. For products with some sales history, you may have enough data to build a predictive model to identify high-potential prospective buyers.

3. This is another area where the survey programs offered by trade publications can be put to use. You may be able to participate in their survey by "buying" a dedicated question that is posed to their readers.

Thorny Problem #24:   Decision Makers

We can't identify the decision maker at a site.

Solution: The interesting thing about B2B data is that it is hard to get and hard to maintain—but usually very valuable. Much of data gathering and maintenance is done by manual processes, and is well worth doing. For missing data elements, like a contact's role in the purchase process, take the following steps:

1. Work with your sales people, who are very likely to know this information about certain accounts.

2. Identify industry colleagues who may have the data. Potential sources include trade publications, trade associations, and—even—competitors.

3. Identify resources that can gather data more efficiently than you can. Trade publications are a perfect example. Collaborate with them for data discovery.

4. Survey your customers.

5. Discuss the problem with your market research colleagues. They may be able to tell you what kinds of titles or job functions are most likely to be decision makers.

Thorny Problem #25:   Purchase Influencers

We can't rank the relative importance of the various parties involved in buying.

Solution: In many companies the buying role changes with the type of product purchased. For electronic equipment, the technical requirements contact may have the highest importance. When it comes to office furniture, on the other hand, the purchasing agent may be the most influential. Model-building can help in this situation because it will take into account both the title and the items purchased. With a series of good models, you should be able to build a predictive list of who is important, from high to low, in buying what.

Thorny Problem #26:   Data Capture

We have trouble coordinating data capture around our company. For example, when we create a questionnaire and finish collecting the responses, someone then comes around and asks us for the answer to an entirely new question.

Solution: Clearly, this is an internal communication problem. One solution is to beat up your colleagues. (Just kidding.) A better solution is to reach out and proactively educate them—regularly—about what data is available in the marketing database, and the completeness levels by data element.

Thorny Problem #27:   Constant Change
The rules that affect data are changing constantly. How can I keep up with fast-moving issues like privacy and hygiene?

Solution: It's your job. Enlist the help of other internal interested parties, like legal, corporate communications, customer service, and sales. Ultimately, you need to keep on top of changes in your industry. But another thing you can do is make sure that your systems are flexible enough to keep up. Change is inevitable, so make the business case for investing in a database solution that gives you the support you need.

Most companies have found that one person can't do this alone, so they have formed cross-functional privacy councils. This is a great way to keep everyone informed of the new laws and to keep communication flowing.

CHAPTER 10

Case Studies in Database Marketing

Makino Jumps Headlong into Database Marketing

In 2004, managers at the North American affiliate of Makino, the Japanese machine tool company, came to the realization that they needed to change the way they did marketing. Makino produces top-of-the-line machine tools and commands premium prices. To build brand awareness and find new customers, Makino Inc., like many industrial suppliers, relied primarily on print advertising and exhibiting at trade shows.

Not that this approach was unsuccessful. Makino is the market share leader in Horizontal Machining Centers, the most commonly used equipment in automotive and aerospace markets. They were enjoying record sales and profits in 2004, but they also understood that the market was changing. They were exhibiting at up to twenty-seven trade shows a year—more than two events per month. Makino's director of marketing, Mark Rentschler, and his boss, CEO Don Lane, decided the the old tactics were not going to give them the scale and efficiency they needed. They would have to find a better way.

So, in 2005, Makino turned to digital and database marketing. The journey was to take them on a path away from trade shows and print and toward laser-targeting of prospects and opportunity. It would also help them develop the ability to deliver messages tailored to particular industries or product segments.

Makino has a well-defined set of sales territories, covered by a wholly-owned distribution company called Single Source Technologies, plus a field sales force of 125 reps, along with a network of independent distributors comprising another 85 to 100 reps.

To support the new marketing approach, the first step was to build a corporate marketing database. They chose to build the database in Saleslogix and set it up to fit their existing sales territory structure. To start, it was populated with existing customers, imported from their legacy system. They also added other existing data sources, like subscribers to their custom publications, inquirers from trade shows, and select records from the customer service system. The current customer quantity flowing into the new database represented about 6,000 accounts.

Next up was adding prospects—and here's where the process became interesting. The new marketing strategy was all about efficiency, so the Makino team set about the job of identifying their actual prospect account universe. In North America, Makino has been most successful with three industry targets: automotive, aerospace, and dies and molds.

With access to a sizable amount of industry research, plus the aid of a trade publisher in their category, they figured the total universe of metal-cutting accounts that fit the Makino range of product and solutions to be about 55,000 companies.

But to reduce waste and optimize their marketing investments they wanted to cull this down to the "must-have" targets. So within that universe, they looked for companies that buy a lot of machine tools (this data coming from UCC filings, government records about machine installs, and lease expiration dates). They also talked to the sales team, to identify the companies the reps most wanted as customers. Then, they looked for category leaders, companies with marquee brands, like GE and Caterpillar. Finally, they added in 12-year dormant past Makino customers, as prospects for reactivation. Altogether, this highly desirable target prospect universe added up to another 8,000 accounts.

Like most B2B marketers, Makino needs to talk to many kinds of contacts at an account. They sell not only tools, but also a variety of engineering solutions. So, for each account, they might need as few as two contacts or as many as twenty to thirty contacts, like the plant manager, maintenance manager, engineers, senior managers, and executives.

With this data preparation work completed, the sales team had its work cut out. The must-have prospects were divided up among the sales reps and distributors, by territory, at the rate of about three or five prospects per rep. "This is a manageable number," says Rentschler. "We are asking each rep to pay particular attention to these prospects. This effort is critical to our market share objectives."

The marketing team also got to work. The first big push was a series of webinars, designed to attract both customers and prospects and demonstrate Makino's technical prowess. "We were an early adopter of webinars," notes Rentschler. "We were doing three a month. What we intended as thought leadership also became excellent lead generation tactics. People started adopting our metal-cutting solution, and that gave our salespeople an easy platform to kick off a conversation. And then the sales rep would add additional contact information to the database." Makino now has over 150 archived webinars in its content library, which each month generates hundreds of new leads.

Makino's sales cycle can be long, as much as three to five years, so the communications stream includes ongoing emails and other messages, with invitations to webinars, events, and trade show exhibits plus ongoing relationship-builders. "We are a content-generating machine," says Rentschler. "A newly-minted engineer or someone from a new foreign direct investment company in the U.S. will be searching—titanium machining, for example—and they will find us. We give them a lot of tactics—ads, white paper downloads, case study, webinar. And eventually we'll get a request for a quote."

Makino's Facebook page has a whopping 36,000 followers, thanks to great content and promoted posts. The Facebook site is among the top ten referring sources for the Makino website. "These are mostly Makino loyalists," says Rentschler. "But also lots of industry people, who follow us as a thought leader." The team is planning to connect these contacts to the target accounts in the marketing database.

Ongoing data maintenance is always a challenge. "Data hygiene is our one weak link," says Rentschler. "We work hard at trying to scrub the data. Thanks to our three custom publications, which have circulations of 18,000; 9,000; and 3,500, we can update the files with the undeliverable returns. Our local sales engineers will also flag and purge names as they learn about contacts leaving a company. During the Great Recession, we did a lot of purging as the manufacturing industry shrank."

When adding new accounts, the sales reps are asked only to do the basic contact management, i.e., entering contact name, phone, and email. Marketing will add other fields to the new record, like the URL, targeting information, competitive product installs—nine fields altogether. A local college intern is often assigned to track down the extra data. Currently, the database contains 115,000 active users. Reflecting the market realities, the universe of accounts has been going down slightly, but the business is growing overall. Makino has experienced four consecutive years of record sales revenue in North America. Furthermore, marketing expenses as a percentage of total revenue has been declining. That's the benefit of targeted marketing.

Staples Models Customer Behavior to Optimize Retention Marketing Investments

The office supplies giant Staples sits on a trove of customer data: nine million active business customers in a pool of twenty-four million active customer records. As reported by Jim Foreman, director of analytics and customer insight, Staples surrounds this customer information with a plethora of tools:

- D&B's data interchange, from which fields are appended once a company signs up for the Staples Rewards loyalty program. Two out of three enrollees are, on average, matched and appended, with as many as 160 attributes.
- The marketing automation module from SAS.
- A data warehouse and a "Marketing Data Mart" where the customer information can be analyzed.

Foreman's mission is to predict and thwart customer churn, or avoid what he calls the "break-up." He uses database marketing techniques to achieve this goal.

In Foreman's view, the two key drivers of churn are misaligned customer expectations and unmet customer needs. He thus crafts his marketing effort to accomplish the following outcomes:

- Better align with customer expectations
- More deeply engage customers by evolving the company's relationship with them
- Demonstrate an ongoing understanding of customer needs and how to best fulfill them
- Reduce the likelihood of break-up
- Proactively identify customers who may be on the path to break-up

If an effort to overcome these problems, Foreman's team applies three approaches:

1. **Listen**, using qualitative analysis, to hear the views of the customers themselves. Tools used here include surveys, focus groups, and social media sentiment analysis. "Customers are surprisingly willing to share their feelings—good or bad—and their reasons for taking certain actions," says Foreman. This is especially critical in "passive" break-up situations, like what you find in retail— where the customer simply stops buying—compared to "active" relationships, like subscriptions—where the customer must proactively notify the seller of the desire to quit or cancel, and the seller has a chance to talk them out of it.
2. **Learn**, using descriptive analytics, to understand past customer behavior. Foreman finds that there is much rich but under-leveraged data at Staples

that can be mined for insights on customer engagement and attrition risk, including firmographics; RFM and transaction history; coupon and discount usage; promotion history and response data; and "big data," like clickstream and online browsing. Using techniques like visual analytics, deciles, and clustering, Foreman's team profiles customer segments and tests various marketing stimuli to motivate desired behaviors, like reactivation and purchase.

3. **Anticipate**, using predictive models to uncover future possible customer behavior. "At some point you reach a ceiling with descriptive analytics," Foreman notes. "Eventually you have to migrate to predictive modeling." For example, a "tenured attrition model" was built to score long-time but recently inactive customers by their likelihood of attrition. The strongest predictive variables included RFM, categories purchased, coupon usage, website browsing behavior and tenure.

One particularly productive marketing strategy was developed based on a cross-decile model using both attrition factors and profitability (see Exhibit 10.1). Foreman mapped the deciles on two dimensions and developed outbound contact strategies accordingly.

Exhibit 10.1: Staples's Attrition and Profitability Model

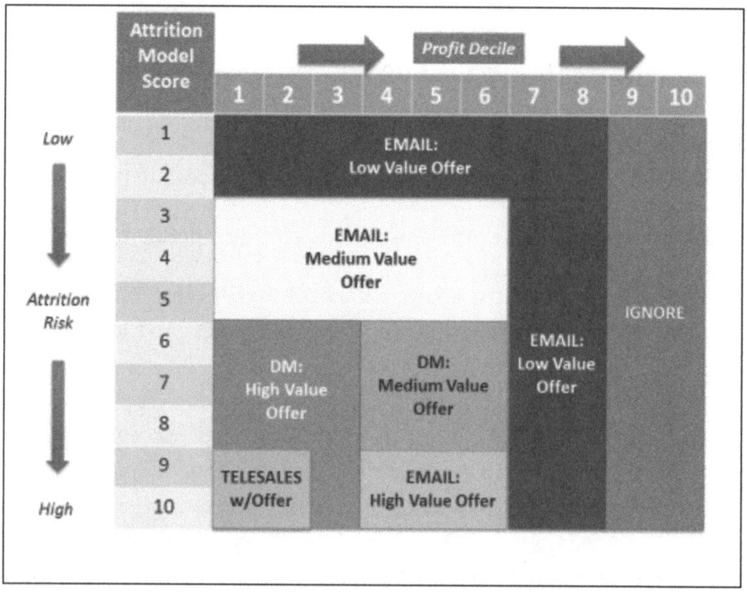

Staples's marketing communications strategies mapped by customer profitability and expected attrition rate. Used with permission.

First, they excluded the two least profitable deciles, on the grounds that further marketing investment there was unproductive. Then, they mapped a series of communications strategies, with less generous offers sent by email to prospects at lower risk of attrition and with lower profitability. Finally, the mapping wrapped up with more generous offers and more intrusive media (direct mail and telemarketing) to the most profitable customers who were at the highest risk of attrition. In short, a neat way to match the marketing investment to the segment where it will have the highest return.

The results of the contact outreach? Overall, Staples achieved ROI increases averaging 29 percent with this new contact and offer strategy. Forman observes, "The cost associated with this strategy was statistically flat to our previous strategy of giving the same offer to everyone regardless of decile. However, in this case, that same investment is being leveraged more tactically, with more marketing dollars being spent on the segments most likely to deliver a better return, and less—or none—being spent on low-profit or lower-risk groups."

SaaS Company Five9 Focuses Its Customer Acquisition Marketing on Top Customer Look-Alikes

Doug Sechrist is vice president of demand marketing at Five9, a cloud contact center software company based in San Ramon, California. Five9's solutions provide everything businesses need to run an inbound and/or outbound center for sales and marketing, customer service, or outsourcing, including sophisticated management tools for reporting, recording, workforce management, quality monitoring, and CRM integration.

With responsibility for demand generation, Sechrist is immersed in database marketing. "Our approach starts with crafting a data strategy and operationalizing it," says Sechrist. "First, we target the right accounts. We look at past wins, and the attributes of those customers. We examine those who buy and later become long-term clients."

In short, Five9 is creating an ideal customer profile and going out in the marketplace to find similar accounts, a process known as look-alike modeling. In their search for look-alikes, they identified 6,000 to 7,000 prospects. "We focus our demand generation marketing on those look-alikes," says Sechrist.

Attributes that tend to be predictive in the look-alike modeling include:

- Number of employees in the call center
- Presence of a customer service or outbound sales and marketing team
- Use of an outbound collections department internally
- Use of similar technologies, whether SaaS or on premise

- Past purchase of cloud-based software
- Competitive technologies installed
- Use of "adjacent" or complementary technologies, like a workflow management system

Five9 also looks at individual personas among their customer base, using a similar process. First they identify the attributes and behaviors of top buyers, using the rich detail that can be found on LinkedIn or other social sites. The personas support the crafting of relevant messages at the right time to sell call center software.

To get a steady stream of look-alike contacts, Sechrist uses Leadspace, which builds models and then scrapes fresh contacts from various websites. Leadspace contacts are scored based on the desired persona attributes, and then ranked and prioritized for use by the sales team.

In an effort to invest marketing resources wisely, Sechrist built a tiered system of lead distribution.

- Tier 1, comprising the highest paid and most skilled reps, gets the most relevant matches to the Five9 ideal customer profile and the highest quality type of leads.
- Tier 2 is the lead development team, given the next level down of relevant qualified accounts and qualified leads.
- Tier 3 goes to outsourced programs that help to validate interest and provide a foot in the door to pitch the Five9 solution. These programs include campaigns with vendors such as By Appointment Only and Simply Direct's survey service, which puts together a custom database of prospects based on specific titles and account attributes, and sends short email surveys to senior executives therein.

The next evolution of this program aims to leverage additional technologies and processes to identify target accounts as they visit the Five9 website or search on relevant terms in Google or other search engines. Once Five9 can identify such accounts, they can trigger the appropriate content to be delivered to the right persona at the right time, and subsequently engage with buyers that not only match the ideal customer profile, but are exhibiting buying signals for Five9 solutions.

Predictive Modeling Identifies Profitable Small Business Targets for Community First Credit Union

Retail banks are typically very skilled at working with medium-sized to large business customers. They understand the client needs, and have excellent sales and marketing processes in place to serve them. The same can be said for their consumer customers.

But when it comes to small businesses, especially very small businesses, retail banks often have a hard time figuring out how to find profitable customers and serve them well. "Banks have a love-hate relationship with SMBs," says Tony Coretto, managing director at the bank advisory and solutions firm Novantas, Inc. "SMBs represent triple the value of a consumer account, so they are by nature an attractive market for banks. But they are always the red-headed stepchild, sitting in limbo between consumer and enterprise."

In the years since the economic downturn, the opportunity in this market segment has captured the attention of the retail banks. Coretto and his partners at Novantas, having had experience helping large, money-center banks develop SMB marketing strategies over a fifteen-year period, has been at the forefront. They were recently retained by Community First Credit Union (CFCU), in the Jacksonville, Florida area, to create a strategy to market profitably to SMBs within their seven-county trading area.

"Looking at the small business market, you find chaos," says Coretto. "Companies with less than $20 million in revenue are all over the map. This category can contain mom and pop stores, SOHO (small office, home office) businesses, small manufacturers, B2B services firms—it runs the gamut. Each has different financial needs for their business."

When it comes to very small businesses, in the $1 million to $5 million revenue range or even smaller, it's even more difficult. Many of these small companies have merely transactional relationships with their financial institutions, and are thus not the most attractive targets for retail banks. The job Novantas takes on is finding the profitable needles in that haystack.

CFCU enjoys very strong brand recognition among consumers in the geography they serve. Their hope is to leverage that brand recognition to build a strong small business franchise. At the outset, they had very few small business customers. They set an ambitious goal to triple the base by 2018.

Initially, the Novantas team reviewed CFCU's product line-up, and found some gaps. "Simply put, the CFCU product line was too consumer-focused," says Coretto. "They had a very small base of small business customers, and not a lot of experience with the market segment outside of a successful commercial real estate loan practice." To grow in the small to medium-sized business space, CFCU needed to develop a more appropriate set of products, like business-specific checking accounts with more features businesses need to help them run and manage their operations. The Novantas team worked with CFCU over a year-long period to analyze the business market and the competitive landscape to help them develop a better product mix.

With the right products in hand, the next step was to build a prospecting model based on data from third parties (such as Infogroup, D&B, and Acxiom), to identify the biggest opportunities for strong growth in each segment. A discussion with the client revealed particular segments predetermined to avoid, like restaurants, jewelry stores, and pawn shops. "There's no sense in analyzing segments the bank already knows they don't want to target for future acquisition because those relationships are not very profitable," points out Coretto. Further analysis of the data and discussions with the client narrowed the target further; in CFCU's case, this was companies within a specific band of annual revenues, target geographies, and business duration.

The prospecting model was used to profile the businesses in CFCU's seven-county trading area. In addition, Novantas used their own proprietary small business banking "wallet model" of the typical banking relationships found among companies with the same size, SIC, employee size, location, and other variables. The goal was to identify targets with a need for various banking services—like certain levels of savings and checking, commercial lines of credit, and auto loans—and to determine what the size of that relationship was likely to be. The resulting prospect universe was then ranked and segmented by potential profitability, and Novantas developed highly targeted acquisition campaigns. "For the higher value segments, we knew we could invest more, so we used more expensive campaign media, like dimensional mail," says Coretto. "We also targeted different offers to different segments for greater offer relevance, uptake, and conversion."

In addition to the wallet model, Novantas employed a behavioral model that analyzed engagement patterns of existing customers, to identify opportunities to deepen and extend the customer relationship. "Variables that we considered for the behavioral model included wire transfers, remote deposits, and deposit and payment frequency. We used this approach to help identify a subset of consumer customers who were doing a lot of transactions out of their consumer checking accounts, as potential targets for a commercial checking product, reasoning that they might be running a small business out of their consumer account based on the volume and type of transactions we observed." This allowed more targeted, effective marketing communications to be sent.

Such a behavioral model can also be applied to defection prevention or identifying further opportunities for cross-sell, based on trigger events observed. "What we're trying to do is move toward a life cycle relationship management system, just as consumer marketers do," says Coretto. "Customer journey mapping works in B2B, too. As a business launches and grows, its banking needs are fairly predictable, over time. A bank using this approach can better serve their customers' banking needs over time, and grow a more profitable banking relationship as their customers' businesses grow."

Finally, Novantas also used techniques and models to understand which of CFCU's current consumer customers were also small business owners. From separate analytical work, the Novantas team knew that between 5 and 15 percent of a typical financial institution's consumer customer base are also small business owners, and that of that group, fewer than half have their business relationships with the same bank. So there is a tremendous opportunity to cross-sell small business banking products and services to business owners in the current consumer customer base.

To size and identify this opportunity for CFCU, Novantas created an analytic database of all small business and consumer customers as well as all prospects in target geographies. They then overlaid the consumer base with executive home address data to create linkages to small businesses not already served, but owned or managed by existing consumer customers. The objective was to find opportunities in four areas:

1. Customers who have a small business account and also have a consumer account.
2. Customers who have a small business account but do not have a consumer account.
3. Customers who have a consumer account, are a small business owner, and already have small business accounts with CFCU.
4. Customers who have a consumer account, are a small business owner, and do not have a small business account with CFCU.

Initial segmentation analysis revealed that approximately 7 percent of the consumer base were owners of small businesses in the bank's target footprint (within the expected range of 5 percent to 15 percent) and its industry or sales sweet spot, and thus serviceable and acquirable by CFCU.

Novantas's initial recommendation was to begin an aggressive cross-sell push into this target, based on the facts that CFCU already:

- Enjoyed strong brand recognition and familiarity with the credit union's products and services among this group.
- Had deep knowledge of their customers.
- Had sustained and profitable relationships with the target population.

At this writing, the modeling strategy is showing strong signs of success. The team segmented the small businesses owned by CFCU's consumer customers according to sales size, industry, and product potential based on the Novantas commercial financial wallet models. They then designed and implemented a multi-channel outbound campaign with offers on small business checking and credit lines, commercial mortgages, and loans. The campaign used direct mail, email, and telephone contact. Creative and messaging took advantage of what the bank knew about the target as a customer, based on the existing consumer-side relationship.

The results delivered more than double those of similar campaigns run in the same time period, targeting "pure" prospect businesses (those without a pre-existing consumer-side relationship) in the geography:

- A 1.4 percent conversion rate versus 0.6 percent on pure business prospects.
- Average acquired small business checking balances more than double those of pure business prospects with no pre-existing consumer-side relationship.
- Average acquired small business line or loan balance of more than double pure business prospects with no pre-existing consumer-side relationship.
- A ROMI of over 110 percent during the first nine months of the program.

Yellowbook Uses Data to Improve Advertising Sales Results

Yellowbook (yellowbook.com) is one of the leading publishers of yellow pages directories. It originated on Long Island in the 1930s and expanded nationally over the last seventy-five years.

When it comes to their B2B database, the company wears two hats. One database is, in effect, their product, meaning the company listings that comprise the yellow pages content, a database containing tens of millions of records.

But the other database, used for marketing, targets the businesses that advertise in the yellow pages, and comprises about a million accounts to whom Yellowbook actively sells. This marketing database contains contact history, both inbound and outbound, and firmographic information. According to Cathy Carleton, director of database marketing at Yellowbook, the most important data element is response behavior, which she analyzes for campaign selection and to track churn.

The marketing database is organized at the account level, with a unique identifier generated in house using a random number generator. When purchasing third-party data, they use an identification system created by Polylogics Consulting, a firm that provides production management software to the directory industry.

Key applications of the marketing database include campaign selection and modeling for propensity in such areas as:

- Attrition
- Up-sell
- Likelihood to use Internet products (an area of intense focus after the launch of yellowbook.com)
- Optimum product mix

Originally, Carleton used an outside agency, Fulcrum Analytics, to build its propensity models. But recently she brought the process in house, using SPSS. Carleton finds modeling more challenging than ever before. "It takes as much as three years to refine a model, but since customer behavior changes so fast today, it's hard to keep up."

Their most important segmentation variables for database marketing at Yellow Book are:

1. The business category (called "headings"), like plumbers and law firms.
2. Geographic area, since most of the print editions are geographically focused.
3. Current yellow pages advertising behavior.

Other challenges include:

- De-duplication. With leads generated from many sources, it can be difficult to match records effectively.
- Staff limitations. Carleton has a team of five, but only two are dedicated to the database.
- Prospect identification. Carleton says, "The hard part is identifying what record is an independent business and which ones are part of a larger firm. We get some help from D&B data and we use some fuzzy match algorithms, but inevitably some errors get through."
- Email list hygiene. Yellowbook is using more and more email today, but finds it problematic when an ad contact leaves the firm and the email bounces. "With direct mail, the piece is usually delivered to the new replacement employee," Carleton notes. "With email, when the employee leaves, the email is dead." Yellowbook is now using FreshAddress for email cleanup.
- Sales force data entry. With 4,500 to 5,000 sales reps, it's a nightmare to provide technology that is easy and clear enough for the sales force to key enter effectively. A new automation tool is being rolled out now.

Other than regular weekly monitoring of campaign results, Carleton keeps track of four key metrics, and reports on them monthly to the advertising managers:

1. Response rate
2. Conversion ("sell in") rate
3. Retention rate
4. Revenue

The biggest lesson learned at Yellowbook has been the importance of targeting. Salespeople need leads and are eager for the net to be cast as widely as possible. At the same time, a database marketer knows that a tight focus will increase response, lower the cost per lead, and improve conversion rates. So it's an ongoing conversation. "It has taken years for the database marketing team to earn the trust of the sales force, but now they are beginning to get it," says Carleton. "Used to be, a salesperson would say, 'Just put a piece in every account in my territory,' but now they are more comfortable leaving it to us to decide whom to contact."

Edmund Optics: The Story of Two Data-Driven Campaigns

Edmund Optics® (EO) is a global distributor and manufacturer of industrial optical components and assemblies. Headquartered in Barrington, New Jersey, and with offices and factories in Japan, China, Singapore, South Korea, Taiwan, Germany, France, Finland, and the U.K., Edmund Optics employs over 750 people worldwide.

Edmund was founded in 1942 by Norman and Paulette Edmund as a mail-order supplier of surplus equipment, like microscopes and telescopes. In 1984, their son Robert Edmund created two separate company divisions: Edmund Scientific, to concentrate on educational and hobby applications, and Edmund Industrial Optics, to focus on precision components for industrial applications. By 2001, Robert repositioned the company, now called Edmund Optics, to focus exclusively in the B2B arena. Under Robert's leadership, Edmund Optics has grown to be a market leader in its category.

Today, the company goes to market in two ways, by catalog/e-commerce and by direct selling. EO mails nearly two million catalogs a year, in nine languages, which carry 27,200 products, over 55 percent of them manufactured by EO and the remaining sourced from third-party manufacturers. The more complex custom optics and high-volume OEM business is sold by a global fifteen-person field sales team, enhanced by an inside sales group and a team of sales engineers.

The company's legacy in mail order has meant a rich legacy of data-driven marketing. EO manages a customer file of over 169,000 names at 91,000 accounts in the U.S., and 338,000 names around the world. The marketing database is built in SQL Server, linked to SAP for supply chain, Microsoft Dynamics for CRM, and Exact Target for email deployment.

Let's look at two recent examples of how data is applied to the EO marketing mission.

Prospecting for Aspheres

An asphere is a semi-spherical lens used in industrial applications like ophthalmology, cell sorting, cell counting, and cell purification. As such, it is a niche product within the niche of industrial optics. The marketing challenge is to find companies and engineers that may be in the market for this product. The sales cycle for a product like this is long, and so is the manufacturing process. So the EO U.S. marketing team needed to fill the pipeline with leads to keep the factories busy.

The first step in their recent aspheres marketing push was to build a predictive look-alike model, called a "migration model." EO's list brokerage partner, Merit-Direct, "froze" the record of EO's existing asphere buyers at the stage just prior to their asphere purchase and built a predictive profile of the accounts. The objective was to find similar characteristics among these buyers, i.e., identify what they had in common prior to their migration to an asphere purchase.

Could they find possible asphere prospects among house-account companies that are buying similar products, but not currently buying aspheres? Says Kirsten Bjork-Jones, director of marketing communications, "We expected so. These are the sites that the data is telling us *should* be buying aspheres."

The migration model included more than 200 predictive variables, the top five being:

1. Recency in the number of months (since their last transaction)
2. Site tenure, meaning how many months the site has been on file
3. Revenue spent on lenses to date
4. Number of lifetime orders a site has placed through the email channel (EO receives many of its large OEM orders through email)
5. Prior three-year revenue

According to database manager Allison Lloyd, the migration model was applied to the rest of the EO house file and produced 1,625 contacts at 990 organization in the top demi-decile. EO also did some digging into the Hoover's database, using SIC codes close to subjects like ophthalmology, or searching under "ophthalmology" or "cell sorting/purification/counting" as keywords. The Hoover's data-mining exercise yielded thirty-eight sites, including both customers and prospects. The next step was to attach useful contacts at those sites based upon title, honing in on titles containing "engineer" or "manufacturing." These sites were cross-referenced with the sales team, who began calling these high-potential sites.

The marketing team then set about preparing an ophthalmology-related case study for use in a specialized direct mail campaign. Over the summer of 2014, EO conducted a multi-touch outbound campaign to encourage these prospect to buy aspheres. "We only needed one or two orders to make this campaign pay for itself," notes Bjork-Jones.

The campaign began with a split test in banners on the EO home page and email to a house-file segment, to identify the better of two messages (see Exhibit 10.2). One message was around speedy access ("Need Aspheres Fast?") and the

Exhibit 10.2: Edmund Optics Split Test of Email Messages

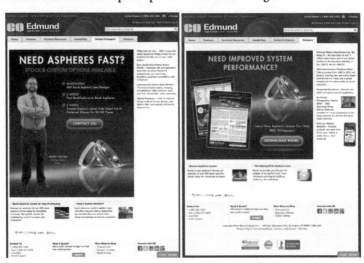

A/B split email messages testing quick product access to improved system performance.

other focused on customer application needs ("Need Improved System Performance?"). The speed message proved to be the stronger of the two, and was thus used in the rest of the campaign.

Next, an email went to the rest of the target audience, with a dedicated landing page.

The campaign has resulted in a 21 percent increase in new asphere business, which includes nearly 300 additional units per month and a new OEM custom design worth more than $450,000.

"Alpha Modeling" for a New Customer Welcome Kit

When any customer places an order with Edmund Optics, they automatically receive a thank-you email. But when the order comes from an entirely new account, EO recognizes the opportunity to make new customers feel especially welcome and to launch the start of a long relationship. Thus, new customers receive a welcome kit in the mail containing an eight-page welcome message, plus the business card of Ray Willis, the phone-based sales rep who is going to be following up with the new customer a few weeks later.

Recently, EO decided to take the welcome kit to a new level, by segmenting new customers by their expected lifetime value and creating customized welcome kits, using digital variable printing, for the top tier of freshly acquired accounts.

MeritDirect suggested using a process that had worked for their other clients called Dynamic Lifetime Value (DLTV), also known as "alpha modeling."

First, MeritDirect profiled EO's best customers to understand the nature of those customers' first orders, by such factors as order size and product assortment, plus firmographics like industry and employee size. The DLTV model included more than 300 attributes, about half of them transactional, from EO's side, and half characteristics elicited from MeritDirect's massive database of B2B company buying behavior across the U.S. The top five variables predicting customer lifetime value for EO turned out to be:

1. Revenue on the first order.
2. Contains title of engineer.
3. Address type (business or consumer).
4. Revenue in the photonics product category.
5. Revenue in the optics product category.

Now, all incoming new-to-file accounts are assigned an "alpha score," which predicts how they are likely to buy over time. In practical terms, the way it works is that EO sends the prior week's orders to MeritDirect, which runs them through the model and attaches a score. The scored accounts are then sent to Quad Graphics, which sends a significantly more personalized welcome kit to the top two deciles identified by the DLTV model.

Produced on demand by digital variable printing, the welcome kit features images of the product categories—optics versus imaging, for example—that appeared in the new customer's first order. The copy is also customized, based on purchase specifics. For example, a customer who ordered imaging lenses would get a different message from one who ordered imaging components. Examples of two customized kit are shown in Exhibits 10.3 and 10.4.

Exhibit 10.3: Edmund Optics Customized Welcome Kit for Optics Products

Kit inside spread featuring optics.

Exhibit 10.4: Edmund Optics Customized Welcome Kit for Imaging Products

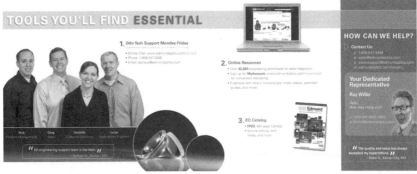

Kit inside spread featuring imaging.

The kit contains a customized brochure in a four-color envelope, featuring a friendly-looking EO team member on the cover welcoming the new customer into the family (see Exhibit 10.5).

Included among the images is the specific EO inside sales rep—Ray Willis—who will be managing the new account. The printer produces and mails the kits

Exhibit 10.5: Sample Cover of Customized Edmund Optics Welcome Kit

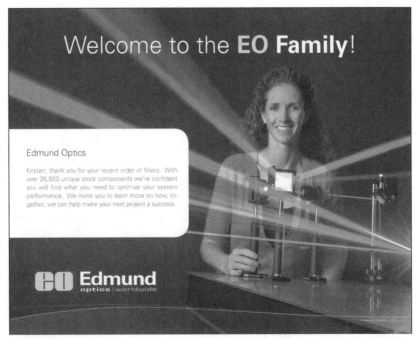

Welcome kit cover.

bi-weekly. So far, about twenty welcome kits have been produced and mailed in the U.S. pilot region. The kits cost about $20 each to produce and mail.

A week later, Ray Willis, the inside sales rep highlighted in the brochure, phones the account to extend the welcome. The new model-driven welcome kit process had been preceded by a pilot program that had been managed by hand. The pilot showed a satisfying lift in second orders, so the team has high hopes that the new automated process with custom copy and illustrations will pay off.

Michelin North America Supports Its Dealers with Data-Driven Marketing

In the early days of 2008, when financial experts were just starting to argue about whether the U.S. was in a recession, Michelin North America rolled out a sales program that would provide exactly the kind of support its network of dealers and distributors would desperately need by year's end.

A designer, manufacturer, and seller of tires for a variety of markets—including consumer, agriculture, aircraft, and heavy truck—Greenville, South Carolina-based Michelin N.A. sells tires directly and via a partnership with distributors and independent dealers. The main source of support for this three-party business union is the company's Alliance Associate Dealer (AAD) program, a sales incentive program that offers premiums to participants who hit sales goals.

"We sell tires to lots of different companies and lots of different kinds of companies. Our independent dealers are the most important to us in many ways," says Bob Schaffner, Michelin N.A.'s manager of distribution development—wholesale. "First of all, they're the ones who've helped us build our business for the last fifty years. They still represent 60 percent of the market in terms of consumer choice. … If we're going to be successful, we have to be successful with our independent tire dealer organizations."

According to trade publication *Modern Tire Dealer*, more than two-thirds of the 29,000 independent tire dealers in the U.S. are single stores, and a little fewer than half of them are family-run. These retail operations are the most vulnerable to economic and competitive influences, says Schaffner, and require unique approaches that fit their particular businesses. Through the AAD program, "we have to give them the tools in order to be successful. And we can spend the money. But if the money is not translated into a program that they can participate in, it's going to be wasted," he emphasizes.

Looking for Wear and Tear

Rolling back several years to the start of this dealer-program overhaul finds Michelin N.A. facing a couple of challenges. One, as the distributors administered the

AAD program, it gradually lost its Michelin identity. Two, the process largely was paper-based, which made it difficult to manage uniformly and efficiently. As a result, all parties to the program couldn't see the same information at the same time, creating knowledge gaps that left sales opportunities on the table.

"We wanted a Michelin-branded Alliance Associate Dealer program. We also wanted to administer this in a unified fashion across the country, where every dealer would be treated essentially the same—that is, per the terms of the contract. We also wanted to relieve the burden of administration from our distributors so that they could focus on their core competency, which is stocking and delivering tires and providing their own services," says Schaffner.

So in 2006, Michelin N.A.'s wholesale division began its program transformation with the relaunch of its paper-based sales agreement as an online contract. "By putting this contract online, we're then able to take that input to the contract, or the numbers, and evolve them into [our] online reporting tool, the eStatement," Schaffner explains.

The next part of the process, the development of the eStatement, would take all of 2007—plus a great deal of manpower—to execute. "We had as many as 150 people internally working on this project," says Schaffner, in addition to database marketing expertise from DATACORE Marketing, a marketing services company located in Westwood, Kansas, and feedback from the distributors and dealers.

Building the Data Engine

The linchpin of the dealer program for the dealers, distributors, and Michelin N.A. is reporting. Essentially, that's what the eStatement is: an online report that shows Alliance Associate dealers:

- Their progress toward their contracted purchase commitment
- How much money they've earned in the program
- Details on their transactions

"Every element of the AAD program is articulated through the eStatement," Schaffner states.

The data underpinnings consist of a daily electronic data interchange of dealer transactions from the distributors to Michelin N.A. The tire manufacturer then consolidates dealers' purchases from multiple distributors and sends this data stream on to DATACORE, where it's incorporated into the program database, bounced off Michelin N.A.'s business rules, and published via the eStatement that dealers access through the interface DATACORE hosts for Michelin N.A.

According to DATACORE president and CEO Jeff Yowell, his firm receives four million transactions annually that feed daily updates of more than 4,000 eStatements. To make this possible, DATACORE first needed to develop sixteen different file transfers between itself, Michelin N.A., and the distributors. For data to be collected and compiled efficiently, Yowell notes, Michelin N.A. had to compel numerous parties to adapt their operations to new and different processes and policies, a massive undertaking that undoubtedly required a certain amount grace under pressure.

On a monthly basis, DATACORE sends Michelin N.A. "a payment file based on the dealers who hit their objectives. We send cash payment to these dealers directly in their bank accounts," Schaffner explains. He adds that the majority of distributors report transactions nightly and the eStatement is updated daily, giving dealers the most current information on which to base their business decisions—a critical need for independent tire retailers who have to manage risk while remaining competitive. The other key component of the online reporting tool is the direct cash payments, reducing the time a dealer is waiting on program incentives.

Yowell explains that all of the data elements being tracked in the AAD program impact dollar amounts and payouts. So, despite the automated nature of the eStatement, this information requires continual monitoring.

Running on All Cylinders

The retooled AAD program has been running for a little more than two years, enough time for Michelin N.A. to see several benefits to its new approach.

Prior to the eStatement, the company's area sales managers operated with less precision when it came to communicating with dealers in their territories. They didn't always have current data on where a dealer stood relative to its sales goals and how much money it was making, so the managers were "very limited in what they could actually talk about with the customer," Schaffner explains. "They could talk about product launches, promotions, training and things like that, but they couldn't really talk about the business facts." Now, the sales managers can pull up their dealers' eStatements and reach out to them with ideas for how to better leverage the AAD program. "It allows for a more consultative relationship between Michelin and the customer—the dealers really appreciate that," Schaffner says. "We can take action before the end of the month, not go back and ask a dealer why he missed his goal by ten tires."

The online tool also helps Michelin N.A. more easily carry out relevant sales promotions. For example, Schaffner points out, before the eStatement, the company would create promotions that it hoped also would be appealing to the distributors who oversaw the dealers' efforts. With the transactional insight available to all stakeholders, Michelin N.A. is able to "execute sales programs for the dealer that draws tires out of the distributor's inventory, which is exactly what we want," he explains.

From the distributor side of the program, the eStatement offers other complementary advantages. Michelin N.A. talked to these constituents before the data project got off the ground to learn how to better address their needs. A key discovery was the importance of customer loyalty to distributors' profitability. In response, Michelin N.A. built into the AAD program a requirement for dealers to purchase a minimum percentage of tires from their primary servicing distributor, which is the co-signer of the dealer's purchasing contract. This feature "ensures the distributor gets the maximum value of the program and that the funds going back to the dealer don't contribute to a price war," says Schaffner.

Other key benefits of the online reporting tool include reduced program administration costs—due to the distributor no longer bearing this responsibility—and greater visibility into the dealers' progress toward sales goals, which also is of importance to the distributor. As Schaffner puts it, "At the end of the month, when [a distributor] looks at their sales to AADs, they can say, 'I need to go talk to Joe, because he's only four tires away from hitting his goal. We need to sell him those four tires,' which might turn into eight or twelve or twenty tires."

And certainly, the eStatement has made a big difference to tire dealers in the AAD program. With 24/7 access to their account details, they're able to fully leverage the ability to sell new Michelin products and expand sales of existing products. "The end result is we want our dealers to be advocates for our brands," says Schaffner. "And advocacy means it must be a good business decision to sell our tires, not just a good purchase decision for the consumer."

More Miles to the Gallon

So far, the AAD program is meeting, if not exceeding, Michelin N.A.'s performance expectations. More than 3,000 dealers have signed on, accounting for more than 4,000 points of sale for the company's Michelin, Goodrich, and Uniroyal tire brands. And the number of customers has grown in excess of 50 percent. What's more, Schaffner reports, in last year's tough economy, Michelin increased its market share, with its AAD program outperforming the overall U.S tire market.

But again, it's the end result for the independent tire dealer that means the most to Michelin. "I've had small dealers who've had a very difficult time competing against the big box stores, the national retailers, call me to thank me for this program because they can now be competitive—not matching price, but they're close enough that the customers who want to shop there will not leave. So the profitability is greatly improved, their price competitiveness has improved and we've seen our sales improve as well," says Schaffner.

Going the Distance

While getting this program revamp on the ground and going was a worthy challenge, the work is not over yet. With so many stakeholders and so many moving parts involved, opportunities abound to make adjustments that can further improve performance.

For example, as Michelin N.A. has increased its understanding of the volume of data available and its value to dealers and distributors, it's developing new product screens for dealers, applying the information to forecasting models, and supplying the area sales managers with more detailed insights for planning and management purposes.

Further, according to Schaffner, the success of the program has "attracted a lot of attention" from other business lines at Michelin, such as the agricultural segment and even overseas operations. "Down the road," he notes, "we could be implementing this program for these business lines."

DATACORE's Yowell points out that Michelin N.A.'s AAD program has two sides to it—one operations-related and one marketing-related. Operations-side innovations connect to aspects like price book updates and audits, personally identifiable information, and reporting functionality. The marketing-side innovations lean more toward customized communication opportunities, such as emails personalized with dealer data at the individual level—progress status, advantages to meeting program goals, dollars available to hit goals, etc. And such messaging could be set up to deploy on a trigger basis.

"This started as a sales program for Michelin," Yowell says. "But with the data being generated, so many opportunities exist to drive a wide variety of communication objectives."

Given Michelin N.A.'s emphasis on the independent dealer's success, any future initiative will need to meet the core criterion of making the tire business easier for the dealer. "In our work, we count tires and we count money," Schaffner says. "We want our dealers to be more focused on selling tires than on buying tires."

Assembling the Moving Parts

A few key challenges exist in managing this sweeping type of data project. Here, DATACORE Marketing president and CEO Jeff Yowell outlines the basic steps involved:

1. Identify every stakeholder, implementer, and other influencer of the program.
2. Clearly define the roles and responsibilities of each party.
3. Develop an internal communication plan for the project development.

4. Develop a transition plan for migrating each current process to the new process.

5. Create a communication plan for external stakeholders (e.g., Michelin N.A.'s dealers and distributors).

Source: Case study by Hallie Mummert. Used with permission from *Target Marketing*.

EU Services and Digital Impact: Two Services Companies Using Data Innovatively to Assess Customer Value

Customer valuation, customer segmentation by value, and differentiated treatment of customers—these notions were invented in the world of direct marketing. Business-to-business direct marketers have used lifetime value, RFM, and value-based segmentation as decision tools for years. But when we move out of the nice, neat traditional world of mail-order merchandise, measuring the value of a customer gets complicated.

Consider business-to-business services. Companies like agencies, printers, utilities, lawyers and accountants, that are selling services to other businesses, can certainly benefit from understanding the profitability of their various customers and clients. Insight into customer value assists decision-making at all levels of the company. Sales can decide which manager to assign to the account. Customer service can vary the perks and privileges. Finance can negotiate better pricing when the contract comes up for renewal.

But customer valuation in business-to-business presents a number of obstacles that are not necessarily faced by traditional mail order companies, for whom RFM is like mother's milk. For one, the numbers are not immediately available—or obvious. Far from calculating a simple sum of the products purchased, less the cost of goods sold, services marketers must consider issues of fixed versus variable cost and how to allocate overheads appropriately to each account. Then there's the question of data collection: is it worth requiring employees to keep time sheets so that their labor can be applied to each customer accurately?

Another hurdle to customer valuation in B2B is the extra work involved. Management is likely to be focused on the financial reporting required by Wall Street or the IRS. They won't be looking to add to the burden.

Perhaps the largest obstacle is the sensitive nature of information about customer profitability. No company wants this data to fall into the wrong hands. How would customers react were they to discover their relative contribution to their vendor's bottom line? Worse yet, what competitor wouldn't want to go poach your best customers, if they only know who they were?

EU Services

Despite the obstacles, business services companies are making great strides in assessing the value of their customers. EU Services, an integrated printing and mailing services company in Rockville, Maryland, has taken a very practical approach to the matter. Every year, the senior management team gets together and analyzes the entire customer base, to look at the contribution level of each account. Since every printing and mailing job is custom-bid, allocations and cost collection are not a problem.

But EU Services recognizes that a simple ranking of accounts by contribution margin does not tell the whole story. So, over the past several years, they have developed a five-part assessment strategy based on the following criteria:

1. Revenue dollars
2. Payment terms—Whether the account pays in 30, 60, or 90 days, or requires some other consideration.
3. Pricing terms—Meaning the extent to which the client's jobs tend to be complex (thus premium priced) or standard, commodity orders (a simple #10 direct mail package on standard paper stock, for example, versus an annual report using special inks and finishing, and requiring a press check)
4. The "impact on the organization"—Based on the input of fifteen different department managers on how much work is required across the company to support the account.
5. The "relationship"— Meaning the opportunity for a long-term partnership, as assessed by the salesperson on the business (for example, is the customer outsourcing jobs to EU Services piecemeal, or might the account be expected to give EU Services a sizable share of its printing and mailing business over time?)

The first three criteria are generated out of the marketing database, through a program developed in house, and each account is assigned a score based on where it falls in a range. The final two are more subjective and gathered manually. Once all the inputs are assembled, the account scores are cross-tabulated with year-end expenses, and a "contribution to overhead" number is established for each account.

According to Sylvia Konkel, former VP of marketing at EU Services, the combination of five criteria allows the company to compare accounts of all kinds on an equal footing. "We have some very large accounts, representing millions of dollars in revenue a year. And we also have many customers who only spend $25,000 with us annually. For peak efficiency, we need a mix of customers. This valuation strategy allows us to compare apples with apples."

EU Services uses the contribution numbers to develop optimal account management strategies for the following year. "We sit with the sales reps and discuss each account," said Konkel. "We are all looking for ways to add more value. Occasionally, we conclude that a certain account requires alternate solutions, so we weed out those customers whose expectations we cannot meet."

Their main challenge in developing the process was deciding on the right criteria to include—and reject. The important thing was to create a complete profitability picture of the account that could not be skewed by anomalies like volume. Konkel notes that it took seven years of experimentation to settle on a set of criteria that provided the right level of feasibility and flexibility.

The accounts are then classified into two groups: the top 10 and the top 100 accounts. Only the senior management team is privy to the final ranking order, due to its sensitivity from customer and competitor points of view. But all employees are made aware of who the top 100 customers are, so that everyone in the company can be united in serving them well. Top accounts will be assigned dedicated support by an experienced account manager, plus a senior management contact from among the VP ranks. Other service offerings, like customized training, annual account review meetings, and special perquisites are also made available for top accounts. "Our objective is to serve our customers as well as we know how," said Konkel. "The valuation process gives us a tool to provide that service more effectively."

Digital Impact

Another example of customer valuation at work comes from Digital Impact, the Silicon Valley online marketing services company, now owned by Acxiom. DI is known as a full-service provider, best suited to companies that seek to build their customer relationships with highly targeted communications programs and need customized support. DI's profitability thus rests on management's ability to steer its way between revenue—set by pricing—and costs, which are primarily driven by staff time and technology usage.

Like most business-to-business companies, DI has good visibility into revenues and variable costs on each account, thanks to its marketing database and ERP systems. Some are direct expenses—the services staff, for example, keeps time sheets to assign their hours to a customer, so their fully loaded costs are applicable. Some of the technology, too, like dedicated servers or IP addresses, can be accurately associated with a particular customer. Other direct expenses, like bandwidth or computer hardware, are allocated by the volume of email the customer runs through the system.

According to David Oppenheimer, former CFO, the major application of DI's customer profitability analysis is in salvaging money-losing clients. "When we have an account that is unprofitable to us, but whose potential is high, what we want to do is bring that account into profitability. We will analyze the whys and wheres of the losses, and figure out how to price and structure the new contract to service the relationship profitably."

A classically-trained finance professional, with a long career in aerospace before moving into marketing services, Oppenheimer is well aware of the importance—and the difficulties—of customer valuation. When it comes to allocations, for example, the expense ratio will vary with the number of clients. "Eliminating an unprofitable customer is an important strategy for business management," he noted. "But you have to get rid of the costs as well. Otherwise, they will just be allocated to the remaining customers, with a negative impact on the company's overall profitability."

On the pricing side, another vexing issue is applying the right cost to incremental volume. If you have excess capacity, it makes sense to price on the margin, that is, looking at only the variable direct costs incurred by the usage—whether it's staff time or technology capacity. That way, you can bring in profitable new business and absorb otherwise unused overhead. But what happens when that capacity is used up? The length of the contract then becomes an important factor. Oppenheimer wrestles regularly with decisions about the best ways to view costs to support decisions about customer value optimization.

DI regularly ranks its customers by profitability, and develops strategies to optimize the value of each account. A highly profitable account, for example, would be targeted for additional cross-selling of service offerings. An account falling near the bottom of the list is examined for its opportunity. Is it a strong reference account? Is it running high volume through the system? Customer valuation thus allows a disciplined and rational approach to account management.

CHAPTER **11**

The Fast-evolving Future of B2B Database Marketing

New tools, new technologies, and most important, new buying behavior among businesses—these changes are accelerating the pace of B2B database marketing's evolution. Here are some predictions about where things are headed, many of which are already underway.

1. The end of the database "build."
Digital marketers today are taking greater advantage of "real-time" data, delivering immediate responses to interactive behaviors between customer and marketer. Increasingly, the ability to manage such data points efficiently will make the traditional marketing database too stagnant and unresponsive to be useful. We are not there yet—the idea is still experimental. But the "always-on" future is beginning to be visible, where your storefront is always available for any kind of customer interaction.

2. The total customer view.
The Internet has been with us since the early1990s, and by now has certainly impacted every scrap of B2B marketing. But the next stage of its evolution will be to simply go away, as a thing in itself. Digital marketing will become so mainstream that it will be called simply marketing. We will no longer make a distinction between online and offline. We will understand and interact with the customer from all sides, in a seamless whole. And the data will be the enabler of the relationship.

3. No more campaigns.
A bold prediction comes from Gary Skidmore, a strategic advisor to many companies in the B2B database marketing world: "The future lies in ongoing marketplace dialogue," he says. "That means no more campaigns. Sure, you can have a special offer, but it will be part of your never-ending interaction with customers and prospects, across multiple platforms."

4. The merging of B2B and B2C.
As business buyers roam the Internet, marketers are able to treat them increasingly like individuals, versus company representatives. One outcome of this is the increasing likelihood that B2B practitioners can do predictive marketing the way it's done at Amazon or Netflix, and has been done for decades by consumer database marketers. "B2me," is the appealing term for this direction coined by Joseph Puthussery of Cisco.

Jeffrey Rohres, VP of marketing insights at Salesforce.com, puts a slightly different spin on this matter, with his intriguing point that B2C is increasingly taking a page from the B2B playbook. "Look at e-commerce and social media," he says. "Just as businesses have long had direct relationships with their vendors, so are manufacturers pulling an end run around their retail channels and building a direct connection with the consumer." In short, consumer marketers are also learning from B2B.

5. Faster access to new tools and approaches.
Just as the buyer behavior is changing, so is marketers' ability to react. Thanks to cloud-based services, laptops, and mobile phones, all you need to set up a company and launch a new idea in the marketplace is speed. IT departments that were needed to establish security, storage, networks, bandwidth, applications—these are all available instantly in the cloud today. Business marketers will find it easier than ever to take advantage of market opportunity.

6. The rise of the marketing technologist.
As marketing technology grows in its sophistication and ease of use, marketers will continue to take advantage, shifting budgets and influence away from IT departments, and requiring a higher level of tech skill and experience in the marketing department. Fortunately, the young marketers coming into the profession are by now mostly "digital natives," for whom technology is a given, and not necessarily a special skill set. "These people grew up with technology, from their cribs. They don't give it a thought," notes Ken Lomasney, COO of the agency UMarketing LLC. So the outlook for talent to manage the new technologies in marketing is bright. And CMOs who come from a brand background must develop a comfort with technology like never before.

7. Sales and marketing symbiosis.

Derek Slayton, CMO of NetProspex, points out that new technologies can only take B2B marketers so far. The next step, he believes, is new organizational structures. Sales and marketing operations will be combined underneath an umbrella that may well be known as the "Go To Market" operation. Better integration will allow sales-people access to necessary data where and when they need it, says John Deighton, professor at Harvard Business School. When a sales rep is in front of a customer, marketing data needs to be easily available on site. And the rep needs an easy way to funnel fresh customer information back to the marketing database.

8. Real-time marketing gets real.

We are fast approaching the holy grail of proactive database marketing, built on al-ways-on, in-the-moment customer interactions. Real-time marketing will be real for business marketers, says Russell Kern of the Kern Agency. "Real-time market-ing is about using data analytics to mine the flood of live data generated by all this activity, in combination with other direct sales, product and brand interactions."

9. The revenge of the nerds.

"Data is the most important thing in marketing today," says Kathleen Schaub, VP at IDC's CMO Advisory Service. "Marketing is becoming almost like a social sci-ence. We are able to collect a lot of data today, but we are still in the early stages of turning it into business value," she notes. The number of people in business intel-ligence functions is rising, but still small. This needs to change in B2B, just as it has in consumer categories like retail and gambling.

10. Big picture automation.

Not just marketing automation, or sales force automation. We are headed to an era of systematically running the sales and marketing function as an integrated whole, with processes automated and running on their own, predicts Joe Caserta of Caserta Concepts, a consultancy in New York that works with a lot of big data, especially in the financial services industry. Bernice Grossman, of DMRSGroup, Inc., echoes the point. "The technology around B2B sales and marketing will morph into a stream-lined integrated system, which will include the marketing database, with lead man-agement, email, mobile and social, across the customer relationship. As a result, the silos between sales and marketing will become a non-issue."

11. A simpler technology picture.

Most marketing technologies claim to make marketers' lives simpler. But at this point, marketing technology has become dizzying in its complexity. In the future, says Nitin Julka, product manager at LinkedIn, more and more of the complexity of running marketing campaigns is going to be automated, in a simpler way, so that marketers can focus on what truly matters—their target audiences, buyer's journeys, and messaging.

12. Complexity moves to the cloud.

One of the ways to make the technology picture less complex is to banish it all to the cloud. Today and increasingly in the future, cloud vendors are providing marketing capabilities. Thus, marketers can concentrate on marketing, and let the cloud vendor manage all the intricacies of database management, system updates, storage and other activities once only provided by internal IT organizations.

13. A sensible balance between data, insight and marketing strategy.

"You can have all kinds of customer data, and still not understand how to communicate persuasively with customers and prospects," notes Howard K. Sewell, president of Spear Marketing Group. "Software and analytics can't tell you the what and the why. We need to respect and harness what the data tells us, but also put it in its place."

14. The end of the list business.

Already, leading data distributors like MeritDirect are reporting a decline in their list management and brokerage units. Marketing data is being generated through new approaches, like inbound marketing and scraping corporate websites and social networks. "The way to be first to market today is not through lists, but through data," says Peter Long, CEO of MCH Strategic Data, Inc. "These new contacts arrive, we welcome them, send a message, and kick off a relationship. That's where B2B prospecting is going."

15. B2C continues to cut the edge in database marketing.

B2B marketing is rarely the leader in advancing database marketing techniques. But it is adept at watching and taking up the new ideas from consumer marketers that apply to business buying, observes David Myron, editorial director at *CRM* magazine. One example is experiments with unstructured data, like that from social media, where consumer marketers are making headway. B2B marketers will likely search and analyze nuggets not only from social media but also from phone conversation content and email content, to identify buying intent, competitive interest and other actionable insights.

16. The freedom to be creative.

As the tools become simpler to use, and we are able to improve the automation of difficult tasks like data collection and hygiene, businesses will continue on the path toward the freedom to apply their data to creative new uses. An example comes from New England Biolabs—producer of specialized enzymes for genomic research—which connected its freezers in customer labs to let scientists open the freezer and scan products for check out using a nearby iPad. NEB also connected the freezers with its own back office systems to drive automated inventory replenishment, and to Salesforce, which lets NEB email customers their receipts and watch usage trends.

17. The rise—and possible fall—of the data scientist.

Formerly known as data analysts and statisticians, those who know how to mine, model and manipulate data for marketing purpose are quickly being elevated to the grander title of data scientist, with commensurate salaries, career paths, and status. But watch out: Marketers may be reducing their dependency on these skills in the near future. New technologies, like Adobe Analytics, are being designed to enable marketers like never before, says Maria Minsker, associate editor of *CRM* magazine. "Marketers can use their data to build models, faster and more cheaply than ever before," says Minsker. "Without the data scientist."

18. Data *is* the business.

The appreciation among stakeholders for the importance of customer data will continue to grow. "Data isn't something we just have stored over there," says Frank Cutitta, CEO of the Center for Global Branding and professor at Northeastern University. "Data is the business. Companies that understand this are ahead of their competitors."

19. The growing influence of marketing.

The sales function has traditionally held the primary B2B revenue responsibility, leaving marketers with a history of frustration at their exclusion from a seat at the senior executive table. That is changing fast, as new tools and measurable communications techniques enable marketing not only to demonstrate financial results, but to take on revenue responsibility. "Salespeople are no longer the only rainmakers," says Thad Kahlow, CEO of the digital agency BusinessOnLine. "Our clients have serious revenue targets hanging over their heads."

20. Accelerating pace of change.

Marketing technology has changed everything in B2B marketing, and marketing everywhere, observes George Wiedemann, CEO of the agency UMarketingLLC. And marketers have reacted quickly, adopting and adapting to the new tools and new behaviors. But technologies will continue to emerge, at a faster pace than ever before, he cautions. So marketers need to be agile, responsive, and flexible.

All these changes will require a new kind of 21st-century marketer, one for whom data to gather insights, manage communications, and measure success is a given in the workday.

Appendices

Since 2005, Ruth P. Stevens and Bernice Grossman have jointly produced a series of white papers and research reports under the umbrella subject of B2B Database Marketing.

In reverse order of publication, the reports include:

"13 Thorny Data Problem That Vex B2B Marketers, and How to Solve Them, 2014 edition" (December 2014)

"A Deep Dive into B2B Prospecting Databases: How Seven Data Suppliers Compare" (October 2013)

"B2B Technology Industry Prospecting Databases: A Comparative Analysis of Nine Data Suppliers" (July 2012)

"B2B Response Databases: A Comparative Analysis" (April 2011)

"Online Sources of B2B Data: A Comparative Analysis, 2010 Edition" (March 2010)

"Online Sources of B2B Data: A Comparative Analysis" (January 2009)

"What B2B Marketers are REALLY Doing with Their Databases" (September 2007)

"Enhancing Your B2B Database with Data Append" (November 2006)

"15 Thorny Data Problem That Vex B2B Marketers, and How to Solve Them" (November 2006)

"Keep it Clean: Address Standardization Data Maintenance for Business Marketers" (February 2006)

"Outsourcing Your Marketing Database: A 'Request for Information' is the First Step" (March 2006)

"Our Data is a Mess! How to Clean Up Your Marketing Database" (October 2005)

Some material from these reports has been used in various chapters in this book. The reports can be accessed in their entirety online at www.ruthstevens.com/white-papers or www.dmrsgroup.com. We are reproducing seven of the most relevant papers here, in reverse chronological order, for your convenient reference. Some of the titles may have been adjusted for clarity.

Appendix 1
A Deep Dive into B2B Prospecting Databases: How Seven Data Suppliers Compare

In a departure from past studies, in 2011 Bernice Grossman and Ruth P. Stevens decided to research the depth of data available to B2B marketers for prospecting purposes. Our thinking was that, while marketers certainly seek coverage of their market segment, they also can benefit from the availability of a rich variety of data elements in any given account record. This is especially true of marketers who build predictive models or look for particular variables by which to segment and refine their data selections.

We identified a variety of suppliers, of both complied and response files in business markets, who offer considerable richness in prospecting records. Invited to participate were:

• ALC	• Infogroup	• Salesforce.com
• D&B	• Mardev DM2	• Stirista
• Harte Hanks	• NetProspex	• Worldata
• HG Data	• OneSource	• ZoomInfo
• IDG	• ReachForce	

We were very pleased that seven suppliers joined the study, and we extend our gratitude to them. The participants who contributed information on their "deep data" are:

• ALC	• Infogroup	• Salesforce.com
• Harte Hanks	• OneSource	• Stirista
• HG Data		

The scope and intent of the study

To get at the question of how much data richness is available about specific target accounts, we needed a different approach from that used in our earlier research on the completeness and accuracy of compiled and response databases as a whole. Where possible, we tried to maintain some semblance of comparability with prior studies.

As with our earlier data studies, we invited the participants to provide a description of their offering and how it differs from that of their competitors. We then provided them with a list of the fields we might have expected to see in a company's data record, ranging from contact information to firmographics, like year established, industry codes, employee size and so forth. We then invited participants to share any additional fields that they offer.

To get at the question of coverage, we also asked them to tell us the number of records for which each data element was available. And to put all vendors, large or small, on a level playing field, we asked them to report on the percentage of their file that the counts represented. With this data point, readers will have a better idea of the likelihood that they will be able to get any given element. For example, a supplier might have 100% of its file with SIC, but only 3% of its file with the year the firm was established.

Recognizing that many marketers use these data elements as a way to predict the value of the target company to their marketing efforts, we asked the vendors to identify the fields that have the most predictive value for their clients. And, because model-building often produces surprising results, we asked the vendors to share any variables that proved to be unexpectedly useful for marketers.

In an effort to get some insight into the question of the accuracy of the deep data available, we asked the participants to provide sample records from five well-known firms: USG, Macy's (Federated Department Stores), Monsanto, MetLife and Dell. We expect our readers can eyeball the data and draw their own conclusions. Just as vendors often determine the validity of a field by the number of times it appears in disparate sources, we expect a field that is consistently reported by multiple vendors might likely be accepted as accurate.

In a "be careful what you ask for" moment, we quickly realized that the data supplied by participating vendors is far too voluminous and complex to publish in full in this white paper. In fact, two of the participants specialize in compiling detailed profiles on the technology installed in companies, driving the number of fields on each company record into the thousands. So, we are reporting only partially on the data submitted here—for example, answers to the simpler questions, and answers that allow for easy comparative viewing. The heftier answers are available in a spreadsheet where readers can access and view the enormously rich and varied "deep data" that illustrates the abundance of prospecting data available to marketers today.

The field counts reported

We provided a list of 30 fields that one might expect to see in a detailed company record. Participants were asked to tell us the equivalent name they use for these fields, and share their counts and the percentages those counts represented.

We also asked them to add the additional fields on their files, and this is where things became interesting. In some cases, we received thousands of additional fields from participating vendors. Clearly, there is a lot of data out there for marketers to access.

Due to space limitations, we are only showing the comparative counts and percentages on the 30 suggested fields in this document. Please see the accompanying spreadsheet for complete details of the fields submitted by the participating vendors.

Here are the counts provided against the list of suggested fields, in response to the question, *Please provide a list of the data fields you offer in a corporate record at the headquarters level (U.S. only). Below, we list some typical fields one might expect on a company record.*

Suggested fields	ALC	Harte-Hanks	HG Data	Infogroup	OneSource	Salesforce	Stirista
Company name	3,141,702	3.5 million+	515,892	5,014,165	13,768,972	65,628,022	17,834,322
Address line 1 (HQ)	9,609,502	3.5 million+	515,892	4,960,699	13,056,617	62,888,082	17,834,322
Address line 2 (HQ)	2,512,341	3.5 million+	515,892		3,002,933		
City	9,609,502	3.5 million+	515,892	5,014,165	13,768,963	65,628,027	17,834,322
State	9,609,502	3.5 million+	515,892	5,014,165	13,768,940	65,628,027	17,834,322
Zip+4	9,609,502	3.5 million+	515,892	5,014,165	13,768,811	65,628,027	17,834,322
Telephone (HQ)	9,128,747	3.5 million+	130,024	5,011,866	13,704,068	39,813,350	17,834,322
Toll-free number		3.5 million+		189,995	514,469		10,834,322
Website URL	6,166,315	1 million+	515,892	1,255,372	3,713,227	3,416,525	17,834,322
Number of sites		3.5 million+	515,892		15,575,747	542,408	
Number of employees	8,535,854	3.5 million+	515,892	4,955,824	13,594,378	51,408,468	16,688,823
Number of contacts	9,609,502	3.5 million+	515,892		26,284,391	9,171,024	17,834,322
Year established		500,000+		409,742	819,592	50,697,517	13,488,432
Fiscal yearend	1,488,913	500,000+			63,527		
Sales volume (total company)	8,618,739	3.5 million+	515,892	18,904	11,555,800	48,892,522	16,688,823
NAICS	426,729	3.5 million+		5,011,181	13,768,268	65,627,946	16,688,823
SIC	10,489,831	3.5 million+	515,892	5,014,165	13,768,268	65,628,028	16,688,823
Female executive/owner indicator	2,967,576	N/A		930,283	N/A	65,620,591	1,723,993
Foreign parent indicator		3.5 million+		2,046			
Fortune Magazine ranking	189,065	1,000		975	998	56,051	1,683,992
SOHO business indicator	12,952,458	???		1,158,796	2,497,938	65,453,753	
Franchise indictor		N/A		15,680	N/A		
Growing/Shrinking indicator		3.5 million+		46,545	7,264		
High-tech business indicator		3.5 million+		90,647			
Import/Export code		N/A		18,975	N/A		
New business code		N/A		1,750,944	N/A		
Public/Private indicator	71,582	N/A		5,014,165	8,715	65,627,018	
Stock exchange ticker symbol	71,362	N/A		7,240	8,679	7,145	
Public filing indicator		N/A		14,865	6,629		
Import / Export business indicator		N/A		18,975	N/A		

The field count percentages reported

Here are the percentages by which each field appears in each vendor's file, in response to the question, *Convert the counts to a percent of your total number of company records, to indicate how likely a marketer is to be able to get that data. This information also allows us to provide a reasonable comparative context for files of differing sizes.*

Suggested fields	ALC	Harte-Hanks	HG Data	Infogroup	OneSource	Salesforce	Stirista
Company name	33%	100%	100%	100%	100%	100%	100%
Address line 1 (HQ)	100%	100%	100%	99%	95%	96%	100%
Address line 2 (HQ)	26%	100%	100%		22%		
City	100%	100%	100%	100%	100%	100%	100%
State	100%	100%	100%	100%	100%	100%	100%
Zip+4	100%	100%	100%	100%	100%	100%	100%
Telephone (HQ)	95%	100%	25%	100%	100%	61%	100%
Toll-free number		100%		4%	4%		61%
Website URL	64%	~34%	100%	25%	27%	5%	100%
Number of sites		100%	100%		113%	1%	
Number of employees	89%	100%	100%	99%	99%	78%	94%
Number of contacts	100%	100%	100%	100%	100%		100%
Year established		~25%		8%	6%	77%	76%
Fiscal yearend	19%	~25%			0%		
Sales volume (total company)	90%	100%	100%	0%	84%	75%	94%
NAICS	5%	100%		100%	100%	100%	94%
SIC	109%	100%	100%	100%	100%	100%	94%
Female executive/owner indicator	31%	N/A		19%		100%	10%
Foreign parent indicator		100%		0%			

Fortune Magazine ranking	2%	100%	0%	100%	0%	9%
SOHO business indicator	100%	100%	23%	18%	100%	
Franchise indictor		N/A	0%			
Growing/Shrinking indicator		100%	1%	0%		
High-tech business indicator		100%	2%			
Import/Export code		N/A	0%			
New business code		N/A	35%			
Public/Private indicator		N/A	100%	100%	100%	
Stock exchange ticker symbol	1%	N/A	0%	0%	1%	
Public filing indicator	1%	N/A	0%	76%		
Import / Export business indicator		N/A	0%			

Predictive fields reported

Respondents provided very interesting insights into the "deep data" fields that had proven to predict valuable insights for their clients, in response to the question, *Based on the experience of you and your customers, please identify the 5 fields that are most predictive of marketing results.* We found these fields, and the associated commentary, enlightening. Readers may wish to test some of these fields as selects and/or model-building elements, keeping in mind the noticeable differences among the various vendors' approaches to data acquisition and usage.

Field   Comments

ALC

Field	Comments
Executive Title/ Job Function	The ability to target the right executive with the job function that meets the targeting criteria for a client's product/service is paramount. We are continually vetting new, unique sources of data to enable us to increase the depth of our reach into America's corporations. With our latest update, we increased the following key titles in our Executive Masterfile database—and added new, highly sought-after titles. (See chart below.)
Industry	ALC's Executive Masterfile provides the opportunity to test market segments by a multitude of business firmographics, including Industry, Annual Revenue, Company Size, etc.
Employee Size	
Sales Volume	
Fortune Flag	For access to the largest companies, ranked by revenue, ALC hand-compiles a database containing the Fortune1000 and Top 2000 companies—allowing marketers to reach the influential players in the American economy.

Harte Hanks

Field	Comments
IT Spend Totals	IT Spend provides modeled totals for common IT budget areas. Total IT Spend information is a discrete number that is most commonly used to size and segment marketing lists for targeted campaigns. IT budgets are also insightful when linked to other planned information to determine if a site is the right size for a specific product set. They are based on local currency.
IT Technology Installation Totals	Harte Hanks continues to expand upon the types of technologies modeled in the CiTDB. Modeled amounts for these technologies are developed through statistical analysis of data obtained from a representative survey of 7,000 business sites in the United States. Extensive data cleaning, outlier checking and variable transformations are performed which, in conjunction with validation tests on hold-out data, help ensure that the models yield accurate estimates.
Vendor Presence	Vendor presence provides additional information on the products installed at the site. For example, information about the specific series of server or type of software will be offered in this section. Determining the product specifics to include or exclude in a campaign list can increase response rates, and help segment potential companies for product-specific messaging.

IT Initiative Models	IT Initiatives include all the planned IT purchases that are discovered by the Harte Hanks syndicated interviews. There are several premium initiatives available in CiTDB 2011 using the same scoring method as in the Presence Install section.
Key purchase indicators such as Cloud Computing	Leveraging over 40 years of experience in the B2B technology market, Harte Hanks Market Intelligence has developed a series of scores that predict the likelihood that a specific technology is present or planned at a business location. These scores are based on Harte Hanks Market Intelligence's quantity and depth of technology installations, planned purchases and business initiatives throughout the United States and Canadian markets. Marketing departments may improve their marketing ROI by aligning marketing resources with the most profitable segments of the market for their product or service. Each score is divided into 5 tiers, (1–5), with 5 being the highest tier that predicts the most likely locations to have the install or be in the purchase cycle of the stated category.

HG Data

Vendor	HG Data customers are using the combination of vendor, technology, technology last verified, and intensity to create predictive models to forecast:a) purchases cycles for how frequently a customer's purchase or upgrades a certain type of product (e.g., IT infrastructure replacement cycles)b) if a customer is likely to switch vendors based on changes to their environment (e.g., if a customer has recently purchased more laptops or tablets, how likely are they to switch endpoint security/ anti-virus vendors)c) likelihood to move from one product to another product (e.g., how likely is a small business to move from excel to Quickbooks to ADP).
Technology	
Technology last verified	
Intensity (number of confirmations)	
Technology verification history	

Infogroup

Employment Size (location and corporate)	(No commentary was provided.)
Primary Industry / SIC	
Franchise Code	
Sales Volume (location and corporate)	
Credit Code	

OneSource

Venture Capital	Venture Capital Triggers provide information on organizations that are getting new money and have a need or desire to spend. These organizations have cash on hand that is usually spent on marketing initiatives, new and expanded technologies and hiring initiatives in an effort to increase growth, which will justify the recent external investment and increase the probability of additional rounds of funding. Additionally, companies receiving venture capital funding represent companies that are up-and-coming in a given industry, which may characterize an opportunity that can be harvested as the organization grows in size and reputation.
Executive Changes—By Function	Executive Change Triggers allow you to track key decision makers and provide insight into new opportunities as well as possible threats to existing accounts. When a decision maker departs from an existing account it can represent a threat if that individual was a champion of your product, while it could inversely represent an opportunity if that departing individual was seen as blocking your organization's entry into the account. Additionally, when a new executive appears at a target account they usually operate as an agent of change for the organization, often purchasing new technologies to help achieve stated targets and demonstrate their worth at company. Executive Change Triggers are categorized by job function providing a direct path to executive contacts and decision makers that would be most interested in a given product or service.
Hiring Initiatives	Hiring Initiative Triggers depict a sign of positive growth and potential for sales opportunities. Often companies that are hiring new employees are developing new products or attempting to sell and support a new product on the market. These organizations mostly have new revenue targets associated with the new head count, which characterizes the need for a whole range of services from marketing to increased software and hardware licenses.
Prospectability	Prospectability is a OneSource proprietary score which identifies how good a particular prospect is for a given company/sales rep at a given point in time. Factors in determining the score include: is the company in the target company's / sales's reps target territory, do we have the name of the contact in the job function that is normally targeted, is supplementary information available to help with making contact and targeting the messaging (e.g., email, direct dial, contact biography info, social media, etc.), and the number of recent Sales Triggers occurring for a given prospect based on the personalization setting for the particular company / sales rep.
Contact in Job function being targeted	While having the traditional company data points, such as size of company (employees, revenue, etc.) and industry the company is, are as always required to help target marketing efforts, it is particularly helpful to know the right person to be contacting at those companies which is why we have put a focus on the quantity and quality of contacts we provide in our products.

Salesforce.com

Marketing Pre-screen	Based on the standard Commercial Credit Score, but grouped into risk ranges.
Marketing Segmentation Cluster	Marketing Segmentation Clusters represent 22 distinct, mutually exclusive profiles resulting from a cluster analysis of U.S. D&B data.
Primary 4 Digit SIC Code	The first-listed SIC code represents the primary operations of the business. (Provides insight into how the business operations and the potential need for a product or service).
Primary 4 Digit SIC Code description	A narrative description of the operations or activities of the business. Relates to the primary four-digit 1987 US SIC.
Employees Total	The total number of employees in the business organization; it should include subsidiary and branch locations. (Provides insight into the potential need for certain services or products based on the employee size, e.g., software licenses, office furniture, phone lines, etc.)

Stirista

Title	(No commentary was provided.)
Level	
Department	
Revenue	
SIC	

Unexpectedly predictive fields

We were also fascinated by the fields submitted in response to the question, *Please tell us if there were any additional fields that surprised you with their predictive ability, and add any relevant discussion or background information.* We asked this question given our own experiences with unexpectedly predictive fields, like the famous story of a compiler's having included the data field "size of Yellow Pages ad" when gathering business listings from Yellow Pages content years ago, only to learn that clients actually found the field useful. Apparently, a large ad in the Yellow Pages—presumably representing size of marketing budget—turned out to be indicative of responsiveness to marketing messages from other sellers. We hoped that participants would reveal similarly unexpected opportunity for fellow marketers.

Field	Comments

ALC

Location Type	Headquarters vs. Branch vs. Plant, etc.—help marketers better target the right decision makers in the corporate family tree.
SOHO	Small business executives have shown to be quick to respond to both business and consumer offers. ALC's Small Business Selector allows marketers to reach business owners and executives at businesses with 50 or less employees—at both home- and business-based companies.
eCommerce Enabled	With over 395,000 companies that have eCommerce-enabled websites, ALC's eBusiness Intelligence database allows marketers to connect with corporations conducting sales on the internet.
Keyword Advertisers	Our eBusiness Intelligence file provides detailed data about a company's website complexity and popularity—and a unique view into corporations who self-identify through keyword SEO and SEM.

Harte Hanks

The Installation Likelihood Score (fields ending with "ILS") is an indicator that a given business location has a specific technology installed at that location. It can help you more effectively target key market sub-segments, thereby matching your message and offer to an audience that has a real need for your solutions.	Harte Hanks Market Intelligence has leveraged decades of experience and knowledge acquired from monitoring the business technology market to develop its installation likelihood and purchase likelihood scores. These scores are driven by data collected from a variety of sources including ongoing purchase intent surveys conducted by Harte Hanks Market Intelligence with tens of thousands of businesses annually. These data are combined with sophisticated statistical models to predict critical likelihoods about what kinds of technologies businesses have and are planning to purchase. The result is an unmatched level of predictive accuracy and reliability which can be applied to EVERY business in the Harte Hanks Technology Database.
A Purchase Likelihood Score (fields ending with "PLS") is an indicator that a given business location has a plan to purchase a specific technology or service. It can help you more precisely target key sub-markets with expertise and offers that will make a real difference in your response and close rates.	(No commentary was provided.)

Infogroup

Business Status Code (e.g., Headquarter vs. Branch)	This variable leads to decisions regarding granularity of the variables to be used.
Contact Title	Professional title of the contact. This variable indicates the depth of information that we obtained.
Growing Business Indicator	This variable reflects trends based on historical employment size.
Wealth Code	This variable illustrates areas surrounding the business.
Call Status Code	Infogroup's own call disposition code indicates authenticity of the business record.

OneSource

Custom Triggers	Custom Triggers leverage the power of OneSource's news searching capabilities, combining standard trigger events with a wide range of news search criteria to identify and alert on target events that are predictive of a discrete Sales opportunity. Custom Triggers can be created using Companies, Business Topics, Industry, Geographic information and free-text search criteria. OneSource can't predict the special and specific needs of all users, but the robust search filters available for Custom Trigger creation provide the tools needed to hone in on the events that drive specific companies' business success.
Combined searching on company, executive, and trigger events	In addition to allowing our customers to create their own Custom Trigger types we go a step further and allow customers to search on any combination of criteria for companies, executives, and trigger events allowing our customers to target their marketing efforts more precisely. As one example, our customers can easily generate a list of companies within a certain industry, geography, or size that have recent triggers showing they are growing, and have experienced a change in Sales and Marketing leadership.

Salesforce.com

Sales Volume	The total annual sales/revenue for this business in local currency. Not available on branch locations. (Ability to understand the potential ROI of a solution or service)
Global Ultimate DUNS	The D-U-N-S® number of the highest parent of a corporate family. Global ultimate records carry their own case D-U-N-S® number in this field so that a common sort and/or match area is available for all family members. Provides the ability to understand the entire family relationship and to predict potential growth through whitespace analysis. (Applies to the two items below)
Domestic Ultimate DUNS	The D-U-N-S® Number for the domestic ultimate, which is the highest family member in the same country as case business record as you walk up this 'branch' of the tree. A case may be its own domestic ultimate.
Parent DUNS	The D-U-N-S® Number for the Parent/Headquarter.

Stirista

Gender/Country of Origin	We often find that catering to particular audience, for instance, mentioning that this email is for female executives, can provide better results as it tends to let the recipient know that we know something beyond the business card info. Stirista is the only major file with ancestry, gender, etc., coded for 95%+ of all executives.

The sample company records reported

The complete records for the five prominent companies turned out to be far too large to share in this document, as they are recorded in the accompanying spreadsheet. In some cases, the records were too complex to be transferred to a spreadsheet, so they are accessible by another set of links within the accompanying spreadsheet. HG Data provided a detailed record for only one of the requested companies. The company records were submitted in response to the question, *Please pull your entire record of each of these 5 enterprises, and share what you have in each field. You may list each field in Column A. For the address, use the headquarters site location.*

Observations about the data

This study reveals that enormous richness about individual accounts is available to B2B marketers today. In fact, we might say that B2B has caught up with consumer, and then some, when it comes to the variety and quantity of fields available.

To us, the big news in this study is the prospecting opportunity this new data richness offers to B2B marketers. With this level of coverage and variety of fields now available, marketers should try their hands at modeling for look-alikes to their top current customers, if they are not already doing so. We suspect that look-alike models may very well unearth interesting and profitable new prospecting segments that most of us would never have expected.

We also notice in this study that each vendor sources and views the data differently. For example, ALC, which works off of response files, presented its company data from the perspective of the top contact, like CEO, of the firm. Harte Hanks and

HG Data, which focus on installed technology, submitted files of enormous volume, given that each technology brand and product is listed individually. This is a good reminder to us all how important it is not only to explore a variety of vendors, but to dig deeply about their data sourcing and compilation practices.

Advice to business marketers ordering from B2B prospecting databases

Based on our conclusion that no single vendor is likely to give you access to your entire target audience, our general recommendation about data depth is that you use multiple vendors to gain the richness you need.

Our specific guidelines for business marketers seeking deep data about their targets:

- Given the wide variances in data quantity and quality, it's essential that you investigate thoroughly the data sources and maintenance practices of the vendors you are considering.
- Specify exactly what you mean when ordering data. Don't make any assumptions that the vendor's definition of a term is the same as yours.
- Inquire about when they update their records, so you can get at the freshest data on the most essential elements.
- Conduct a comparative test before you buy. Every vendor is different. For example, if you happen to experience a low match rate with a particular vendor, it doesn't much matter to you how many wonderful fields they offer.

We hope our research is useful to business marketers who are renting or buying data on prospective accounts. This information will serve as a guide as you conduct your due diligence.

Appendix 2
B2B Technology Industry Prospecting Databases:
A Comparative Analysis of Nine Data Suppliers

Building on the general enthusiasm surrounding our past three studies on the accuracy and completeness of B2B compiled and response data, we decided to conduct similar research on the data available in the large and active technology marketing sector.

We found a sizable quantity of suppliers offering compiled data, response data, or a combination, to marketers who are trying to reach technology buyers. Invited to participate were:

• ALC	• Demandbase	• InsideView	• Stirista
• Broadlook	• Discoverorg.com	• Mardev-DM2	• TechTarget
• CardBrowser	• Harte Hanks	• MeritDirect MeritBase	• UBM
• D&B	• IDG	• NetProspex	• Worldata
• Data.com	• Infogroup	• ReachForce	• ZoomInfo

We were very pleased that nine suppliers joined the study, and we extend our gratitude to them. From those who declined, three reasons surfaced. As with last year's response data study, some managers of response databases felt that only their list-owner clients could make the decision to participate, and the complexity managing all those permissions was too great. Some database owners felt that our methodology favors vendors with large volumes of data, and the strengths of those that compete on quality versus quantity would not be made evident in our study. We understand both of these lines of reasoning, and hope we can figure out refinements to our study that will overcome these limitations in the future. In the case of a few other vendors, further discussion revealed that they do not offer data for rent or append, but instead make it available through a proprietary platform—thus being ineligible for inclusion.

One relatively unusual aspect of the world of technology marketing is the proliferation of specialty data providers who dig deep into the characteristics of target accounts, particularly among very large enterprises with vast technology budgets. These vendors invest in capturing useful information like the specifics of the account's current installed technology, and their buying processes, buying roles, budgets and purchase intentions. These vendors may not offer as many records as others, but each record is very richly detailed. Examples of such vendors are SalesQuest CRUSH Reports, iProfile.net, and InsideView. This kind of information is extremely valuable for key account planning. But is a considerably different animal from the prospecting databases studied here.

The nine participants who contributed information on their tech-buyer data are:

• Data.com	• Infogroup	• Stirista
• D&B	• Mardev-DM2	• Worldata
• Harte Hanks	• NetProspex	• ZoomInfo

Our sincere thanks to them, and to everyone else who considered participating.

The scope and intent of the study

We followed the same approach as used in our earlier research on compiled and response databases, to get answers to the concerns of business marketers about data volume, completeness and accuracy. By using a similar research methodology, we also hoped to provide some apples-to-apples comparison among the contents of response databases, compiled databases, and industry-specific databases, over time.

As with our earlier data studies, we asked the vendors to provide company counts in a selection of target industry sectors, plus contact counts for specific companies, and complete records on individual business people.

We specified the same ten industries as in prior studies, and asked the vendors to tell us how many companies they had in each of the ten, as indicated by SIC.

For the contact data, we made two changes from prior studies. First, we doubled the number of companies for whom contact counts were requested. While we used the same set of well-known large firms in each of the ten industries as in the 2010 and 2011 studies, we added another list of ten smaller firms, in the same ten industries, to broaden the understanding of vendor data by company size. This change we made in response to requests by several readers of past studies who are interested in targeting small/medium businesses versus large enterprises.

Second, to get at the tech-buyer question, we specified that the contact counts be limited to IT professional contacts. We offered the participating vendors the following list of technology professional titles, as examples of the types of contacts we expected them to include in their counts.

Examples of IT professional titles

Architects	LAN Administrators	Solution Engineers
Business Analysts	LAN Managers	Solutions / Services - Technical
CIO's	Network Administrators	Sales Reps
Computer Operations Managers	Network Directors	Storage - SAN Administrators
Computer Operators	Network Engineers	Systems Administrators
CTO's	Network Managers	Systems Analysts
Data Modelers	Network Support	Systems Engineers
Database Administrators (DBA's)	NOC Specialists	Systems Managers
Database Analysts	NOC Team Leaders	Systems Programmers
Database Managers	Programmers	Technical Consultants
Datacommunications	Project Leaders Technology	Technical Liaison
Datacommunications Managers	Project Managers Technology	Technical Support
Datawarehouse Architects	Quality Assurance	Telecommunications
Desktop Support Managers	Quality Assurance Managers	Telecommunications Managers
Directors Technology	Sales Support Engineers	VP's Technology
Disaster Recovery Specialists	Security Specialists	WAN Administrators
Help Desk	Software Developers	Web Developers
Help Desk Managers	Software Development Managers	Web Masters
Infrastructure Analysts	Software Engineers	Wireless Communications

We also recruited ten IT professionals in a variety of industries, who agreed to lend their names and contact information. We are grateful for their generous support of this study.

Individual contacts in the study

Industry	Name	Title	Company
Software	Rick Graham	President	Dual Impact Inc.
Financial Services	Michael Spencer	Director, Information Technology	Barclays Capital
Marketing	Dan Spiegel	Vice President of Engineering	AdMarketplace
Optical Equipment	Jeff Harvey	Director of IT	Edmund Optics, Inc.
Technology	Dominic Dimascia	VP, Technology Delivery Services	GSI Commerce
Manufacturing	Doug Lee	Reporting Manager	Pasternack Enterprises, Inc.
Not-for Profit	Andrew Lazar	Senior Technical Business Analyst/Database Developer	American Institute of Chemical Engineers
Electronics	Al Logiodice	Platform Manager, Store.Sony.com Development	Sony Electronics
Healthcare Technology	Arthur J Fisher	Marketo & SalesLogix Marketing DBA	GE Healthcare
Communications	Michael Green Sr.	Manager, Database Marketing Level	3 Communications, LLC

We asked only one qualitative question, inviting the vendors to explain their competitive positioning in the marketplace.

The positioning statements

Here is how the vendors described themselves in response to the following question: *Provide a statement of no more than 150 words that describes your tech data product/service, including how you are positioned, meaning your competitive differentiation. In short, this question is, "Who are you, and how are you different?"*

Data.com

Launched in September 2011 at Dreamforce, Salesforce Data.com is democratizing data by delivering instant access to the business data companies need right inside salesforce.com. We provide the data foundation customers need to succeed as a social enterprise by helping them easily find new customers and clean their data right in the cloud. Data.com delivers the data foundation with accurate crowd-sourced contact information and the leading company information from Dun & Bradstreet. Data.com draws on a community of over 2 million strong members which make over a million updates a month, all in real-time to address the pace of change in business data. Data.com stands alone as social, transparent, collaborative and integrated directly in salesforce.com—powering marketers to grow their business with complete and quality business data.

D&B

D&B Professional Contacts provides high-quality contact information—including email addresses and direct dials—on more than 60 million U.S. business professionals. Our database includes 900+ standardized job titles spanning sole proprietorships and multi-billion dollar enterprises. Customers selling into IT organizations have access to IT contacts as well as other business stakeholders who may be involved in the purchasing decision. D&B takes rigorous steps to ensure the accuracy of our data, vetting information through a rigorous quality assurance process, and linking each contact to a unique company identifier, the D-U-N-S® Number. This connection between contact and company offers key insight—such as employee count and sales—that puts a prospect's technology purchase in context. No one else offers this comprehensive view of contacts and the business they're in.

Harte Hanks

Harte Hanks is the industry's most trusted source for detailed information and insight into today's business technology buying market. Our flagship product, the Ci Technology Database™ (CITDB), tracks technology installations, purchase plans and key decision makers at more than four million locations in 25 countries in North America, Latin America and Europe. Detailed profiles include:

- Technology purchase plans including budget, need, timing, preferred vendor and key decision-maker.
- Installed technology and primary manufacturers for more than 45 products including computer hardware, software, networks, storage and telecommunications
- Site and enterprise-level IT budgets and IT staffing estimates
- Detailed contact information on IT and business decision-makers including functional responsibility.
- Plus, 65 descriptive fields including address, telephone, number of employees, annual revenue, industry classifications, DUNS number and fiscal year end. Put the power of the Ci Technology Database to work for you. Contact the technology experts at Harte Hanks at 1-800-854-8409 or visit www.citdb.com for more information.

Infogroup Targeting Solutions

Infogroup Targeting Solutions helps companies increase sales and customer loyalty through analytically driven consumer and business data and database marketing solutions. With exclusive access to the Data Axle™, we build multichannel solutions using contextually relevant information on 230MM individuals and 24MM businesses. We incorporate the highest quality, most accurate and comprehensive compiled and third-party information rich data. Our response generated data sources contain millions of records of leading IT executives and professional IT buyers within the US and Canada. Additionally, our B2B response driven powerful databases are rich in IT & technology related buyer information. We provide solutions and services to support marketers' and sales' efforts throughout the entire marketing and sales cycles by integrating cross-channel data from disparate sources to provide insights that ultimately increase efficiency, productivity and target the most responsive customers and prospects to drive the highest ROI.

Mardev-DM2

Mardevdm2 DecisionMaker® Databases are more than just a masterfile. They are custom built, multi-channel databases that start with all of our individual, high quality, direct response lists and end with custom built, single-source databases that provide marketers with both "deep data" selectivity and larger volumes of names. Selectable by specific detailed title and level, buying authority, software, hardware, number of PCs, laptops and printers as well as other IT related site data. It is this combination of depth, quality and coverage, that differentiates Decisionmaker from other masterfiles, improving marketing outcomes for our varied client-base. Partners include BuyerZone, CFE Media's Consulting Specifying Engineer, Control Engineering, Plant Engineering, Financial Media Group, Ward's Business Directory, IBIS, Lexis Nexis's Corporate Directories, Martindale Hubbell, Advertiser and Agency Redbooks, Reed Business Information, RS Means and many other highly reputable controlled circulation and media partners.

NetProspex

NetProspex is the only B2B data provider with a proprietary verification process to ensure clean, accurate, and up-to-date contact information. NetProspex drives customer acquisition by partnering with B2B marketers to deliver targeted prospect lists, data cleansing, and profiling analytics that help to uncover data insight and optimize lead generation results. Voted Best Lead Generation Solution by the SIIA, NetProspex maintains a deep database of millions of crowd-sourced business contacts verified by CleneStep™ technology. Thousands of B2B organizations rely on NetProspex to acquire and maintain clean, accurate prospect information to fuel high-performing marketing campaigns. More information at www.netprospex.com or on Twitter @NetProspex.

Stirista

Quite often the term 'social media' is used as a buzzword, but we rarely see practical usage and integration of the data with actionable email addresses. Stirista combines information from public profiles and websites and connects that information with an email database. This helps IT vendors identify exactly what technologies and products the IT buyers interested in even before someone makes a pitch to them. By figuring out, for instance, that an IT department specializes in .NET and is part of an online discussion forum for .NET, one can safely assume that a conference on Linux would not be of much interest to that individual. Stirista knows something beyond the fact that someone is an IT director and that makes the data exponentially more powerful. It not only helps with enhanced targeting capabilities but also decreases the potential of lost revenue and time due to incorrect messaging.

Worldata

Worldata is the leading data agency firm in the U.S. As the largest buyer and user of 3rd party permissioned email media, Worldata has unique abilities that our clients leverage including: reduced costs, special data availability and overall best practice knowledge. Our primary focus is with the Email, Direct Mail and Tele-marketing categories. We help marketers to execute prospect marketing programs, data hygiene initiatives and overall direct marketing strategies. More than 800 customers worldwide from all types of businesses and organizations—from enterprise technology, publishing, and online education to business services, nonprofits, and associations—use Worldata to leverage data assets, procure key datasets and find overall solutions to customer and prospect data initiatives. For more information contact Jay Schwedelson at 800.331.8102 x176 JayS@Worldata.com.

ZoomInfo

ZoomInfo is a B2B directory of over 50 million people throughout 5 million companies that includes contact information such as phone numbers, email addresses, and mailing addresses as well as the most in-depth profiles on individuals. The core of our technology is our patented web-crawling tools which help us compile all of our information. We also have a community of thousands of contributors who allow us to scan their email signatures in exchange for viewing our data. Our missions is to be able to map the business landscape in near real-time, and our technology is close to being able to give business professionals a 30-day snapshot so that our data is as up-to-date as possible. In terms of IT titles, our database consists of over 1,814,000 IT titles throughout 189 industries as well.

The company counts reported

Here are the company counts in each of the ten industries reported by the vendors in response to the question, *State the number of U.S. firms you have on your file in each of these 10 SICs. Also state (Y/N) whether you code firms with NAICS.*

SIC	32	56	28	64	73	81	80	82	35	48	Comments
	Stone, clay and glass products	Apparel and accessory stores	Chemical and allied products	Insurance agents, brokers & services	Business services	Legal services	Health services	Educational servoces	Machinery, except electrical	Communications	Do you code firms with NAICS? (Y/N)
Data.com	22,141	8,832	4,946	81,634	164,279	78,184	25,541	17,753	51,298	43,494	Yes	
D&B	40,391	308,890	53,049	307,131	5,799,337	488,019	1,454,473	360,850	127,086	200,884	Yes	
Harte Hanks	13,555	2,630	24,803	72,568	372,699	33,784	507,566	216,088	60,140	56,319	Yes	
Infogroup	45,355	335,512	59,776	444,584	4,306,799	598,841	2,189,964	457,247	155,251	242,965	Yes	
Mardev-DM2	34,080	154,213	45,065	834,340	2,866,125	531,718	955,738	299,494	111,255	111,116	No	*
NetProspex	10,049	7,753	14,358	45,909	261,998	46,892	75,625	74,899	45,687	35,761	No	**
Stirista	1,937	2,893	12,704	15,296	78,682	29,642	63,639	176,019	15,019	23,668	Yes	
Worldata	27,075	172,644	35,490	200,317	3,412,525	439,812	1,203,994	327,309	86,600	137,566	Yes	
ZoomInfo	3,813	42,213	23,655	52,906	284,518	80,908	81,689	155,291	19,088	36,431	No	***

* Most of our database participants are response lists and the demographics are self reported. Because of this not all of our records are SIC coded. We have our own detailed business activity to allow our customers to target their marketing efforts.
** SIC codes are available down to the 8-digit level.
*** We have some companies with NAICS codes but not many.

The contact counts reported

Here are the counts for contacts at ten each large and small companies in response to the question, *Provide the total number of contacts with IT-related titles you have at each of these 20 firms, U.S. only, including headquarters and all branch locations. For a list of the kinds of titles we are interested in, see below* (see p. x for the list).

Large enterprises	Data.com	D&B	Harte Hanks	Info group	Mardev-DM2	Net Prospex	Stirista	Worldata	Zoom Info
Andersen Windows	91	179	25	29	9	45	33	189	17
Nordstroms	238	379	19	494	3	250	983	1,117	90
Monsanto	276	351	95	621	448	453	869	928	289
MetLife	1,665	2,630	241	2,088	1,000	753	2,258	2,287	370
Accenture	9,465	4,610	49	4,826	3,332	3,310	8,052	1,701	2,242
Baker & McKenzie	93	119	22	136	139	177	135	451	44
Methodist Hospital System	107	120	12	53	113	89	155	344	516
ETS (Educational Testing Service)	163	190	4	265	218	217	145	133	27
Dell	1,473	1,756	83	3,928	2,096	1,287	1,512	2,319	3,220
Verizon	776	3,024	551	5,088	6,001	2,683	701	3,879	1,611
Small/medium enterprises									
Overly Door Company	3	6	0	4	5	5	4	5	2
Haggar Clothing Company	5	0	40	14	16	10	7	188	9
Frontier Pharmaceutical, Inc.	0	0	0	1	0	0	4	0	0
Hicks Insurance Group	0	0	0	3	0	0	3	0	0
Cadence Management Corporation	0	0	1	2	4	3	2	0	1
Henderson Legal Services, Inc.	0	0	1	1	1	1	2	0	0
Tri-anim Health Services, Inc.	1	0	3	5	6	7	4	9	0
Kumon Learning Centers	0	12	5	101	0	7	15	21	0
Device Technologies, Inc.	1	2	0	112	3	1	5	1	3
Reel-o-Matic, Inc.	0	0	0	4	0	2	2	0	2

Here are the figures on complete counts for each industry, in response to the question, *Provide the number of "complete" contact records among the IT professionals you have at each firm. Complete means including full name, address, title, phone, and email.*

Large enterprises	Data.com	D&B	Harte Hanks	Info group	Mardev-DM2	Net Prospex	Stirista	Worldata	Zoom Info
Andersen Windows	91	169	12	17	2	45	33	167	12
Nordstroms	238	371	3	249	1	250	983	994	40
Monsanto	276	310	30	354	48	453	869	813	113
MetLife	1,665	2,584	139	1,424	166	753	2,258	1,978	254
Accenture	9,465	4,589	19	4,119	269	3,310	8,052	1,432	205
Baker & McKenzie	93	111	11	248	25	177	135	405	14
Methodist Hospital System	107	111	6	194	18	89	155	293	362
ETS (Educational Testing Service)	163	184	2	183	41	217	145	88	1
Dell	1,473	1,699	44	1,298	224	1,287	1,512	2,016	1,171
Verizon	776	2,830	168	1,801	578	2,683	701	3,287	736
Small/medium enterprises									
Overly Door Company	3	6	0	2	0	5	4	4	2
Haggar Clothing Company	5	0	39	6	4	10	7	134	1
Frontier Pharmaceutical, Inc.	0	0	0	2	0	0	4	0	0
Hicks Insurance Group	0	0	0	18	0	0	3	0	0
Cadence Management Corporation	0	0	0	1	0	3	2	0	0
Henderson Legal Services, Inc.	0	0	1	1	1	1	2	0	0
Tri-anim Health Services, Inc.	1	0	1	7	0	7	4	6	0
Kumon Learning Centers	0	12	4	94	0	7	15	17	0
Device Technologies, Inc.	1	1	0	23	0	1	5	1	2
Reel-o-Matic, Inc.	0	0	0	4	0	2	2	0	1

The contact records reported

Here are the records for our ten individual business people, in response to the following directions. *Please pull the record of each of these 10 IT professionals as it currently appears on your file. Submit the record in its entirety. Note: Please do not use any other data sources (e.g., tele-verification, or Internet search) to research these names. We have secured permission from these 10 people to include their data in this research, and we have told them they will not be contacted or researched in any way by the participating suppliers.*

Contact Record: Dominic Dimascia

	First name	Last name	Title	Company	Address 1	Address 2	City	State	Zip	Office Phone	Email
Correct record	Dominic	Dimascia	VP, Technology Delivery Services	GSI Commerce	935 First Avenue		King Of Prussia	PA	19406	(610) 491-7221	dimasciad@gsicommerce.com
Data.com	Dominic	Dimascia	Vice President Technology Delivery Services	GSI Commerce, Inc.	935 1st Ave		King Of Prussia	PA	19406-1342	+1.610.491.7000	dominicd@gsicommerce.com
D&B	Dominic	Dimascia	Vice President Technology Delivery Services	Gsi Commerce, Inc.	935 1st Ave		King of Prussia	PA	19406		DIMASCIAD@GSICOMMERCE.COM
Harte-Hanks											
Infogroup	Dominic	Dimascia	Vice President Technology Delivery Services	GSI Commerce, Inc.	935 1st Ave		King Of Prussia	PA	19406	610-491-7000	
Mardev-DM2	Dominic	Dimascia	VICE PRESIDENT TECHNOLOGY DELIVERY SERVICES	GSI Commerce	935 1ST AVE		KING OF PRUSSIA	PA	19406-1342	610 491 7000	
NetProspex	Dominic	Dimascia	Vice President Technology Delivery Services	GSI Commerce, Inc.	935 1st Ave		King Of Prussia	PA	19406-1342	(610) 491-7000	dimasciad@gsicommerce.com
Sirista	Dominic	Dimascia	eCommerce Executive	GSI Commerce, Inc.	935 1st Ave		King Of Prussia	PA	19406	6104917000	dominicd@gsicommerce.com
Worldata	Dominic	Dimascia	VP, Technology Delivery Services at GSI Commerce	GSI Commerce, Inc.	935 First Avenue		King of Prussia	PA	19406	(610) 491-7000	dimasciad@gsicommerce.com
ZoomInfo											

Contact Record: Arthur Fisher

	First name	Last name	Title	Company	Address 1	Address 2	City	State	Zip	Office Phone	Email
Correct record	Arthur J	Fisher	Marketo & SalesLogix Marketing DBA	GE Healthcare	40 IDX Dr		South Burlington	VT	5407	802-859-6476	jay.fisher@ge.com
Data.com											
D&B											
Harte-Hanks											
Infogroup											
Mardev-DM2											
NetProspex	Jay	Fisher	Database Administrator	General Electric Company	PO Box 1070		Burlington	VT	5402	802 859-6476	jay.fisher@ge.com
Sirista											
Worldata											
ZoomInfo	Arthur	Fisher		GE Healthcare LTD	So. Burlington, Vermont, United States	800 Centennial Avenue, P.O. Box 1327	Piscataway	New Jersey	8855	(732) 457-8000	

-Contact Record: Rick Graham

Correct record	First name	Last name	Title	Company	Address 1	Address 2	City	State	Zip	Office Phone	Email
Correct record	Rick	Graham	President	Dual Impact Inc.	241 Forsgate Drive	Suite 208	Jamesburg	NJ	8831	(732) 656-0745	rick@computercare.com
Data.com	Rick	Graham	IT Department	Dual Impact Inc	109 S Main St		Cranbury	NJ	08512-3174	+1.609.448.4449	rick@computercare.com
D&B	Rick	Graham	President	Dual Impact Inc	241 Forsgate Dr Ste 208		Jamesburg	NJ	08831	7326560673	
Harte-Hanks	Rick	Graham	President	Dual Impact Inc	241 Forsgate Dr Ste 208		Jamesburg	NJ	08831-1385	(732)656-0673	
Infogroup	Richard	Graham	President	Dual Impact	241 Forsgate Dr # 208		Jamesburg	NJ	08831	732-656-0673	rick@computercare.com
Mardev-DM2	RICHARD	GRAHAM	PRESIDENT	DUAL IMPACT	3762 SUMMER ROSE DR		ATLANTA	GA	30341-1690	732 656 0673	
NetProspex	Rich	Graham	President	Computer Care	241 Forsgate Dr.	Ste 208	Jamesburg	NJ	8831	732-656-0745	rick@computercare.com
Sirista	RICK	GRAHAM	IT DEPARTMENT	DUAL IMPACT INC	241 FORSGATE DR STE 208		JAMESBURG	NJ	8831	7326560673	rick@computercare.com
Worldata	Rick	Graham	President	ComputerCare, Inc.	241 Forsgate Drive	Suite 208	Jamesburg	NJ	08831	(800) 248-0122	RICK@computercare.com
ZoomInfo											

Contact Record: Michael Green

Correct record	First name	Last name	Title	Company	Address 1	Address 2	City	State	Zip	Office Phone	Email
Correct record	Michael	Green	Sr. Manager, Database Marketing	Level 3 Communications, LLC	100 S Cincinnati Ave	Suite 1200	Tulsa	OK	74103	918-547-0602	mike.green@level3.com
Data.com	Michael	Green	Database Marketing Manager	Level 3 Communications, Inc	1025 Eldorado Blvd	Boulevard	Broomfield	CO	80021-8254	+1.720.888.1000	michael.green@level3.com
D&B											
Harte-Hanks	Mike	Green	Sr. Manager, Database Marketing - Level3	Level 3 Communications				OK		(918) 547-0602	Mike.Green@Level3.com
Infogroup											
Mardev-DM2											
NetProspex	Michael	Green	Database Marketing Manager	Level 3 Communications Inc.	1025 ELDORADO BLVD		BROOMFIELD	CO	80021	(720) 888-1000	michael.green@level3.com*
Sirista	MICHAEL	GREEN	SR. MANAGER, DATABASE MARKETING	LEVEL3 COMMUNICATIONS	100 S CINCINNATI AVE		TULSA	OK	74103	9185476000	michael.green@level3.com
Worldata	Michael	Green	Senior Manager, Database Marketing	Level 3 Communications, Inc.	1025 Eldorado Boulevard		Broomfield	CO	80021	(720) 888-1000	michael.green@level3.com
ZoomInfo	Mike	Green	Senior Manager, Database Marketing	Level 3 Communications, Inc.	Tulsa, Oklahoma, United States	1025 Eldorado Boulevard	Brofield	Colorado	80021	(918) 547-0602	mike@level3.com

* Michael Green has opted out of the NetProspex database, but his record is on the file.

Contact Record: Jeff Harvey

	First name	Last name	Title	Company	Address 1	Address 2	City	State	Zip	Office Phone	Email
Correct record	Jeff	Harvey	Director of IT	Edmund Optics, Inc.	101 E. Gloucester Pike		Barrington	NJ	8007	800-363-1992 x6825	JHarvey@edmundoptics.com
Data.com	Jeff	Harvey	Marketing Manager	Edmund Optics, Inc.	6464 E Grant Rd		Tucson	AZ	85715-8801	+1.856.573.6250 x6825	jharvey@edmundoptics.com
D&B	Jeff	Harvey	Marketing Manager	Edmund Optics, Inc.	Edmund Scientific Co	101 E Gloucester Pike	Barrington	NJ	08007	8565473488	
Harte-Hanks											
Infogroup	Jeff	Harvey	Director of IT	Edmunds Optics Inc.	101 E Gloucester Pike		Barrington	NJ	08007	800-363-1992	jharvey@edmundoptics.com
Mardev-DM2	JEFF	HARVEY	DIR-IS	EDMUND INDUSTRIAL OPTICS INC	101 E GLOUCESTER PIKE		BARRINGTON	NJ	08007-1380	856 573 6250	
NetProspex	Jeff	Harvey	IT Director	Edmund Optics Inc	101 EAST GLOUCESTER PIKE		BARRINGTON	NJ	8007	(856) 573-6250	jharvey@edmundoptics.com
Sirista	JEFF	HARVEY	DIRECTOR OF IS	EDMUND OPTICS, INC.	101 GLOUCESTER PIKE		BARRINGTON	NJ	8007	8565736250	jharvey@edmundoptics.com
Worldata	Jeff	Harvey	Director of Information Systems	Edmund Optics Inc.	101 East Gloucester Pike		Barrington	NJ	08007	(800) 363-1992	jharvey@edmundoptics.com
ZoomInfo											

Contact Record: Andrew Lazar

	First name	Last name	Title	Company	Address 1	Address 2	City	State	Zip	Office Phone	Email
Correct record	Andrew	Lazar	Senior Technical Business Analyst/Database Developer	American Institute of Chemical Engineers	3 Park Avenue		New York	NY	10016	646-495-1336	andrl@aiche.org
Data.com	Andy	Lazar	Senior Information Technology Support and Director	American Institute of Chemical Engineers (AIChE)	3 Park Ave		New York	NY	10016-5901	+1.800.242.4363	andrl@aiche.org
D&B											
Harte-Hanks											
Infogroup											
Mardev-DM2	ANDREW	LAZAR	SENIOR PROFESSIONAL	AMERICAN INSTITUTE OF CHEMICAL ENGINEERS	3 PARK AVE		NEW YORK	NY	10016-5991	646 495 1377	
NetProspex											
Sirista	ANDREW	LAZAR	DIRECTOR APPLICATIONS AND DATABASE DEVELOPMENT	AMERICAN INSTITUTE OF CHEMICAL ENGINEERS (AICHE)	3 PARK AVE FL 19		NEW YORK	NY	10016	6464951336	andrl@aiche.org
Worldata	Andrew	Lazar	Technical Business Analyst/Database Developer	American Institute of Chemical Engineers	3 Park Avenue		New York	NY	10016	(800) 242-4363	andrl@aiche.org
ZoomInfo											

Contact Record: Doug Lee

	First name	Last name	Title	Company	Address 1	Address 2	City	State	Zip	Office Phone	Email
Correct record	Doug	Lee	Reporting Manager	Pasternack Enterprises, Inc.	17802 Fitch		Irvine	CA	92614	949-261-1920 x139	doug@pasternack.com
Data.com											
D&B	Doug	Lee	Reporting Manager	Pasternack Enterprises, Inc.	17802 Fitch		Irvine	CA	92614	8667278376	DOUG@PASTERNACK.COM
Harte-Hanks											
Infogroup	Doug	Lee		Pasternack Enterprises Inc	17802 Fitch		Irvine	CA	92614	949-261-1920	
Mardev-DM2	DOUG	LEE	REPORTING MANAGER	PASTERNACK ENTERPRISES INC	17802 FITCH		IRVINE	CA	92614-6002	949 261 1920	
NetProspex	Doug	Lee	Reporting Manager	Pasternack Enterprises Inc	1851 Kettering		Irvine	CA	92614-5617	(949) 261-1920	doug@pasternack.com
Sirista	DOUG	LEE	REPORTING MANAGER	PASTERNACK ENTERPRISES, INC.	PO BOX 16759		IRVINE	CA	92623	8667278376	doug@pasternack.com
Worldata	Doug	Lee	Reporting Manager	Pasternack Enterprises, Inc.	17802 Fitch		Irvine	CA	92614	(949) 261-1920	doug@pasternack.com
ZoomInfo											

Contact Record: Al Logiodice

	First name	Last name	Title	Company	Address 1	Address 2	City	State	Zip	Office Phone	Email
Correct record	Al	Logiodice	Platform Manager, Store.Sony.com Development	Sony Electronics	16500 Via Esprillo		San Diego	CA	92127	858-942-5347	al.logiodice@am.sony.com
Data.com											
D&B											
Harte-Hanks											
Infogroup											
Mardev-DM2	AL	LOGIODICE	MANAGER WEB CRM AND CUSTOMER SERVICE SYSTEMS	SONY STYLE	1745 W BERNARDO DR		SAN DIEGO	CA	92127-1907	858 942 8000	
NetProspex	Al	Logiodice	Manager Platform Development SonyStyle.com	(310) 244-4000	10202 WASHINGTON BLVD		CULVER CITY	CA	90232-3119	(310) 244-4000	al.logiodice@am.sony.com
Sirista											
Worldata	Al	Logiodice	Platform Manager	Sony Electronics, Inc.	16530 Via Esprillo		San Diego	CA	92127	(858) 942-2400	al.logiodice@sony.com
ZoomInfo											

Contact Record: Michael Spencer

	First name	Last name	Title	Company	Address 1	Address 2	City	State	Zip	Office Phone	Email
Correct record	Michael	Spencer	Director, Information Technology	Barclays Capital	745 Seventh Avenue		New York	NY	10019	(212) 412-2890	michael.spencer@barclayscapital.com
Data.com*	Michael	Spencer	E2E Infrastructure Architect	Barclays Capital Inc.	Unit 5 9	2 Churchill Place	London		E14 5RB	+44.2071161000	michael.spencer@barclays.co.uk
D&B											
Harte-Hanks											
Infogroup											
Mardev-DM2											
NetProspex	Michael	Spencer	E2E Infrastructure Architect	Barclays Capital Inc.	200 PARK AVE L0WR 3A		NEW YORK	NY	10166	(212) 412-4000	michael.spencer@barcap.com
Sirista	MICHAEL	SPENCER	E2E INFRASTRUCTURE ARCHITECT	BARCLAYS CAPITAL INC.	200 PARK AVE L0WR 3A		NEW YORK	NY	10166	2124124000	michael.spencer@barcap.com
Worldata											
ZoomInfo											

* Jigsaw only accepts complete records. A member reported in 2009 that this contact is no longer with the company. We are also able to confirm that this is an undeliverable email. Hence this contact is in the Jigsaw Graveyard.

Contact Record: Dan Spiegel

	First name	Last name	Title	Company	Address 1	Address 2	City	State	Zip	Office Phone	Email
Correct record	Dan	Spiegel	Vice President of Engineering	AdMarketplace	3 Park Avenue	27F	New York	NY	10016	631-219-6710	dspiegel@admarketplace.com
Data.com	Dan	Spiegel	Vice President of Engineering	adMarketplace	3 Park Ave	Fl 27	New York	NY	10016-5902	+1.212.925.2022	dan@admarketplace.com
D&B											
Harte-Hanks											
Infogroup											
Mardev-DM2											
NetProspex	Dan	Spiegel	VP Engineering	adMarketplace	3 Park Ave	27th Floor	New York	NY	10016	212-925-2022	dan@admarketplace.com
Sirista	DAN	SPIEGEL	VP; ENGINEERING	adMarketplace	3 Park Ave	Fl 27	NEW YORK	NY	10016	2129252022	dan@admarketplace.com
Worldata	Dan	Spiegel	Vice President of Engineering	adMarketplace	3 Park Avenue	27th Floor	New York	NY	10016	(212) 925-2022	dan@admarketplace.com
ZoomInfo											

Observations about the data

This study revealed several unexpected angles about tech data. For one, we were surprised at how many IT professionals can be found at large enterprises. Paradoxically, we also notice that individuals in certain very large companies may be relatively difficult to reach—judging from the large holes in several of the ten individual records. We hypothesize that the level of secrecy—some might call is paranoia—at some large enterprises may encourage some IT professionals to keep a low profile.

For another, the contact counts reported raise a critical issue for business marketers. It's apparent that IT titles are growing fuzzier over time. Consider some of the titles used by our ten individuals: "Platform Manager," "Reporting Manager," "Vice President of Engineering." It's well nigh impossible from these titles to conclude that the person is in an IT role. Marketers may need to broaden the variety of titles they specify to capture a wider set of targets.

Finally, the wide variation in company counts reported per SIC reminds us that many vendors use proprietary industry categorization methodologies. This means that marketers need to be aware of the lack of standardization in determining how to classify any given company. This represents is a larger, ongoing problem in B2B database marketing, and an issue we will try to address in a future study.

As we expected, the data reported was fairly accurate, with only a few minor errors. When there were errors, they were not fatal for marketing purposes: The mail or email would still be deliverable, and the telephone call would eventually get to the prospect, in most cases.

Like earlier studies, the data field with the most problems—either missing or less accurate than other data elements—was email address.

When looking at the volume of complete records versus all contact records, keep in mind that vendors like Data.com, Stirista and NetProspex offer only data that is complete by our definition.

We also caution readers of this study against drawing conclusions about the capabilities of any particular vendor based on the comparative records of the ten individuals. This is not a statistically projectable sample in any respect—not only because it is too small, but also because these are simply ten people we happen to know and could persuade to lend their names. What we can conclude, however, is that important fields like direct phone number and email address tend to be fluid in this vertical. And that the fast-moving tech industry is characterized by high levels of turnover in jobs, skills and companies.

The wide fluctuations in company counts and contact counts lead us to the conclusion that no single vendor provides access to all the prospecting companies and all the prospective contacts that marketers of technology may be looking to reach.

Advice to business marketers ordering from technology industry prospecting databases

Based on our conclusion that no single vendor is likely to give you access to your entire target, our general recommendation about technology industry vertical data is that you use multiple vendors to gain the breadth of market coverage you need.

Our specific guidelines for business marketers seeking to reach tech-buyer targets:

- Given the wide variances in data quantity and quality, it's essential that you investigate thoroughly the data sources and maintenance practices of the vendors you are considering. In tech data particularly, quality trumps quantity.
- Specify exactly what you mean when ordering data. Don't make any assumptions that the vendor's definition of a term is the same as yours.
- Find out how your vendor gets at SIC, and whether they use some kind of conversion algorithm.
- Ask your vendor for details on how they define and source title and job function information, and how they are dealing with the new titles that have come into use in recent years. Also inquire about when they update their records, so you can get at the freshest data on this essential element.
- Conduct a comparative test before you buy. Here are three approaches you can try:
  —Send each potential vendor a sample of records from your house file and ask them to add data fields. Include a few dozen records on which you know the "truth," to assess accuracy of what comes back.
  —Order a sample of names with phone numbers from a prospective vendor, and then verify the accuracy of the records by telephone.
  —Order 5,000 records from a single state, from multiple vendors. Ask the vendors to deliver the file in ZIP sequence. Examine them. A high incidence of identical records among the vendors will be a strong indicator of likely accuracy.

We hope our research is useful to business marketers who are renting or buying data on technology buyers. This information will serve as a guide as you conduct your due diligence.

Appendix 3
B2B Response Databases: A Comparative Analysis

As a result of general enthusiasm about our past studies on the accuracy and completeness of the compiled data available on B2B markets, we were asked to conduct similar research on the data found in the response databases that have come on the scene in recent years.

The timing of this suggestion was excellent, because response databases are maturing as a prospecting resource, and marketers are getting accustomed to sourcing names from these pre-deduplicated amalgamations of response lists, often called "master files," versus renting from a batch of individual lists, as was the predominant list rental method in the past.

So, we invited as many managers of response databases as we could find to participate in the study. Invited to participate were:
- Direct Media's Data Warehouse
- Edith Roman's BRAD and BEN databases
- IDG
- Mardev-DM2's Decisionmaker database
- MeritDirect and Experian's b2bBase
- MeritDirect's MeritBase
- Statlistics
- Worldata

We think it's fair to say that all were intrigued by the opportunity and generally inclined to join. However, by the time our deadline rolled around, only three vendors were included. Why? For one thing, Infogroup decided to make a single submission combining the records of the various response databases living under the Infogroup umbrella (Direct Media's Data Warehouse, and the Edith Roman databases). For another, several response database managers determined that only their list-owner clients could make the decision to participate, and the complexity managing all those permissions was too great. Concerns were also expressed about competing on accuracy at the contact level. One database manager explained to us, for example, that any given contact in his file could come from scores of list sources, each with its own degree of accuracy, and all of which were maintained in the coop database.

As a result, our study includes the following:
- Infogroup
- Mardev-DM2
- Worldata

Our sincere thanks to them, and to everyone else who considered participating.

The growth of response databases

Business marketers have been the happy beneficiaries of the rise of cooperative databases in the last decade. Some of these have been built by independent list management companies, who persuade their management clients to allow their lists to be added to the database, and rented that way. Some cooperative databases have been built by owners of multiple lists, such as large B2B trade publishers.

These databases offer many appealing features:

- Names from multiple list owners are collected, de-duplicated, and in some cases appended with additional firmographic or behavioral data.
- Marketers may select names based on useful variables like company size, title, and geography, across all the lists, without worrying about individual minimum list order quantities.
- List owners are paid by usage on a name-by-name basis. Since list purchase is easier for marketers, in theory, owners' list revenues are higher than they could get by limiting rentals to the traditional list-by-list basis.
- Since records come from multiple sources, they may tend to be more accurate than single-sourced data.

A note about private cooperative databases

While the MeritBase and the Mardev-DM2 Decisionmaker are prominent examples of coop databases, another type of cooperative database is also available today, this one private and available only to members. A leading example is Abacus's B2B Alliance. Only list owners who join the Abacus coop and put their names in may take names out of the database. The identity of member companies is kept confidential. Because of the inaccessibility to non-member marketers, we did not ask Abacus or other similar private database cooperatives to participate in the study.

The scope and intent of the study

We followed the same approach as our recent research on compiled databases, to get answers to the concerns of business marketers about data volume, completeness and accuracy. By using a similar research methodology, we also hoped to provide some apples-to-apples comparison between the contents of response databases and compiled databases.

As with our compiled data studies, we asked the vendors to provide company counts in a selection of critical industry sectors, plus contact counts for specific companies, and complete records on individual business people.

We specified the same ten industries as in the compiled studies, and asked the vendors to tell us how many companies they had in each of the ten, as indicated by SIC. For the contact data, we used the same set of well-known firms in each of the ten industries as were used in the 2010 compiled data study.

We also recruited ten new business people in a variety of industries and in various job categories to agree to serve as this year's guinea pigs. We are grateful to these brave souls for their generous support of this study.

Individual contacts in the study

Industry	Name	Company	Title
Retail	Susan Sachatello	Lands' End	Chief Marketing Officer
Technology	Theresa Kushner	Cisco Systems	Director, Customer Intelligence
Not-for-profit	Jim Siegel	HealthCare Chaplaincy	Director, Marketing and Communications
Optical equipment	Stan Oskiera	Edmund Optics, Inc.	Vice President, Operations
Publishing	Michael S. Hyatt	Thomas Nelson	President and Chief Executive Officer
Legal services Assistance	John E. Tobin, Jr.	New Hampshire Legal	Executive Director
Healthcare	Brian A. Nester	Lehigh Valley Health Network	Senior Vice President, Physician Hospital Network Development
Education	Russell Winer	New York University	William Joyce Professor of Marketing;
Stern School of Business		Chair, Department of Marketing	
Tech services	Dale Mesnick	Smart Solutions, Inc.	Treasurer
Industrial	Bill Bullock	Turbosteam	General Manager

We asked only one qualitative question, inviting the vendors to explain their competitive positioning in the marketplace.

The positioning statements

Here is how the vendors described themselves in response to the following question: *Provide a statement of no more than 150 words that describes your online B2B data product/service, including how you are positioned, meaning your competitive differentiation. In short, this question is, "Who are you, and how are you different?"*

Infogroup

Infogroup is the leading provider of data and interactive resources that enable targeted sales, effective marketing and insightful research solutions. Among Infogroup's assets are powerful B2B response driven databases. These assets allow access to over 100 million key decision-makers penetrating virtually every business site in the US and Canada. They contain over 25 million executive email addresses, and enable users to choose from over 48 buying influence selectors including multi-buyers, job function, industry, products purchased, and more. Infogroup's assets have over 1,500 "list specific" response-generated data sources and are enhanced with firmographic and transactional data elements for targeted campaigns based on our expert strategic guidance. With over 100 million buyers and 32 million buying sites, our solutions are designed to maximize ROI for our customers. They are sourced from responder lists of mail order catalogers, publishers, book buyers, seminar and conference attendees and association memberships.

Mardev-DM2

For B2B marketers who need to expand their domestic or worldwide market footprint or accelerate their sales, Mardev-DM2 delivers a targeted audience of buyers and the global marketing services that most effectively reaches them. Unlike companies who provide compiled or standard company data, Mardev-DM2 delivers a level of detail within our data that enables better targeting at the individual level and far surpasses the quality of most data providers. In addition, Mardev-DM2 takes a consultative, creative and objective-based approach to each new client project, whether for B2B postal, email or telemarketing data, lead generation and nurturing programs, or fully integrated strategic marketing services. We meet each client where they are and work with them to develop a complete marketing program—from planning to execution to measurement—to ensure the best ROMI and overall success. A few of our core industries include: IT/Computers, Building/Construction, Manufacturing, Insurance/Finance, Engineering, Electronics, Legal, HR/Training, Foodservice/ Hospitality.

Worldata

Worldata is the leading data agency and list brokerage/ management firm in the U.S. Our ability to source, negotiate and utilize the latest technologies gives us a competitive advantage over the general list rental buying marketplace. Our primary focus is with the Email, Direct Mail and Telemarketing categories. We help marketers to execute prospect marketing programs, data hygiene initiatives and overall direct marketing strategies. More than 800 customers worldwide from all types of businesses and organizations—from enterprise technology, publishing, and online education to business services, nonprofits, and associations—use Worldata to leverage data assets, procure key datasets and find overall solutions to customer and prospect data initiatives.

The company counts reported

Here are the company counts in each of the ten industries reported by the vendors in response to the question, *State the number of U.S. firms you have on your file within each of these 10 SICs.*

		Infogroup	Mardev-DM2	Worldata
32	Stone, clay and glass products	43,318	82,416	20,571
56	Apparel and accessory stores	297,473	15,319	18,137
28	Chemical and allied products	54,807	224,308	62,210
64	Insurance agents, brokers & services	365,758	1,082,065	72,267
73	Business services	3,190,830	894,257	84,703
81	Legal service	546,267	892,825	123,712
80	Health services	2,059,979	329,153	1,315,999
82	Educational service	524,256	450,560	657,129
35	achinery, except electrical	152,375	405,674	206,547
48	Communications	203,792	173,422	192,266
	Do you code firms with NAICS? (Y/N)	Y	Y	Y

The contact counts reported

Here are the counts for contacts at each of ten well-known companies, in response to the question, *Provide the total number of contacts you have at each firm, U.S. only, including headquarters and all branch locations.*

	Infogroup	Mardev-DM2	Worldata
Andersen Windows	330	107	0
Nordstroms	349	5	531
Monsanto	6,527	1,679	1,288
MetLife	12,073	11,625	1,722
Accenture	34,355	6,803	472
Baker & McKenzie	2,128	1,082	320
Methodist Hospital System	1,010	767	201
ETS (Educational Testing Service)	2,333	515	89
Dell	7,060	8,872	1,446
Verizon	30,684	18,353	2,938

Here are the figures on complete counts for each industry, in response to the question, *The number of "complete" contact records you have at each firm. Complete means including full name, address, title, phone, fax and email.*

	Infogroup	Mardev-DM2	Worldata
Andersen Windows	158	41	0
Nordstroms	284	2	331
Monsanto	340	880	988
MetLife	1,468	1,965	1,472
Accenture	5,660	1,048	302
Baker & McKenzie	1,779	430	237
Methodist Hospital System	321	224	176
ETS (Educational Testing Service)	318	213	66
Dell	852	2,991	1,099
Verizon	1,937	3,881	2,019

The contact records reported

Here are the records for our ten individual business people, in response to the following directions. *Please pull the record of each of these persons as it currently appears on your file. Submit the record in its entirety. Note: Please do not use any other data sources (e.g., tele-verification, or Internet search) to research these names. We have secured permission from these 10 people to include their data in this research, and we have told them they will not be contacted or researched in any way by the participating suppliers.*

Contact: Susan Sachatello

	Correct data	Infogroup	Mardev-DM2	Worldata
First name	Susan	Susan	SUSAN	
Last name	Sachatello	Sachatello	SACHATELLO	
Title	Chief Marketing Officer	Senior Vice President Marketing	SR VICE PRESIDENT MARKETING	
Company	Lands' End	Lands' End, Inc.	LANDS' END, INC.	
Address 1	5 Lands' End Lane	1 Lands End Ln	LANDS END LN	
Address 2				
City	Dodgeville	Dodgeville	DODGEVILLE	
State	WI	WI	WI	
Zip	53595	53595	53595-0001	
Office phone	608-935-4169	608-935-9341	608 935 9341	
Email	susan.sachatello@andsend.com	susan.sachatello@landsend.com	SUSAN.SACHATELLO@LANDSEND.COM	

Contact: Theresa Kushner

	Correct data	Infogroup	Mardev-DM2	Worldata
First name	Theresa	Theresa	THERESA	Theresa
Last name	Kushner	Kushner	KUSHNER	Kushner
Title	Director, Customer Intelligence	Director of Customer Intelligence	DIRECTOR	DIRECTOR, CUSTOMER INTELLIGENCE
Company	Cisco Systems	Cisco Systems, Inc.	CISCO SYSTEMS INC	Cisco Systems, Inc.
Address 1	170 West Tasman Drive	170 W Tasman Dr BLDG 8	170 W TASMAN DR	170 W Tasman Dr
Address 2		SJ08-3	SJ08-3	
City	San Jose	San Jose	SAN JOSE	San Jose
State	CA	CA	CA	CA
Zip	95134-1706	95134	95134-1700	95134-1706
Office phone	408-526-8774	408-526-8774	(408) 526-8774	408-526-8774
Email	thkushne@cisco.com	thkushne@cisco.com	THKUSHNE@CISCO.COM	thkushne@cisco.com

Contact: Jim Siegel

	Correct data	Infogroup	Mardev-DM2	Worldata
First name	Jim	Jim		JIM
Last name	Siegel	Siegel		SIEGEL
Title	Director, Marketing and Communications	Director Marketing & Communication		DIRECTOR OF MARKETING AND COMMUNICATIONS
Company	Healthcare Chaplaincy	The Healthcare Chaplaincy Inc.		THE HEALTHCARE CHAPLAINCY INC
Address 1	315 East 62nd Street	315 E 62nd St FL 4		307 EAST 60TH STREET
Address 2	4th Floor			
City	New York	New York		NEW YORK
State	NY	NY		NY
Zip	10065-7767	10065		10022-1505
Office Phone	212-644-1111 x141	212-644-1111		212-644-1111 ext. 141
Email	jsiegel@healthcarechaplaincy.org	jsiegel@healthcarechaplaincy.org		jsiegel@healthcarechaplaincy.org

Contact: Michael S. Hyatt

	Correct data	Infogroup	Mardev-DM2	Worldata
First name	Michael S.	Michael S	MICHAEL	MICHAEL
Last name	Hyatt	Hyatt	HYATT	HYATT
Title	President and Chief Executive Officer	President, Chief Executive Officer	CHIEF INFORMATION OFFICER	PRESIDENT AND CHIEF EXECUTIVE OFFICER
Company	Thomas Nelson	Thomas Nelson Inc	THOMAS NELSON, INC.	THOMAS NELSON INC.
Address 1	P.O. Box 141000	501 Nelson Pl	141000 PO BOX	501 NELSON PL
Address 2		PO Box 141000	501 NELSON PL	NASHVILLE
City	Nashville	Nashville	NASHVILLE	NASHVILLE
State	TN	TN	TN	TN
Zip	37214	37214	37214-3600	37214-3600
Office Phone	615.902.1100	615-889-9000	615 889 9000	615-902-1100
Email	mhyatt@thomasnelson.com	mhyatt@thomasnelson.com		MHYATT@THOMASNELSON.COM

Contact: Stan Oskiera

	Correct data	Infogroup	Mardev-DM2	Worldata
First name	Stan	Stan	STAN	Stanley
Last name	Oskiera	Oskiera	OSKIERA	Oskiera
Title	Vice President, Operations	Vice President of Operations	VP OPERATIONS	VICE PRESIDENT OPERATIONS
Company	Edmund Optics, Inc.	Edmund Optics, Inc.	EDMUND OPTICS INC	Edmund Optics
Address 1	101 E. Gloucester Pike	101 East Gloucester Pike	101 E GLOUCESTER PIKE	101 E. Gloucester Pike
Address 2				
City	Barrington	Barrington	BARRINGTON	Barrington
State	NJ	NJ	NJ	NJ
Zip	08007	08007	08007-1331	08007
Office Phone	856-547-3488 ext. 6887	856-547-3488	8565473488	856-547-3488
Email	soskiera@edmundoptics.com	soskiera@edmundoptics.com		soskiera@edmundoptics.com

Contact: John E. Tobin, Jr.

	Correct data	Infogroup	Mardev-DM2	Worldata
First name	John E.	John	JOHN	JOHN
Last name	Tobin, Jr.	Tobin	TOBIN	TOBIN
Title	Executive Director	Executive Director	EXECUTIVE DIRECTOR	EXECUTIVE DIRECTOR
Company	New Hampshire Legal Assistance	New Hampshire Legal Assistance	NEW HAMPSHIRE LEGAL ASSISTANCE	NEW HAMPSHIRE LEGAL ASSISTANCE
Address 1	117 North State St.,	117 N State St	3117 N STATE	117 North State St.
Address 2				
City	Concord	Concord	CONCORD	Concord
State	NH	NH	NH	NH
Zip	03301	03301	03301	03301
Office Phone	603-224-4107 x 2816	603-223-9750	603 668 2900	603-224-4107 ext.2816
Email	jtobin@nhla.org	jtobin@nhla.org	JTOBIN@NHLA.ORG	JTOBIN@NHLA.ORG

Contact: Brian A. Nester

	Correct data	Infogroup	Mardev-DM2	Worldata
First name	Brian A.	Brian		BRIAN
Last name	Nester	Nester		NESTER
Title	Senior Vice President	Doctor of Osteopathy		SVP PHYSICIAN PRACTICE
Company	Lehigh Valley Health Network	Lehigh Valley Health Network		LEHIGH VALLEY HOSPITAL EMERGENCY
Address 1	Cedar Crest and I-78,	PO Box 689		240 S CEDAR CREST BLVD & I-78
Address 2	P. O. Box 689			EMERGENCY MEDICINE
City	Allentown	Allentown		ALLENTOWN
State	PA	PA		PA
Zip	18105	18105		18105
Office Phone	610-402-7544	610-402-8111		610-402-8111
Email	Brian.Nester@lvhn.org	brian.nester@healthnetworklabs.com		Brain.Nester@LVH.COM

Contact: Russell Winer

	Correct data	Infogroup	Mardev-DM2	Worldata
First name	Russell	Russell		Russell
Last name	Winer	Winer		Winer
Title	William Joyce Professor of Marketing; Chair, Department of Marketing	Professor; Chair Marketing		Chair, Marketing Department
Company	Stern School of Business	NYU-Stern School Of Business		NEW YORK UNIVERSITY
Address 1	40 West 4th Street	40 W 4th St		44 West Fourth Street
Address 2	Tisch Hall 806	Tisch Hall Marketing Dept		Stern School of Business
City	New York	New York		New York
State	NY	NY		NY
Zip	10012-11	10012		10012
Office Phone	212.998.0540	212-998-0100		212-998-0540
Email	rwiner@stern.nyu.edu			rwiner@stern.nyu.edu

Contact: Dale Mesnick

	Correct data	Infogroup	Mardev-DM2	Worldata
First name	Dale	Dale	DALE	DALE
Last name	Mesnick	Mesnick	MESNICK	MESNICK
Title	Treasurer	Senior Manager; Finance Executive	VICE PRESIDENT	TREASURER
Company	Smart Solutions, Inc.	Smart Solutions, Inc.	SMART SOLUTIONS INC	SMART SOLUTIONS INC
Address1	23900 Mercantile Road	23900 Mercantile Rd	23900 MERCANTILE RD	23900 MERCANTILE RD
Address2				
City	Cleveland	Cleveland	CLEVELAND	CLEVELAND
State	OH	OH	OH	OH
ZIP	44132	44122	44122-5910	44122-5910
Office phone	(216) 765-1122, ext. 8227	216-765-1122	216 765 1122	2167651122
Email	dmesnick@smartsolutionsonline.com	dmesnick@smartsolutionsonline.com		dmesnick@smartsolutionsonline.com

Contact: Bill Bullock

	Correct data	Infogroup	Mardev-DM2	Worldata
First name	Bill	William	BILL	WILLIAM
Last name	Bullock	Bullock	BULLOCK	BULLOCK
Title	General Manager	General Manager	GENERAL MANAGER	GENERAL MANAGER
Company	Turbosteam	Turbosteam LLC	TURBOSTEAM CORP	TURBOSTEAM CORPORATION
Address1	161 Industrial Blvd	161 Industrial Blvd	161 INDUSTRIAL BLVD	161 INDUSTRIAL BOULEVARD
Address2				
City	Turners Falls	Turners Falls	TURNERS FALLS	TURNERS FALLS
State	MA	MA	MA	MA
ZIP	01376	01376	01376-1611	01376-1611
Office phone	(413) 676-3016	413-863-3500	413 863 3500	413-863-3500
Email	Bbullock@turbosteam.com	bbullock@turbosteam.com	WBULLOCK@TURBOSTEAM.COM	WBULLOCK@TURBOSTEAM.COM

Observations about the data

Having done two successive annual studies on the accuracy and completeness of B2B compiled data, we brought with us certain assumptions as we prepared for a study on response data. Most direct marketers expect that, while compiled data provides better market coverage but is less accurate, response data is more accurate but gives you less breadth of coverage.

Just as we were surprised at the results of our compiled data studies, which showed better than expected accuracy, we are now surprised at the response data we looked at, which is broader than we anticipated. The number of companies reported by SIC, and the number of contacts per company, were impressive. Comparing the counts with last year's compiled data (which is not quite fair, since a lot can happen in B2B data in one year) we would say the response databases are holding their own, certainly debunking our long-held assumption that response files give limited market coverage. When it comes to the individual contacts, less than a handful were missing records or particular data elements.

As we expected, the data reported was fairly accurate, with only a few minor errors. When there were errors, they were not fatal for marketing purposes: The mail or email would still be deliverable, and the telephone call would eventually get to the prospect, in most cases.

The data field with the most problems—either missing or less accurate than other data elements—was email.

We generally conclude that:

- The data available in response databases is quite similar in accuracy and completeness to compiled data.

As was shown by our past studies, data varies by vendor, and each vendor has its strengths and weaknesses.

Advice to business marketers ordering from response databases

Our advice to marketers about response data is similar to that on compiled data. We urge caution when ordering data from these databases. Marketers should develop a detailed ordering methodology, to increase the likelihood that the data they receive is what they were seeking.

Our guidelines:

- Given the wide variances in data quantity and quality, it's essential that you investigate thoroughly the data sources and maintenance practices of the vendors you are considering.
- Specify exactly what you mean when ordering data. Don't make any assumptions that the vendor's definition of a term is the same as yours.
- Be very specific about industry selections. Find out if the vendor uses SIC, or some kind of conversion algorithm.
- Keep an eye out for vendor specialization by industry. Companies and con-

tacts vary widely by vendor. For additional market coverage we suggest that you explore industry specialty files for both prospecting and data append purposes.

· Conduct a comparative test before you buy. Here are three approaches you can try:

—Send each potential vendor a sample of records from your house file and ask them to add data fields. Include a few dozen records on which you know the "truth," to assess accuracy of what comes back.

—Order a sample of names with phone numbers from a prospective vendor, and then verify the accuracy of the records by telephone.

—Order 5,000 records from a single state, from multiple vendors. Ask the vendors to deliver the file in ZIP sequence. Examine them. A high incidence of identical records among the vendors will be a strong indicator of likely accuracy.

We hope our research is useful to business marketers who are renting or buying response data. This information will serve as a guide as you conduct your due diligence.

Appendix 4
B2B Compiled Data Sources: A Comparative Analysis

Access to complete and accurate information about customers and prospects is more important than ever to business marketers. In recent years, much has happened in the world of B2B compiled data. Suppliers who compile business data via the Internet continue to grow their files, and develop new ways to package and present their information. But the traditional B2B data compilers have seen declining sales and considerable restructuring and consolidation during the economic downturn.

In light of these changes, Bernice Grossman and Ruth P. Stevens decided to conduct an update of their 2009 research about online sources of B2B data. We invited a variety of well-known and reputable vendors to answer a series of questions about their data and their business practices.

We would like to express our deep appreciation to the five vendors who agreed to participate:

- Demandbase
- D&B Selectory
- Infogroup
- Jigsaw
- NetProspex

The scope and intent of the study

We followed the same approach as in 2009 in order to address the perennial questions that concern business marketers about data volume, completeness and accuracy. We asked the vendors to provide company counts in a selection of critical industry sectors, plus contact counts for specific companies, and complete records on individual business people.

We specified the same ten industries as in the 2009 study, and asked the vendors to tell us how many companies they had in each of the ten, as indicated by SIC. For the contact data, however, this year we selected a different set of well-known firms in each of the ten industries.

We also recruited ten new business people in a variety of industries and in various job categories to agree to serve as this year's guinea pigs. We are grateful to these brave souls for their generous support of this study.

Individual contacts in the study

Industry	Name	Company	Title
Environment	Stephen A. Wallis	AIRxpert Systems	Chairman
Business Services	Deborah Sliz	Morgan Meguire LLC	President & CEO
Not-for-profit	Jim Siegel	HealthCare Chaplaincy	Director, Marketing and Communications
Education	Michael Devitt	City University of New York	Distinguished Professor, Philosophy Program
Transportation	Michael Cox	Aviacargo Inc.	President
Government-Administration	Marilyn Sescholtz Veterans Affairs	Department of	Psychiatrist
Retail	Bill Williams	Harry & David	CEO
Financial Services Investment Management	Michael Christie	Christie/Coghlin	Managing Partner
USPS	Cathrine E. Moriarty	USPS	Marketing Specialist
Technology	Dominic Dimascia	GSI Commerce	VP, Technology Delivery Services

The positioning statements

Here is how the vendors described themselves in response to the following question: Provide a statement of no more than 150 words that describes your online B2B data product/service, including how you are positioned, meaning your competitive differentiation. In short, this question is, "Who are you, and how are you different?"

Participating vendor	
Demandbase	Demandbase offers the only online database of business contact information that integrates the highest quality data from the industry's top sources (Jigsaw, InfoUSA, D&B, Harte Hanks, LexisNexis, Hoovers, and dozens of others). More than 8 million business contact records with email have been pre-validated and can be searched online am using thousands of powerful filter combinations. A simple user interface, pay-as-you-go pricing, automated de-dupe, and closed-loop web monitoring technology to track responses has made Demandbase #1 for more than 30,000 sales and marketing professionals in just 2 years. Any marketing or sales professional looking for an easier way to target a market or prospect within a sales territory, should try Demandbase. It is free to get started, there are no minimums, and complete business contact information can be added to Outlook, CRM, or any marketing automation system.
D&B® Selectory®	D&B® Selectory® helps sales and marketing professionals find new customers and grow their sales by building targeted lists, profiling existing customers and running direct marketing campaigns from their desktop. Selectory offers its users unlimited searching, viewing and printing of detailed, location-specific company and contact information. Selectory provides access to 23 million businesses—16 million in the U.S. and Canada, and 7 million others worldwide. Selectory allows you to: build targeted lists using up to 40 search criteria, download information for campaigns or for importing into CRM applications, no need to deal with a list broker, build a list in minutes, pinpoint the best opportunities in your target market, lookup company and contact details before making the call, add tags or notes, and keep all your sales data in a single place.

Participating vendor	
Infogroup	Infogroup is the leading provider of data driven and interactive resources for targeted sales, marketing and research solutions. Sales and marketing professionals know they can rely on Infogroup's flexible suite of solutions to add insight to every stage of the sales and marketing process and to achieve results. Infogroup offers comprehensive information through multiple solutions including: 1) idExec, for online access to 2 million executive decision-makers at 900,000 public, private, non-profit, and government organizations in 172 countries. 2) OneSource®, a recognized leader in global business information services, delivering unparalleled company, executive and industry intelligence and content from over 2500 information sources. 3) Our signature US Business Database of 14 million US businesses. The US Business Database is phone verified and is not a derivative of another product or application. As a result, the coverage of the Infogroup US Business Database is intended to represent all active business sites.
Jigsaw	Jigsaw is the fastest growing data provider in the world, and the industry leader in Data as a Service (DaaS) and business information. Jigsaw uniquely leverages user-generated content contributed by its global business-to-business community of one million members, as well as world class data hygiene and validation technologies. Jigsaw is the only company in the Industry to use "Native App" sharing where users of CRM systems share data with Jigsaw and extend the reach of the Jigsaw community. Jigsaw gives individuals and companies access to contact information for millions of business professionals and profiles on millions of companies. In addition to delivering low-cost and easy access to high value business information, Jigsaw provides companies with cloud based data acquisition and management services. Jigsaw has won the CODiE award for Best Business Productivity Solution, a CRM Rising Star award, and salesforce. com customer's choice award for Best Sales Intelligence Tool of 2009.
NetProspex	NetProspex is raising the standards of the online contact information industry by being the most accurate resource for business contact information. Business contacts are crowd-sourced from a community of users, and verified by proprietary technology before being published. Continual data scrubbing ensures maximum quality. With over 9 million verified contacts, NetProspex provides accurate contact information on difficult-to-find decision makers across North America. 1. It's growing—new records added each day. 2. It's verified—scrubbed by powerful proprietary CleneStep™ technology and backed by a 100% hard bounce replacement guarantee within 30 days. 3. It's crowd-sourced, providing a deep reach into hard-to-find mid-management decision makers. 4. It's integrated, designed to fuel companies large and small, available on the AppExchange, and perfect for fueling marketing automation and sales pipeline fulfillment.

The company counts reported

Here are the company counts in each of the ten industries reported by the vendors in response to the question, *State the number of U.S. firms you have on your file within each of these 10 SICs.*

		Demandbase	D&B® Selectory®	Infogroup	Jigsaw	NetProspex
32	Stone, clay and glass products	4,114	28,630	26,853	10,446	852
56	Apparel and accessory stores	3,662	203,663	228,194	19,766	1,200
28	Chemical and allied products	5,861	33,852	23,782	16,236	6,616
64	Insurance agents, brokers & services	8,804	221,917	267,784	30,760	11,030
73	Business services	44,471	2,434,988	894,833	297,986	63,039
81	Legal service	26,346	323,037	561,712	69,152	12,156
80	Health service	48,158	902,982	1,829,198	108,780	20,108
82	Educational service	24,350	232,129	288,577	73,196	16,242
35	Machinery, except electrical	15,754	94,318	105,875	53,852	9,737
48	Communications	6,072	119,848	114,099	59,168	5,978
Do you code firms with NAICS?	NAICS conversion file	no	yes	yes, through an SIC to	yes	no

D&B Selectory reported counts on companies whose Primary SIC is as shown. Companies with Secondary SICs in the named categories are not included. About a third of all US companies on the D&B file use multiple name and address combinations for what is really the same company at the same address. However, D&B products neither count separately, nor deliver separately as prospects, multiple variations of the same company at the same address.

Jigsaw uses its own "Jigsaw Industry Code," and overlays SIC from a third party source. In these counts, Jigsaw stated that they included both the "hard match SICS," as well as the mapping of SIC to JIC.

The contact counts reported

Here are the counts for contacts at each of ten well-known companies, in response to the question, *Provide the total number of contacts you have at each firm, U.S. only, including headquarters and all branch locations.*

	Demandbase	D&B® Selectory®	Infogroup	Jigsaw	NetProspex
Andersen Windows	416	104	121	11	36
Nordstroms	644	253	285	852	234
Monsanto	1,332	370	172	1,238	1,251
MetLife	6,250	1,196	1,318	7,088	879
Accenture	22,084	258	131	27,668	784
Baker & McKenzie	453	82	178	2,665	516
Methodist Hospital System	7	65	928	321	454
ETS (Educational Testing Service)	281	75	105	384	224
Dell 2,161	212	199	7,061	2,409	
Verizon	5,583	6,066	1,687	11,544	3,586

Here are the figures on complete counts for each industry, in response to the question, *The number of "complete" contact records you have at each firm. Complete means including full name, address, title, phone, fax and email.*

	Demandbase	D&B® Selectory®	Infogroup	Jigsaw	NetProspex
Andersen Windows	416	104	121	11	36
Andersen Windows	416	104	36	11	29
Nordstroms	644	253	232	852	228
Monsanto	1,332	370	145	1,238	1,081
MetLife	6,250	1,196	630	7,088	852
Accenture	22,084	258	119	27,668	69
Baker & McKenzie	453	82	160	2,665	491
Methodist Hospital System	7	65	396	321	450
ETS (Educational Testing Service)	281	75	33	384	220
Dell 2,161	212	188	7,061	2,379	
Verizon	5,583	6,066	1,755	11,544	3,093

Selectory defines "complete" as meaning contacts having full name, title, address and phone, but not email. They also notes that some records may not have fax number.

The contact records reported

Here are the records for our ten individual business people, in response to the following directions. *Please pull the record of each of these persons as it currently appears on your file. Submit the record in its entirety. Note: Please do not use any other data sources (e.g., tele-verification, or Internet search) to research these names. We have secured permission from these 10 people to include their data in this research, and we have told them they will not be contacted or researched in any way by the participating suppliers.*

THE CONTACT RECORDS REPORTED: STEPHEN WALLIS

	First Name	Last Name	Title	Company	Address	City	State	Zip	Office Phone	Email
Correct Data	Stephen	Wallis	Chairman	AIRxpert Systems	1 John Wilson Lane	Lexington	MA	02421	781-862-4739	steve@ airxpert.com
Participating Vendor										
Demandbase										
D&B Selectory	Stephen	Wallis	President	Airxpert Systems Inc	1 John Wilson Ln	Lexington	MA	02421-6032	781-862-4739	
Infogroup	STEPHEN	WALLIS	OWNER	AIRXPERT SYSTEMS INC	1 JOHN WILSON LN	LEXINGTON	MA	02421	781-862-4739	
Jigsaw	Stephen	Wallis	President	Airxpert Systems Inc.	1 John Wilson Ln	Lexington	MA	02421-6032	1.781.862.4739	s.wallis@ airxpert.com
NetProspex	Stephen	Wallis	President	AIRxpert Systems, Inc.	1 John Wilson Ln.	Lexington	MA	02421-6032	781-862-4739	steve@ airxpert.com

THE CONTACT RECORDS REPORTED: DEBORAH SLIZ

	First Name	Last Name	Title	Company	Address	City	State	Zip	Office Phone	Email
Correct Data	Deborah	Sliz	President & CEO	Morgan Meguire LLC	1225 I Street, NW, Suite 1150	Washington	DC	20005	(202) 661-6192	dsliz@morgan-meguire.com
Participating Vendor										
Demandbase										
D&B Selectory										
Infogroup	DEBORAH	SLIZ	PRESIDENT	MORGAN MEGUIRE LLC	1225 I ST NW #1150	WASHINGTON	DC	20005	202-661-6180	DSLIZ@MORGANMEGUIRE.COM
Jigsaw	Deborah	Sliz	President	Morgan Meguire LLC	1225 I St NW, Ste 300	Washington	DC	20005-5955	1.202.661.6180	dsliz@morgan-meguire.com
NetProspex	Deborah	Sliz	President & CEO	Morgan Meguire LLC	1225 I Street, NW, Ste 300	Washington	DC	20005	202.661.6192	dsliz@morgan-meguire.com

THE CONTACT RECORDS REPORTED: JIM SIEGEL

	First Name	Last Name	Title	Company	Address	City	State	Zip	Office Phone	Email
Correct Data	Jim	Seigel	Director, Marketing and Communications	HealthCare Chaplaincy	315 E. 62nd Street, 4th Fl	New York	NY	10065	212-644-1111 x141	jsiegel@healthcarechaplaincy.org
Participating Vendor										
Demandbase	Jim	Seigel	Director Marketing & Communications	The HealthCare Chaplaincy Inc	307 E 60th St	New York	NY	10022	212 6441111	jsiegel@healthcarechaplaincy.org
D&B Selectory										
Infogroup										
Jigsaw										
NetProspex										

THE CONTACT RECORDS REPORTED: MICHAEL DEVITT

	First Name	Last Name	Title	Company	Address	City	State	Zip	Office Phone	Email
Correct Data	Michael	Devitt	Distinguished Professor at Philosophy Program	City University of New York	Graduate Center of CUNY, 365 5th Ave	New York	NY	10016	212-817-8620	MDevitt@ gc.cuny.edu
Participating Vendor										
Demandbase										
D&B Selectory										
Infogroup										
Jigsaw										
NetProspex										

THE CONTACT RECORDS REPORTED: MICHAEL COX

	First Name	Last Name	Title	Company	Address	City	State	Zip	Office Phone	Email
Correct Data	Michael	Cox	President	Aviacargo Inc.	304 Park Avenue South	New York	NY	10010	212-949-3139	mcox@aviacargo.com
Participating Vendor										
Demandbase										
D&B Selectory	Michael	Cox	President	Aviacargo	304 Park Ave S Fl 11	New York	NY	10010-4305		
Infogroup	MICHAEL J	COX	PRESIDENT	AVIA CARGO INC	304 PARK AVE S, STE 11	NEW YORK	NY	10010		MCOX@AVIACARGO.US
Jigsaw										
NetProspex	Michael	Cox	President, Sales and Customer Service	AVIA Cargo	304 Park Ave. South	New York	NY	10010	216-671-5500	mcox@aviacargo.us

THE CONTACT RECORDS REPORTED: MARILYN SESCHOLTZ

	First Name	Last Name	Title	Company	Address	City	State	Zip	Office Phone	Email
Correct Data	Marilyn	Sescholtz	Psychiatrist	Department of Veterans Affairs	423 E.23rd Street	New York	NY	10010	212-686-7500 x4919	marilyn.sescholtz@va.gov
Participating Vendor										
Demandbase										
D&B Selectory										
Infogroup										
Jigsaw	Marilyn	Sescholtz	Psychiatrist	United States Department of Veterans Affairs	423 E 23rd St	New York	NY	10010-5011	1.212.951.5983	marilyn.sescholtz@va.gov
NetProspex										

THE CONTACT RECORDS REPORTED: BILL WILLIAMS

	First Name	Last Name	Title	Company	Address	City	State	Zip	Office Phone	Email
Correct Data	Bill	Williams	CEO	Harry & David	2500 S. Pacific Hwy.	Medford	OR	97501-2675	541-864-2727	williams@ HarryandDavid. com
Participating Vendor										
Demandbase										
D&B Selectory	William	Williams	President; Chief Executive Officer	Harry & David Holdings Inc	2500 S Pacific Hwy	Medford	OR	97501-8724	541-864-2362	
Infogroup	William H.	Williams	President & Chief Executive Officer	Harry & David	2500 S Pacific Hwy	Medford	OR	97501-8724	541-776-2121	wwilliams@bco. com
Jigsaw	William	Williams	Chief Executive-Officer	Harry and David	2500 S Pacific Hwy	Medford	OR	97501-8724	1.541. 864.2121	wwilliams@ harryanddavid. com
NetProspex	Bill H.	Williams	President, CEO, and Director	Harry & David	2500 S Pacific Hwy	Medford	OR	97501-8724	(541) 864-2362	williams@ harryanddavid. com

THE CONTACT RECORDS REPORTED: MICHAEL CHRISTIE

	First Name	Last Name	Title	Company	Address	City	State	Zip	Office Phone	Email
Correct Data	Michael	Christie	Managing Partner	Christie/Coghlin Investment Management	2 Landmark Square 2F	Stamford	CT	06901	(203) 504-2890	michael.christie@wachoviafinet.com
Participating Vendor										
Demandbase										
D&B Selectory										
Infogroup										
Jigsaw	Michael	Christie	Partner	Wachovia Securites	2 Stamford Plz	Stamford	CT	06901-3263	1.203.504.2890	michael.christie@wachoviafinet.com
NetProspex	Michael	Christie	Managing Partner	Christie/Coghlin Investment Management	2 Landmark Square	Stamford	CT	6901	203-504-2890	michael.christie@wachoviafinet.com

THE CONTACT RECORDS REPORTED: CATHRINE MORIARTY

	First Name	Last Name	Title	Company	Address	City	State	Zip	Office Phone	Email
Correct Data	Cathrine	Moriarty	Marketing Specialist	USPS	475 L'Enfant Plaza SW	Washington	DC	20260-7540	202-268-7498	cathrine.c.moriarty@usps.gov
Participating Vendor										
Demandbase										
D&B Selectory										
Infogroup										
Jigsaw	Cat	Moriarty	Editor	United States Postal Service	475 L Enfant Plz Southwest	Washington	DC	20260-1805	1.202.268.2155	delivermag@usps.com
NetProspex										

THE CONTACT RECORDS REPORTED: DOMINIC DIMASCIA

	First Name	Last Name	Title	Company	Address	City	State	Zip	Office Phone	Email
Correct Data	Dominic	Dimascia	VP, Technology Delivery Services	GSI Commerce	935 First Avenue	King of Prussia	PA	19406	(610) 491-7221	dimasciad@gsicommerce.com
Participating Vendor										
Demandbase										
D&B Selectory										
Infogroup										
Jigsaw	Dominic	Dimascia	Chief Information Officer	Genesis Direct	391 Roberts Rd	Oldsmar	FL	34677-4918	1.813.855.4274	ddimascia@gendirect.net
NetProspex										

Jigsaw classifies a record that has been reported as incorrect by a member of the Jigsaw Community as being in the "Graveyard." This usually means the contact has left the company. The Graveyard status can be changed once the report has been successfully Appealed or Updated. Jigsaw's record for Dominic Dimascia was classified as Graveyard.

Observations about the data

We knew going into the 2010 study that much consolidation had taken place in the B2B data industry. So it came as no surprise that fewer firms participated in our study this year—five, down from ten. Last year, several divisions of both InfoGroup and D&B participated. But this year, both of these firms chose to represent themselves with single reports. One firm from last year dropped out because it had divested its business lists division. Other companies, like ZoomInfo, declined to take the time to participate due to the press of business.

Overall, the results bring us to the same conclusion as last year: The business data available from vendors tends to be relatively accurate, but coverage is extremely spotty.

To be fair, this year we went further afield in selecting the ten businesspeople whose individual records would be requested from the vendors. We included such people as a psychiatrist from the VA, a marketing director at a non-profit, and a Washington lobbyist. All of these people are active buyers of business products and services, and thus of great interest to business marketers. But in many cases, the vendors had no records on them.

Another interesting angle in the data is the wide variance between vendors who build their files from the business level and those who build from the contact level. Jigsaw is an example of the latter, having begun as a business-card swap site. As such, compared to traditional compilers like Infogroup and D&B, Jigsaw has many contacts per company, but relatively fewer companies per industry.

Like last year, individuals with more senior titles tended to attract better coverage. Also like last year, we noticed that we could ask the same question of multiple vendors and get some very different answers, due to differences in interpretation and definition.

With regard to how the reported data has changed year on year, we can make a few observations:

- Inexplicably, some vendors reported vastly lower company counts in the same SICs in 2010 versus 2009.
- Fax number as a data category appears to be in decline. We hypothesize that fax has declined as a marketing tool, possibly because of the rise of scanning.
- On the individual records, we assumed that vendors would provide us with direct phone numbers, but many provided only the general company number.

Advice to business marketers ordering compiled data online

Our advice to marketers based on this year's data has changed little from last year. We urge caution when ordering data from compliers. Marketers should develop a detailed ordering methodology, to increase the likelihood that the data they receive is what they were seeking.

Our guidelines:

- Given the wide variances in data quantity and quality, it's essential that you investigate thoroughly the data sources and maintenance practices of the vendors you are considering.

- Specify exactly what you mean when ordering data. Also drill down in detail to understand what the vendor means. In this year's research, D&B Selectory and Jigsaw were working from a different definition of the term "complete" than ours. Not that either is right or wrong—but it adds to the confusion. As another example, when asking for phone number, be clear about whether you want the general switchboard or the contact's direct dial.
- Be very specific about industry selections. Find out if the vendor uses SIC, or some kind of conversion algorithm. You want to know exactly what you are getting.
- Keep an eye out for vendor specialization by industry. As we saw in this year's study, some individuals in some categories were not included in these large databases. So it's essential for market coverage that you explore industry specialty files for both prospecting and data append purposes.
- Consider whether you want breadth of contacts or breadth of companies—or both. Data source will always be an important factor in this determining which compiler is right for you. To enhance coverage, many marketers find that buying data from multiple vendors is necessary.
- Only use reputable vendors. A number of unscrupulous firms have entered the market claiming they can get you any business names you want, but their data turns out to be stolen, inaccurate, or otherwise not usable.
- Conduct a comparative test before you buy. Here are three approaches you can try:
  —Send each potential vendor a list of 5000 records from your house file and asking them to add data fields. Include a few dozen records on which you know the "truth," to assess accuracy of what comes back.
  —Order a sample of names from a prospective vendor as per above, and then verify the accuracy of sample records by telephone.
  —Give each prospective vendor a set of instructions using very narrow criteria like a certain employee size range and sales volume range in a certain state. Ask the vendors to sort the records in ZIP sequence, and give you the first 1000 records to look at. A high incidence of identical records among the vendors will be a strong indicator of likely accuracy.

We hope our research is useful to business marketers who are renting or buying data online. This information will serve as a guide as you conduct your due diligence.

Appendix 5
Data append comparative analysis

Bernice Grossman and Ruth P. Stevens invited a group of leading business-to-business data services providers to join in a research project to compare their various approaches to data append. Three vendors agreed to participate: InfoUSA Donnelley Marketing Division (now Infogroup), Equifax and MarketModels (now AccuData).

We compiled a sample file of 10,000 "live" records, from a variety of client sources. We expected that they were all records of individuals at business addresses, although we later learned that a sizable number of consumer addresses had crept in. The records comprised 9 fields:

- Last name
- First name
- Business title
- Company name
- Address 1
- Address 2
- City
- State
- ZIP code

We asked the vendors to perform their typical append processes on the data, but not to perform any data hygiene or de-duplication on the file we sent. Our reasoning was that this is an append project. We did not want to introduce an additional variable in the form of data hygiene services that would impact the result.

We asked the vendors to take no more than 14 weeks to do the project (usually 3 weeks is sufficient). Finally, we requested that they do this work at no charge, for the benefit of members of the business marketing community. Our sincere thanks to them all for participating.

Our instructions were to append the following fields, which are very typical of B2B append projects:

- Year Started: When the company went into business
- SIC: Although NAICS is available, many users and vendors still rely on SIC to identify the company's industry category. We asked for primary SIC
- Franchise: Indicates a franchise business like Jiffy Lube
- Headquarters/Site: Does the address reflect a company headquarters or simply a site, meaning, a non-headquarters location
- Number of Employees Total: Number company-wide
- Number of Employees Local: Number at this site
- Sales Volume Total: Sales company-wide
- Sales Volume Local: Sales at this site
- Public/Private
- Minority Owned
- Government
- Educational Institution

Results

As you review the append project results, you'll notice that some data fields were not provided by some vendors. This may be because:

- The data was not available to this service provider.
- The service provider chose not to offer this data element for this project.

Now, let us examine the data as appended by the three participating vendors to the sample file they received.

Table 1. Average Append Rates by Field

The highest level of appendability was achieved for Number of Employees Local, SIC, and Sales Volume Local. The other fields experienced statistically insignificant append rates. Keep in mind, however, that these results are specific to this particular sample data set, so they cannot serve as any sort of benchmark.

	SIC	Headquarters / Site	Number of Employees Local	Sales Volume Local	Public / Private
Average/ received	50.49%	28.95%	50.37%	44.92%	21.53%
Average/ matched	97.83%	59.69%	98.03%	89.22%	44.44%

Table 2. Match Rates

All three vendors identified 9,665 records received. They then attempted to match these records to their own databases, with widely varying results, as seen in this table. Keep in mind that the relative match rate is primarily a function of how the matching process of each vendor interacts with the data sample submitted. On another sample, the relative match rates are likely to be very different. This table illustrates the importance of testing each vendor with your own data sample.

Vendor	Records Matched	Match Rate
InfoUSA	5,982	61.89%
Equifax	4,904	50.74%
MarketModels	4,074	42.15%

When considering the results of matching your data to the vendor's database, there are a number of drivers that may explain how your data performed:

- Some of your records may have contained residential address data. You may want to ask the vendor for residential address counts. In this test, InfoUSA Donnelley Marketing Division voluntarily provided a count of consumer records on our file (see Table 15).
- Company names can be written so many ways—IBM versus International Business Machines, for example. If your files are not standardized, you will experience lower match rates.
- Companies may use many addresses, including post office boxes.
- You may have more duplicates than you thought.
- Your data needs to be cleaned up.

Table 3. Year Started

	Hits	Hits/Received	Hits/Matched
InfoUSA	1,928	19.95%	32.23%
Equifax	2,711	28.05%	55.28%
MarketModels	Not provided	Not provided	Not provided

Table 4. SIC

	Hits	Hits/Received	Hits/Matched
Donnelley	5,982	61.89%	100%
Equifax	4,585	47.44%	93.50%
MarketModels	4,074	42.15%	100%

Table 5. Franchise

	Hits	Hits/Received	Hits/Matched
InfoUSA	560	5.79%	9.36%
Equifax	Not provided	Not provided	Not provided
MarketModels	28	0.29%	0.69%

Table 6. Headquarters/Site

	Hits	Hits/Received	Hits/Matched
Donnelley	2,033	21.03%	33.99%
Equifax	2,654	27.46%	54.12%
MarketModels	3,708	38.34%	90.97%

Table 7. Number of Employees, Total Company

	Hits	Hits/Received	Hits/Matched
InfoUSA	800	8.28%	13.37%
Equifax	Not provided	Not provided	Not provided
MarketModels	Not provided	Not provided	Not provided

Table 8. Number of Employees, Local (at the site)

	Hits	Hits/Received	Hits/Matched
Donnelley	5,628	58.23%	94.08%
Equifax	4,904	50.74%	100%
MarketModels	4,074	42.15%	100%

Table 9. Sales Volume, Total Company

	Hits	Hits/Received	Hits/Matched
USA	697	7.21%	11.65%
Equifax	Not provided	Not provided	Not provided
MarketModels	Not provided	Not provided	Not provided

Table 10. Sales Volume, Local (at the site)

Notice that Equifax and MarketModels identified the same number of hits for both Sales Volume Local and Number of Employees Local.

	Hits	Hits/Received	Hits/Matched
Donnelley	4,047	41.87%	67.65%
Equifax	4,904	50.74%	100%
MarketModels	4,074	42.15%	100%

Table 11. Public/Private

The following four tables are structured on a "yes/no" basis, so a hit means that the vendor had information on whether the company is public or private, minority owned, etc.

	Hits	Hits/Received	Hits/Matched
InfoUSA	1,338	13.84%	22.37%
Equifax	2,281	23.60%	46.51%
MarketModels	2,625	27.16%	64.43%

Table 12. Minority Owned

The determination of minority owned business here is driven by the federal government's very detailed set of characteristics, and may not be entirely consistent with how a marketer would define it.

	Hits	Hits/Received	Hits/Matched
Donnelley	127	1.31%	2.12%
Equifax	129	1.33%	2.63%
MarketModels	534	5.53%	13.11%

Table 13. Government

	Hits	Hits/Received	Hits/Matched
InfoUSA	343	3.55%	5.73%
Equifax	362	3.75%	7.38%
MarketModels	47	0.49%	1.15%

Table 14. Education

This particular file did not happen to contain many educational institutions. But there is one other technique you can use to assess this factor: Compare the Education hit rate against the education SIC codes appended to the file.

	Hits	Hits/Received	Hits/Matched
Donnelley	357	3.69%	5.97%
Equifax	139	1.44%	2.83%
MarketModels	140	1.45%	3.44%

Table 15. Consumer Addresses

While we did not request information about consumer addresses, InfoUSA Donnelley Marketing Division supplied an analysis based on their consumer databases, so we include it here. The relatively high level of consumer addresses on this file is certainly an impediment to perfect match rates. However, it is very common in B2B, due to the preponderance of small office / home office (SOHO) businesses, as well as situations where business customers respond to marketers using their home addresses. If you do find a sizable set of consumer addresses, you may want to conduct additional protocols on that portion of the data.

	Hits	Hits/Received	Hits/Matched
InfoUSA	1,370	14.17%	22.90%
Equifax	Not requested	Not requested	Not requested
MarketModels	Not requested	Not requested	Not requested

Observations and conclusions

This study suggests that large, reputable vendors will provide very similar services when it comes to data append. Results are heavily a function of the nature of the names processed, so it is imperative that you test a sample of your file before selecting a vendor. We did not ask the vendors to clean up the data, so these match-rate results are on the low side of what's possible. The highest hit rates on this particular data set came from SIC, Number of Employees Local and Sales Volume Local. The lowest hit rates were from Government, Education and Franchise. The only ways to measure append accuracy are 1) seed the file with names you already know the truth about, and/or 2) conduct outbound telephone verification on a sample.

This study was conducted in 2006.

Appendix 6
How to Prepare an RFI for B2B Database Outsourcing Services: Results from six prominent providers

Bernice Grossman and Ruth P. Stevens submitted a typical RFI to a field of six well-known providers of B2B marketing database outsourcing services. They were generous enough to answer the questions and allow us to share the information publicly. Our hearty thanks to them all:

Analytic*i*	Harte Hanks
Creative Automation	MarketModels
Donnelley Marketing	MSC

For this project, we dreamed up a fictional B2B company, ACME, which sells—what else?—widgets. On behalf of ACME, we created an RFI document as follows. The document followed the format described above, and described a company that has decided to outsource its marketing database (MDB), and seeks to improve its marketing processes and its profitability as a result. ACME has about 2 million customer records, currently housed on multiple systems. ACME's sales force uses salesforce.com as their automation system.

ACME's Marketing Database Project RFI

Table of Contents

- ACME's objectives
- ACME's current technical environment
- Vendor description
    - —Data center procedures
    - —Subcontractors
- Vendor references
- RFI policy

ACME's objectives for the marketing database (MDB)

ACME marketing identified the following business goals for their marketing database (MDB):

- Become customer-centric by developing a complete view of the customer with all pertinent data.
- Increase effectiveness and efficiency of acquisition and retention marketing with better customer targeting and campaign management.
- Improve overall ROI by marketing to most valuable customers.
- Target individual customers with specific messages designed to best meet their needs.
- Understand customer behavior for each product within channels and across the brands.

They also identified the following functional requirements:

- Provide access for query and analysis by both marketing and sales.
- Integrate the mail and email query and campaign management functions.
- Allow for bi-directional integration of SFA data with the marketing database.
- Provide accurate information on new customers, cost to acquire customers, number of inactive customer, migration of customers between value segments and the cost of migration.
- Use 3rd party data to establish corporate hierarchy links of ownership.
- Enhance customer data through the use of 3rd party firmographics.

ACME's current technical environment

ACME's data currently resides in (ACME's selections appear in **bold**):

- **Oracle data warehouse**
- Siebel
- SAP
- **Mainframe flat files**
- **SQL Server**
- DB2
- Access
- FoxPro
- ACT
- Goldmine
- Onyx
- Pivotal
- **SalesForce.com**
- Yellow Brick
- Proprietary system
- Other (describe)

There are approximately 2,000,000 potentially eligible records on file. This data along with historical information comprises approximately 50 Gb of data representing, the last 3 years. Growth over the next 3 years is expected at a rate of 25% per year.

ACME's file will include business-to-business data from the United States only.

Estimated number of users at ACME will be 20. Users must be able to access the marketing database from their laptops via the Internet.

Vendor description

Please provide a short description of your organization, its business activities and affiliated entities (if any). In your response please address the following points:

- corporate mission statement and customer service philosophy
- years in business
- total number of staff
- key executive bios
- ownership information (company's inception to current)
- organization chart
- documented quality control procedures from data receipt to MDB update
- total # of customer support staff
- total # of technical support staff

- largest (Gig) volume B2B MDB designed
- total number of MDB installations (show B2B # and consumer #)
- system software information
  —release dates (first, last and frequency)
  —programming language, operating system and database engine
  —required third party software
- previous B2B experience
- percent of budget applied to R&D
- confirmation of liability insurance; willingness to provide details
- pending litigation
- MDB staff attrition over the last year
- company privacy policy
- primary industries that you serve
- number/type of user group meetings you hold each year

Data center procedures

Please provide a detailed description of the facility, the process, and the security resident at the hosted data center facility managed by the vendor.

- Available data center locations
- Back up procedures
- Real-time redundancy (servers, HVAC, etc.)
- Disaster recovery and business continuity procedures
- Contingency for downtime and preventive maintenance
- Physical and data security measures
- Connectivity options
- Service levels for problem reporting and problem resolution
- Proof of existing maintenance contracts for hardware and operating systems resident at the vendor's facility
- Ability to provide support 24 x 7 x 365

Subcontractors

The selected vendor will be solely responsible for overseeing and indemnifying all sub-contracted work. Any sub-contractor not listed in the original agreement must be approved by ACME before working on this project. ACME reserves the right to approve all sub-contractors. All sub-contractors must sign a Nondisclosure Agreement in advance of any work or communication regarding the specifics of this work.

Vendor references

Please provide at least three (3) references, B2B organizations at which you have provided products or services in circumstances required to support the design and development of an MDB.

Include the names, titles and telephone numbers of individuals at those organizations who may be called by ACME as references. Please identify clients engaged in the past 6 months as well as those clients of longer duration.

Please include one company who is no longer a client.

RFI policy

ACME is not prepared to pay any costs incurred in the preparation and/or submission of the response to this RFI, the RFP to follow, or the preparation for the presentation/visit to ACME.

How the participating vendors responded

We found considerable differences among the vendors in the areas of infrastructure, size and business focus. In the areas of policy and process, they were quite similar. Here are the details of their answers. Keep in mind that these answers were prepared in the summer of 2005, and are subject to change over time.

	Analytic *i*	Creative Automation	Donnelley Marketing	Harte-Hanks	Market Models	MSC
Years	1999	1969	1972	Over 40	1999	1975
Staff	35	300+ (100 in computer services)	About 500 2,400 at InfoUSA	350 in database group	18 + 15 in tech support	46
Largest MDB	Over 2 terabytes	130 million records	1/2 terabyte	7 terabyte	500 gigabytes	2.5 terabytes 65 million records
Installations	Did not furnish	246 external users	54, of which 12 are B-to-B	Over 100	15	7+ dozens of smaller DBs
Operating System	SQL Server	Mainframe Oracle, SQL Server	Oracle	Oracle and SQL Server	SQL Server	SQL Server and Mainframe
Application Software	Surround, E.piphany, Unica	Proprietary, Oracle Discoverer	Market-Zone with Alterian	Unica, E.piphany	Proprietary	Proprietary
R&D	Did not furnish	$3.5+ million	At least $6 million	Over $35 million & partner R&D	5% per year	15% of gross revenue
Staff Attrition	None	6 in 2003	Low	Extremely Low	None	None in last 7 years
User Groups	4 per year	As needed by clients	Annual User Group meeting	2 Customer Forums per year	No	Not required
24 x 7 x 365	Yes	Yes	Yes, after hours support by Opps staff	Yes	Yes, on call as needed	Yes

As for the areas of great similarity, all of the participating vendors said they have:
- No litigation
- Liability insurance
- Detailed quality control processes
- Excellent privacy policies
- Excellent backup and redundancy capabilities

Observations and conclusions

An RFI is a useful first step in the process of outsourcing a marketing database, especially in the world of business-to-business data, where the content is more complex and the business needs more varied. As we went through this exercise, we developed a number of conclusions and recommendations:

- First and foremost, make sure you are dealing with a vendor who has plenty of experience with B2B data. Further, you may want to select a vendor who already has clients in the same business category as yours.
- Check to be sure all of your questions have been answered in the responses to the RFI. If not, this is a red flag.
- Consider the size of other companies on the vendor's client list. You don't want to be the vendor's smallest client, unless you're sure you'll be very profitable for them.
- You need to scan the mission statements and corporate philosophy documents the vendors provide—even if they are not the most exciting reading—just to be sure you see nothing in conflict with your company's culture.
- Don't expect the RFI to provide details about how your database outsourcing project will be managed. That information needs to wait until the RFP stage. If the RFI response reads as though the vendor has already determined what you need, look elsewhere.

Appendix 7
The data hygiene comparative analysis project

In the spring of 2004, Bernice Grossman and Ruth P. Stevens invited a group of leading business-to-business data services providers to join in a research project to compare their various approaches to data clean up. Four vendors agreed to participate: Acxiom, DataFlux, Donnelley Marketing and Harte Hanks. We compiled a sample file of 10,000 "live" names, containing 12 fields. The names we used came from a variety of client sources. They were all names of individuals at business addresses.

We asked the vendors to perform their typical hygiene processes on the data and send the results back to us within 30 days. We also asked them to answer some questions about their companies and their approaches to data hygiene. Finally, we requested that they do this work at no charge, for the benefit of members of the business marketing community.

As you can imagine, this research project raised several fairly touchy issues. First, we were asking the vendors to open their doors, and reveal the results of their processes as compared to their direct competition. We gratefully acknowledge the courage and openness of the vendors who chose to participate. To reduce the competitive pressure, we are withholding the identity of the specific vendors in the report below (Table 5), which reveals the number of data elements corrected, by vendor.

Second, everyone involved in the project recognized the importance of protecting the privacy of the business people and companies whose names happened to turn up on the sample file. If the vendors were to apply their actual standard data hygiene processes to the file, live data was required. To protect the privacy of those involved, we have decided not to publish the sample records of individual names and addresses after clean up.

Table 1. Vendor definitions of data hygiene

To make sure we were all talking about the same thing, we asked the vendors, "What is your company's definition of data hygiene?"

Acxiom	"Purpose-driven data management practices and/or processes that promote data accuracy. Typically is applied to name and address data content, correction and completion."
DataFlux	"A 5-phase data management cycle, including profiling (inspection), quality (correction), integration (merging and linking), augmentation (enhancement), and monitoring (auditing and control). Understand the data problems: improve the data."
Donnelley Marketing	"A broad range of processes that collectively deliver the highest deliverability of an address: standardizing, correcting, updating and verifying."
Harte Hanks	"The process of solving business problems resulting from inadequate data quality: accuracy, completeness, timeliness, validity."

Table 2. Vendor-described differentiation

We thought readers would find it helpful to understand how the vendors view themselves in comparison with their competition. So we asked the vendors, "What are the 5 most important ways your work differs from your competitors'?"

Acxiom
1. Ability to recognize and parse name, business name, and address components
2. Ability to recognize the difference between business and consumer entities
3. Ad hoc, batch, automated batch and real time support of hygiene solution delivery
4. Abilitec-enabled occupancy database tool
5. NCOA/ChangePlus

DataFlux
1. Integrated data profiling and data quality technologies
2. Technologies developed in house, using the same core engine
3. Forthcoming capability to monitor data quality over time
4. Interface permits business users (non IT staff)
5. All processing done in one pass

Donnelley Marketing
1. Proprietary file of 13 million businesses in the US and Canada, and over 8 million executive contacts and title elements, for verification, appending and addition of missing elements
2. 100% telephone verification of each business record at least once a year
3. Ability to track executives at their home or business addresses
4. OnePass system allows all B2B hygiene to be done in one continuous logical flow
5. Proprietary Mailability Score that ranks each address based on deliverability

Harte Hanks
1. Expertise in multiple vertical markets
2. Ability to provide customizable and flexible client-specific hierarchy of business rules
3. Objective selection of best-of-breed vendors of business files, to suit client needs
4. Integrated access to both USPS advanced postal products and HH proprietary data
5. Broad data management tool set

Table 3. Vendor definitions of "bad" data

To understand any potential differences in the subject matter, we asked, "How do you characterize 'bad' B2B data?"

Acxiom	"Data that fails to meet specific data content requirements and/or cannot be used to fulfill a specific business purpose."
DataFlux	"Any data that does not support the underlying processes or business applications built on that information."
Donnelley Marketing	"There is no right answer. The answer is to look within the customer segment and identify what is 'bad' to them."
Harte Hanks	"Data that fails to support the mission of delivering the right message to the right individual through the right channel."

Table 4. The sample file

Our compiled file of business names and addresses came from a variety of client sources. We aimed for 10,000 names, and resulted in 9,699 usable records.

Each record contained the following fields:
Last name
First name
Phone number
Fax number
Email address
Business title
Company name
Address 1
Address 2
City
State
ZIP code

Table 5. Topline correction counts on the 9,699 records

Each vendor reported slightly different counts, based on match rates and the data the vendors have on hand. You will notice that there are wide fluctuations in the counts on non-postal data, like fax, phone and email. This is because some vendors own current data, while others rent or lease it from third parties as needed by their clients. For this research project, we did not want the vendors to incur any out-of-pocket expense, so data owners delivered higher counts in these categories. Another reason for discrepancies is the way the vendors defined certain fields, like Address line 1 versus Address line 2. What strikes us as we look at these results is how similar they are.

	Vendor 1	Vendor 2	Vendor 3	Vendor 4
ZIP codes corrected	344	479	446	864
ZIP+4s added	8652	9375	8706	9101
Carrier routes coded	9342	9381	9401	9121
Delivery points coded	9333	9324	9203	9101
Street addresses corrected (addr1)	1776	5387	7583	685
Street addresses corrected (addr2)	704	1588	NA	3007
City names corrected	592	472	470	648
State codes corrected	163	472	470	158
Phone numbers appended	2101	4097	NA	4183
Fax numbers appended	0	2931	NA	2834
Email addresses appended	520	861	NA	645
NCOA matches	760	760	778	689
Delivery point validated records	9151	921	9203	9086
CASS certified records	9645	9596	9334	9589

Conclusions and observations

This study suggests that large, reputable vendors will provide very similar services when it comes to postal address standardization and correction, such as ZIP+4 and NCOA (National Change of Address). The marketer should not ask the vendor to change a title or company name—this information must come from the customer. Marketers can request that the vendor provide phone numbers, fax numbers and email addresses, but these are not part of standard data clean up as defined by most vendors. The append rates for these elements will differ by vendor, and no vendor can provide 100% coverage. In short, it's the marketer who must make the final call about customer data accuracy.

Index